*The only way to see beyond your darkness is to be set alight by your inner sun.*

# Awakening You

## Embodying Peace, Love and Freedom on Earth

Also by Isira

**Buddha on the Dance Floor**
(previously published as *A Journey of Awakening*)

# Awakening You

## Embodying Peace, Love and Freedom on Earth

Isira Sananda

LIVING AWARENESS

AWAKENING YOU
Embodying Peace, Love and Freedom on Earth

First published by Living Awareness, 2015
PO Box 447 Frenchs Forest Sydney NSW 1640
ABN 30 596 615 132

© Isira Sananda, 2015
www.isira.com

This book is copyright. Apart from any fair dealing for the purposes of private study, research, criticism or review, as permitted by the Copyright Act 1968, no part may be reproduced by any process without written permission. Enquiries should be addressed to the publisher.

All rights reserved.

National Library of Australia Cataloguing-in-Publication data:

Author: Isira Sananda
Title: Awakening YOU: Embodying Peace, Love and Freedom on Earth

ISBN: 9780994218018 (pbk)
ISBN: 9780994218056 (ebook)

Subjects: Sananda, Isira.
Spiritual life. Awareness. Enlightenment.
Self-actualization (Psychology).

Dewey Number: 204.4
Cover art and design: Muhammad Aamir
Internal design: Caitlin McGee
Contributing editor: Shanti Einolander
Copy editing: Caitlin McGee
Photography: Ankya Klay

**LIVING AWARENESS**
www.isira.com

*To every person, all creatures, and our living mother earth...
in endless love and gratitude*

# ACKNOWLEDGEMENTS

My first acknowledgment goes to Consciousness – as the very essence of that which I am and is all. It is through its power and light that my life has been illumined and graced in every way. Secondly, to creation, to earth and all creatures – for the blessing of life breathed into and through me.

Thank you to every person who has been a part of my journey – family, friends and companions – for all the nurturing and love.

Special acknowledgments to Leelani – my ever-constant support, Caitlin – for all the love, passion and extraordinary help in refining, editing, proof reading and layout, Shanti – for exceptional 'top end' editing and Gareth, Amali and Kirk for all your feedback and advice.

And to the Living Awareness team who hold the same vision of greater peace and awareness in this world – thank you for your selfless support, generosity and dedication – without you I would not have been able to complete this book.

# CONTENTS

| | |
|---|---|
| INTRODUCTION | 1 |
| PART 1: AWAKENING TO TRUTH | 11 |
| Understanding our Fractured Selves and World | 13 |
| Reuniting with Innermost Being | 27 |
| As Within, So Without | 35 |
| The World we Create | 45 |
| The Journey of Awakening | 53 |
| PART 2: AWAKENING YOU | 65 |
| The Microcosm and the Macrocosm | 67 |
| Preparing for Transformation | 79 |
| Breathing | 91 |
| Meditation | 101 |
| Being Centred | 111 |
| Flowing with Energy | 123 |
| Witnessing | 133 |
| Self-Reflection | 147 |
| Practicing Self-Reflection | 161 |
| Being in the Now | 177 |
| PART 3: AN AWAKENING WORLD | 191 |
| Harmony on Earth | 193 |
| Awakening to Love | 205 |
| The Embodiment of Love | 219 |
| In Service of the Whole | 235 |
| CONCLUSION | 247 |

# INTRODUCTION

Where we live is more than a body, a house, or a planet. Where we live is a place of spirit, of love, of sharing and wonder ... a unified field of life. Yet today we experience a world filled with fear and uncertainty, as we, our communities and our environment face unprecedented change. Even in the face of adversity, there is a power and a truth that is ours – one we all belong to, one that is *yours* ...

*You* are powerful beyond measure. You are not your ego, your mind or your beliefs. You are not your job, the clothes you wear or the objects you possess. You are not your fears, your failures or your past. *You* are consciousness.

You are imagination. You are the power to change, to create and to grow. You are a soul of infinite power, love and wisdom. No matter the uncertainty you face, *you* will awaken again. The journey of awakening is to know yourself, to know life, to be centred and connected within yourself and within the world, to live a life of love and harmony.

*Awakening YOU* is about switching the light back on. It's about becoming present to the love and truth that is you, and in doing so, creating a life of harmony. It's about discovering the power that abides inside you – the answers, the solutions, the strength, the peace and the freedom. It's about recognising what is here in every moment, hidden in your seemingly normal existence. It's about discovering how powerful you truly are, that indeed you are capable of generating greater happiness and love, every day, in every way. It's also about reclaiming the most profound relationship of all – *oneness*.

*Awakening YOU* is also about recognising yourself in all things, in each and every moment, and recognising that as *you* awaken, you awaken the world too. As you move into the peace and truth of your being, you bring that peace and truth into the world. As you create greater love and harmony in your own life, you bring greater love and harmony into the world. *Awakening YOU* will show you how accessible this all is, not as a concept but as a *direct experience*. As you awaken into greater awareness and love, you will realise that you are capable of all you truly seek.

## Living in harmony

By its universal definition, harmony is the 'order or congruity of parts to their whole or to one another'. The harmony I speak of in this book is not some utopian dream, a place free of life's tensions, challenges and the natural process of growth, but rather a state in which we as individuals embrace and consciously flow with life's dynamics. In this state, we create a more natural momentum of our being in synchronicity with the natural order of existence, as it truly is. Harmony is the ability to find congruence with our true nature, with each other, and with the world as a whole.

Life itself appears in the same instant to be tumultuous and chaotic yet suspended in profound order. Every single thing is held together and interconnected in this delicate balance. This to me is harmony.

Yet when it comes to our human experience, there seems to be a great struggle to be present with the way things simply are. Peace is a universal desire. We are hard-wired to always seek a state of balance, of harmony. This need underlies our every motivation. Even as children we are aware that all we really want is happiness – to love and be loved – and as such to live in the glow of harmony.

As a child, my awareness of harmony in the environment around me, or the lack of it, was fundamentally present in nearly every moment. I was highly sensitive. In fact I came into this world with such an acute, awake state of awareness that I was both profoundly engaged in the timeless ocean of all-connectedness and a conscious witness to the conflicts that arose in the people around me. I began to realise that not everyone was connected with the existential peace of purely 'being'. Not everyone was at rest in the centre, seeing all things as one all-connected being. My desire grew to communicate 'how things really are' so that the people around me could relax into being-ness and be at peace. This in itself presented many dilemmas. I was considered strange, even delusional. And the more I spoke of such seemingly unreal phenomena, the more confusing things became. Conflict was constantly thick in the air in our household.

Gradually I came to see and comprehend that the mind has a lot to do with these conflicts. I could see that whilst I was flowing, at rest in a vast openness of awareness, most people around me were deeply contracted, fixated in thoughts, and in particular a sense of separation.

I was aware that I am, and all is, awareness (consciousness) itself, and that the body, the mind, and the events of life are phenomena arising within this. Yet around me people were so identified with their thoughts, their bodies and their beliefs. It was as if they were trapped in a turbulent fog, completely blind to the vast perfection and connectedness of their own being with all else. The gift within all of this for me was the very clear recognition that despite any appearing disturbance on the surface of events, an ever-present peace and stillness was always within 'me'.

I began to identify and empathise so deeply with the conflicts and pain of the people around me that it became my 'life mission' to help people understand this dilemma and find a way to return to the inherent harmony that is always here within us and all around us. In a nutshell, I knew 'liberation' was possible.

Of course this dilemma is universal and not only impacts people at the personal level, but it is the very cause of the greater circles of conflict we face today, rippling out through families, societies and the environment.

Throughout this book I will be addressing the nature and cause of these conflicts in our individual and collective lives. Although some of the insights may prove challenging, perhaps even disturbing, the truth is, we really are far more powerful than we ever imagined. These insights are presented not to evoke a sense of alarm or gloom and doom, but to wake you up to the inspiration of your own incredible capacity to face and transform whatever conflicts you meet.

Inevitably we must face some hard truths in order to initiate deeper understanding and take action. Yet even if we were to collectively heap together all of our conflicts, they remain but dust in comparison to the conscious and creative intelligence that abides within each and every one of us.

Let's start with you.

Do you feel like your life is full of conflict? Do you feel that despite your best efforts you still feel challenged in most areas of your life? Are there questions you cannot seem to answer? Are you scared of the changes we are now facing in the world? Do you yearn to understand the meaning behind life and the conflicts you and the world seem to be facing?

If the answer is yes, then you are like so many fellow seekers in this world ... you are a seeker of truth and long to discover a way to deeper and lasting harmony, peace and understanding in your life. You probably also long to make a difference in the world. Seekers of truth have been looking for solutions for aeons yet are still feeling disillusioned by life's ongoing challenges.

However, there *is* a way to rediscover harmony amidst the challenges we all face. First, upfront, here are a few hard truths we must face, embrace, acknowledge and address if we are to achieve the deeper harmony I will speak of throughout this book.

## Awakening, peace and the world

As a global family we are clearly on the threshold of enormous upheaval, which beckons us either to greater fear or to a shift in our consciousness. At this time, it is evident that many of us are looking for answers and feeling disillusioned by the degree of conflict, division and environmental destruction in our own lives and at large.

We have expended great energy on criticising each other and asserting forceful power for the sake of greed, or even in the name of peace. We have vied for a position of the best politics, the greatest truth, the best religion or the right way. Our efforts have focused extensively on the identity and material possessions of our human being-ness and have largely overlooked the essential truth of being human. We have discussed our ideals, politics and philosophies endlessly, only to find that we – and importantly, our leaders – are still trapped in unconscious beliefs and controlling behaviours. We have been, and still are, mostly driven by the ego. In the quest for power we overlook the most essential powers there are to our humanity: consciousness and compassion.

*We* are the people of the world, yet are we conscious of what is happening around us every day? Are we conscious of our actions and their effects? Conscious of the growing imbalances of this world? Conscious of our world heading toward a potential abyss? Are we truly conscious? Where is our compassion? Are we *awake*?

At the end of the day, when we take off the hats and the cloaks of individual identities, we remember that we are all human. It is only when we meet each other as such that we find the place of unity where all images are respected, even in our diversity, and are held as equal, as one. *This place is the heart.*

The heart is where our true human power abides. Here, true wisdom, compassion and cooperation are born. Here, we transcend the ego and awaken consciousness. When we return to the wisdom of our hearts, we see that we are no different from each other. It is when we follow the way of the heart that we find our common spirit where all pretence of superiority or inferiority becomes obsolete. We all have families, we all long for peace and wellbeing and we all strive for our basic dignity of human rights and respect. We are all worthy. We all have a part to play in life.

And, most significantly, *we only have this one world to share.*

A higher awareness waits in the heart of each and every one of us. This awakened one, conscious awareness, is waiting in the ever-present silence within. Awakened consciousness is the universal power that will return us to harmony and oneness. This is our true leader. The true answers we seek can only come from conscious awareness.

With awakening we discover that our true capacity for human greatness begins to emerge as compassion in all its colours: loving kindness, equal rights, respect, and constructive change for growth. We uncover our largely untapped potential for true hope, courage, transcendence and higher vision, even when faced with the greatest adversities. We are able to set out again on a true path, to *return to harmony*. Underneath all our fears and attachments, it is harmony that we seek.

Eventually every human comes to face one of two possibilities: either to accept an existence beset with disillusionment and suffering, or to realise that every soul was born to be happy. This leads us to the single most relevant choice: love or fear. When we choose fear we remain unconscious. When we choose love, we regain greater consciousness.

If we are to create a world of love and harmony, for ourselves and each other, we must make a *conscious* shift from our unconscious behaviours to awakened awareness. We must awaken ourselves, humanity, without ever using violence to achieve any objective. The only way to change the world for the better is by uplifting the consciousness and the heart of each individual, of all people. When critical mass is achieved, the politicians and the business sector will follow. That is when real change will begin.

Only consciousness, which is free of the mind, can reveal our true nature. Ultimately we must renounce the belief in separation and turn from concepts to our own inner being. When we look within we enter a different dimension of seeing. We enter the presence of conscious awareness that releases inner vision – *in*sight. With insight comes true and authentic feeling. With authentic feeling comes experience. And with experience comes knowing. With the experience of knowing, our doubts and the rejection of ourselves as love and peace dissolve.

For this to happen, commitment, application and vigilant self-awareness are required. The habits of maintaining limited beliefs and looking outside ourselves are deeply rooted and compulsive. Rest assured, letting go of these habits is well worth the effort. The prize is the experience of awakening in one's own process, of gaining one's own true Self, something that no other can either give or take away. It is so great and immeasurable in its joy, love and peace that once we are self-realised, whatever appeared as suffering no longer has any relevance. Within the authenticity of our own realisation, we transcend all doubts and we discover that what we were seeking was, is and always will be within us.

I remember being asked, "How do you know you are awake?" That is like asking, "How do you know you've eaten the apple?" Once you have looked at the apple, touched it, smelled it, picked it from the tree and tasted it, do you ask how you know you've eaten the apple? However, without the direct experience, questions remain. We have been taught dependence on someone else's experience. I could tell you, "Believe me, the apple is…" and you could blindly believe what I say but you will still have a seed of doubt until you yourself eat the apple. A master's words or examples are only ever a signpost. The signpost is pointing us towards truth, to awakened awareness. It is never the teacher who sets us free, it is our exploration of what the teacher reflects back to us – our true essence – that leads us to experience and *know* the truth that sets us free.

Discovering our innermost power and awareness is a journey. Yes, by the nature of habit, it seems natural to keep looking for answers with the mind, to keep looking for answers from the past, or to project hope into the future. Yet despite this, every person who has encountered the liberating power of awareness has come to realise the very same thing:

*The where is HERE.*
*The HOW is always in the NOW.*
*The NOW is beyond time, beyond the mind.*
*The NOW is the source and presence of all that is True.*

It is when we meet this, consciously, that everything we have tried to understand, the peace and love we have been seeking, is discovered in the very midst of every living moment.

## This book's invitation to you

*Awakening YOU: Embodying Peace, Love and Freedom on Earth* sheds light on the source of true happiness and how to regain it through very real means. By addressing the underlying causes and symptoms of conflict, *Awakening YOU* shows how you can regain a sense of personal empowerment and a deeper sense of harmony in relation to all of life. It invites *you* to reawaken to all that you truly are, providing penetrating insight, guidance and sure methods that enable you to reconnect with the truth in your own being.

What we must address, however, cannot be based in concepts. It must be based in application. *Awakening YOU* provides a series of clear, conscious tools that lead naturally to a life of happiness, peace, freedom and harmony. With the key insights gained you will achieve a much deeper understanding of your true nature and the potential you have to live a life of love and harmony. You will take a journey back into conscious awareness and oneness. You will discover simple ways to generate direct communion with your true Self and the world around you. You will begin to understand much more deeply that through awakening YOU, the whole world changes with you.

**Part One, 'Awakening to Truth',** is about awakening to universal truths, as the first step in our transformation is to understand and acknowledge these truths. Until we understand that we are living in illusion and with false beliefs, we will continue to be caught in conflict. These universal truths give us the necessary foundation to move beyond the underlying causes of conflict and return to harmony.

Part One provides clear insight into the nature of our human conflicts, their causes and how we have been trapped in a seeming illusion. This book does not suggest there is one single answer or cure to conflict. It does not promise a life free of pain. And it does not suggest that abstract truths have enough power to set you free. Instead, *Awakening YOU* empowers you to identify the symptoms of conflict in your life, to return to the originating cause, and to apply the understanding and tools provided to achieve true transformation at the root of your being.

When you begin to understand how unreal the underlying conditions that cause your suffering really are, you begin to dissolve the power these fears and conflicts have had in your life. You move ever closer to understanding your true nature. This is the beginning of your awakening.

Part One illustrates that conflict is not a sin or a failing of any individual or of humanity. Rather, it is a symptom of an underlying condition – a state of dualistic perception – an illusion that must be addressed before a true sense of love, power, peace or liberation can be achieved. Here is the kernel of truth: The answer – *The* Truth – lies at the very core of our own *beingness*, in the very nature of all that we are.

**Part Two, 'Awakening YOU',** takes you on a practical journey into transformation. It moves the focus from universal truths to *you*. Having understood the basis of these universal truths, you are ready to directly and personally explore how you can practically integrate them into your own life and create from that foundation. Here, you will discover the power of conscious habits and learn how to put greater awareness into action in your own life. Although this process is unique to each of us, the essence of our true nature is the same. Hence there are defined methods that infallibly lead us all to a more harmonious and awakened life.

Using a practical approach based on tried and true methods, Part Two provides a concise and integrated model for conscious insight, self-transformation and awakening. I will share with you the same methods and habits that every enlightened person knows and understands – methods that have contributed to greater harmony in many people's lives.

You will find specific meditations, exercises and techniques that will support you in the process of awakening. The tools shared in Part Two are scientific in nature and distilled from my own experience or, as I eventually came to realise, drawn from lifetimes of experience. I will share with you many insights derived from personal practice and discovery.

I will also give you seven special 'attunements'. These are distinct affirmations that will help you align deeply with greater consciousness and attune yourself to love and truth, thereby creating a very powerful shift in your being.

**Part Three, 'An Awakened World',** brings the exploration full circle. When you understand the causes of conflict and have discovered how to bring truth into your own life, you will see that the positive impact is amplified at a universal scale. You will celebrate the truth that your awakening is inextricably linked to humanity's purpose as a whole: to love, to serve and to awaken. You will discover that *your* process of enlightening informs and influences the collective as we awaken together as a human family. As you change, the world changes with you. Part Three is about changing your life and the world for the better, forever.

*Awakening YOU: Embodying Peace, Love and Freedom on Earth,* assures each of us that there are applicable and entirely natural solutions in our very own lives. It affirms that our vision for greater harmony in our own lives and the world is something achievable. This book is about helping you to achieve extraordinary perspective and balance in your life, by transforming conflict with conscious awareness and conscious habits. It is about awakening YOU. The challenge is that most people have core issues that are so entrenched they simply can't figure out what to do on their own. *Until now . . .*

Part One

# AWAKENING TO TRUTH

In this section I provide clear insight into the nature of our conflicts, their causes and how we have been trapped in a seeming illusion. The root cause of our dysfunction, the illusory belief that we are separate from the rest of creation, creates an unfolding series of symptoms that progressively affect the way we relate to each other and our world. You will see that this dynamic forms the construct of your conditions - the conflicted you. You will also see how intimately connected you are with every other person, with all of life, and that what you see, feel and experience is helping to shape reality. You will begin to see into and beyond your conditions, and come to realise that you are something far greater.

CHAPTER 1

# UNDERSTANDING OUR FRACTURED SELVES AND WORLD

*Harmony makes small things grow. Lack of it makes great things decay.* —Sallust

Today is a good day to return to harmony. Today is the only day there ever is. It is this very day that gives you the opportunity to experience life as it is, free of the past and ready to energise the future with greater awareness.

Whether we realise it or not, all of our activities are driven by a need for harmony. With increased awareness of the extent of conflict that surrounds us, our efforts to understand ourselves and our world are heightened. At some point in our journey we all reach for something better or greater, something that will lead us to a place of greater peace and wellbeing. We seek peace in all the small steps we take, trying to bring greater order to our lives. Yet each of these efforts is pointing to something far more sustainable.

The ultimate place of peace and wellbeing is enlightenment. 'Enlightenment' is a consciously integrated state of harmony. It is the fulcrum of human consciousness, the blossoming of our being into the beauty of wholeness and oneness. It is the return to our most original natural self, that which is free of polarisation. Such a state is arrived at through the crystallisation of all experiences with the aware Self. It is a process of embracing rather than resisting every aspect of our being and life. But it is also a process of shedding our false impressions and habits, the very things that obscure our vision and seem to conceal the underlying harmony of our whole being – physically, mentally, emotionally and spiritually.

Most integral is our aware connection with the true essence of our being, our soul. Without this we gradually become lost in the mental impressions we collect through life. We develop a sense of disconnection from spirit, the universe, each other and ourselves. This signals it is time to understand the underlying *cause* of our conflicts. Only then can we regain a sense of order and the harmony we seek.

## Where conflict starts

**Our spiral of self-destruction, imbalance and unconscious living begins with our perceived disconnection from spirit.**

I say 'perceived' because the truth is we are not really separate from spirit (because everything we are *is* a manifestation of spirit), but we do have a firmly conditioned *perception* of separation from spirit, the source of all life. We base this sense of separation in the limited concept of our individual self.

Essentially there are two different types or dimensions of 'self'. The strongest identification for most people is the ego self – this is made up of false impressions and conditioned beliefs which generate the identity of a separate self. It is who you think you are; for example, your title, your job, your looks, your attainments and your personality. Beyond and deeper than this is the 'true Self' – consciousness. This consciousness is, in essence, spirit. It is who, or *what*, you are at the deepest level. Underlying the phenomena of form, the self you really are remains undefined and unchanged. If you really look for this 'Self' you may be surprised to discover that it doesn't exist in the construct you think of as 'yourself'. The body, mind, life events, beliefs and ideas are always changing, yet despite this 'you' are always here. So who is this 'you'? What is this 'Self'? The more deeply you look, the more mysterious it seems to become. Yet most people are too busy looking outside, as if the external world somehow validates who we are.

When we continue to look outside we lose ourselves in the world and in all that is false – we lose contact with who we really are. We dissociate from our Self as spirit. When we reunite with our innermost being – our essence, which is spirit – we realise our true nature and rediscover all that is real. We re-awaken to our 'true Self' – that which is pure consciousness and love, unbound by time or identity. This reunion liberates us from the conflicts of our falsely identified selves and the illusion of separation.

Humans naturally seek consistency between inner feelings and desires and outer experiences. Yet when a person operates from a state of perceived separateness it is impossible to attain any sense of consistency. Instead, life becomes an emotional roller coaster. This leads to accumulated stress, health disorders and disease (dis-ease). Gradually the feeling of dis-ease grows, along with a deeper rift from our inner being and connection with source. A feeling of lack develops, and along with it, issues with material possessions and resources, especially money. Wherever these issues exist there will be behaviours of control or suppression, manifesting in greed, a disregard for the collective and a disconnection to nature.

The pain of our separation is evident in the way we treat the world inside and outside ourselves. Outside of us, we have an environmental crisis so large it is hard to face with full conscious presence. Inside us, we have our obsessive conditions, which are also very difficult to face. But we have the gift of contemplation, the very thing that makes us distinctly human and can show us the way to true resolution. Our quest to find harmony is our effort to join the inner and outer points together.

It is our journey of rediscovering spirit that makes sense of and unites all things. 'Spirit' is the subtle realm of our being. It is the subtle energy behind all life. It is the infinite conscious 'One' that is aware and eternally present in all things and in every one of us. It is the true 'Self'. Yet despite its omnipresence, we are ironically, tragically and even comically unaware of it because of our lack of attention to our inner being, which is the key to our connection with this consciousness.

Instead our focus is projected externally. We have been taught to identify with our dense physical bodies and our thoughts. As we maintain this conditioning it becomes increasingly difficult to sense our inner self, a subtle being that is pure energy and pure awareness. It is even more difficult to believe in its existence. Our ever-present, ever-denied source remains a mystery, while we hold firmly to the illusory belief that we are separate from our source and from each other. Consequently our whole sense of ourselves, and therefore the world, is built on a divisive foundation.

Nearly everyone suffers from a sense of separation from his or her true Self. This underlies *every* issue we endure as individuals and as a human race. We feel dislocated in ourselves and in life. We feel profoundly disconnected. When we are disconnected, our first condition is one of fear. We are rooted in fear. But as Franklin D. Roosevelt famously declared, "The only thing we have to fear is fear itself." How transformed we would all be if we could realise the depth of this truth! It is because we invest so much 'truth' into the illusion of fear that we continue to be bound to it.

Fear creates our erroneous perceptions – the largest of all being that 'separateness' is real. All our misery, in fact all the misery on the planet, arises due to a personalised sense of 'me', 'us' or 'them', born out of our mistaken perception of separation. It is this personal story that we project onto life and onto ourselves. This covers up the essence of who we really are and manifests in all of our dysfunctional relating. We no longer know our 'true Self' or life. As a result, we are in constant fear, consciously or unconsciously, of the 'unknown'.

Our distorted perceptions then lead us to experience life primarily through our minds. As we experience what we think, we make it our belief system. From our belief system, we continue to think and act in ways that shape our entire experience of life. We live in and through our perceptions rather than reality.

**As we perceive, we believe; as we believe, we think; as we think, we imagine; as we imagine, we behave; as we behave, we have ... exactly what we imagined to be.**

Our sense of separation from our true being, which is oneness, is the central cause that leads us through a spiral of increasingly dysfunctional behaviours. It starts with those that are most central to us individually – the microcosm – and gradually ripples out to those that are part of the bigger collective environment – the macrocosm.

## THE SYMPTOMS OF DISCONNECTION

As humans we all face core issues, individually and collectively. These core issues are primarily a source of conflict and suffering, yet are also avenues for our growth. In many ways they are what defines our humanity. Once we begin to understand these issues, we see a direct relationship between the symptoms and their causes. Essentially there is one underlying *root cause* – our disconnection from our most conscious and unified Self – and six primary *symptoms* that arise out of this condition:

1. Distorted perception and distorted relationships
2. Distorted emotions and dis-ease
3. Materialism
4. Environmental imbalance
5. Collective disconnection and conflict
6. Desire for peace and unity

### Symptom 1: Distorted perception and distorted relationships

The first symptom arising from our perceived disconnection with Self is the belief that we are separate, manifesting in our idea of 'other'. We develop a lens of perception through which everything appears to be outside of ourselves. It is as if we have forgotten how truly connected we are to the whole, and that at the deepest level of our being we are all the infinite cosmos. We live in a kind of 'optical delusion', as Einstein put it. We lose contact with pure awareness, the very source of our Self. We have forgotten that what we truly are is consciousness and that this consciousness is the creator of all things. We are incapable of seeing and knowing that there is *no* outside; that you, me, all of us, everything in existence, is this *one* being.

With the perception of separation, all experiences become polarised between a separate self with 'inside' feelings being affected by 'outside' circumstances. Life is encountered as dualistic. Do you notice how this perceived duality plays out in your own life? How many times do you find your thoughts pulled in two different directions? Or perhaps you are struggling to make the 'right' choice as opposed to the 'wrong' one?

The idea of good and evil is inseparable from dualistic consciousness. The story of Adam and Eve, for example, frames this belief thoroughly.

It reveals how completely we see ourselves as being cast out of wholeness and into divisiveness. The Garden of Eden perhaps symbolises an underlying unity and wholeness that was ours before we took to the act of 'thinking,' or in other words, eating from the Tree of Knowledge. This implies our 'fall from Grace' was a direct result of dualistic, universe-dividing consciousness.

Consequently, we have condemned ourselves to the grief of being truly homeless in our own world – only to be born into sin and deception, to live in conflict, to inflict suffering and to die – cut off from the gift and blessing of the eternal life that is alive in our very soul. In this unconscious cycle, we struggle against all that is natural and whole.

Not only is there a sense of separation from one's own Self or source, but a sense of separation from every other part of creation. And not only is the experience a sense of 'other', but a sense of opposite. Our experience is polarised: it becomes me and you, this and that, right and wrong. Our *perception* of 'other' is a product of the layers of beliefs and concepts we have already accumulated. The 'other' is not even seen *as they truly are*, but rather as the images created by the lenses through which the observer is looking. The more we identify with these accumulated perceptions, the more the underlying belief in separation is validated.

This sense of separation is the source of all fears. Whatever is seen as outside of ourselves is seen as either a threat or as desirable. We seek to reject in order to protect ourselves, or to possess in order to feel more complete. Our experience becomes one of *dualistic relating*... a sense of never-ending struggle. How often do you feel as if life is somehow being *done* to you... rather than *with* you?

From this original rift in our being, we gradually spiral into deeper and deeper dysfunctional states. With the misperception of separation, we first experience a distortion of relating and relationships – *everything* we relate to in life is experienced through polarised perceptions. This knowledge is crucial, because:

**Our whole experience of life is a relating. Every single moment is centred in the way we relate to what is happening.**

What we call 'relationship' is the game of the dualistic mind. From this position there can never be a sense of true unity, harmony, peace or fulfilment. For as long as the person is seen or felt as a fixed and separate 'other,' there will always be a polarity of feelings in order to protect oneself. True relating is lost.

Nearly all of humanity has a perception of relationships based on fixed definitions. Indeed they are established fairy tales. The first feature of the universal myth is that we are all separate, the second is that somewhere out there is a one and only Mr or Mrs 'Right', and the third is that union with that one right person will lead to a life of happily-ever-after. Think about how deeply this fairy tale is embedded in our collective psyche and how often it does not turn out that way. It is a primary quest that leads many people to grief.

When we bring ourselves back to truth, to our true nature, we discover that there truly is no 'other'. Each encounter we have with any individual character is simply an experience with another aspect of our Self. No single moment or form ever stays the same. In other words, there is no everlasting love at the level of form, only at the level of spirit.

This does not mean it is impossible to have fulfilling and harmonious relationships. It does mean that we must give up the illusion – the fairy tale – of relationships, and embrace the journey of *relating*. And where does that begin?

**With our Self, in our innermost being.**

## Symptom 2: Distorted emotions and dis-ease

Having taken on the belief and illusion of separation, humanity lives in a perpetual state of fear and perception of lack. Life is largely perceived as an experience of disappointments, discord and failures. This corresponds with an increasing focus on our physicality as our identity and sole or primary reality. Limited by our focus on the physical world, we see no option but to look for solutions outside ourselves.

When our inner being is starved, we look to feed that sense of emptiness, often with more objects and bigger possessions. We struggle to make transient things permanent. We look for love outside ourselves. We even develop unhealthy ways to try to dampen our increasing pain and dissatisfaction, such as addictions to sex and drugs. Our sense of confusion drives us to look, sometimes knowingly but mostly unconsciously, in all the wrong places. We lose sight of all that truly nurtures us. We struggle against the stream of our true nature.

In this state, there is no thing that can ever truly fill or fulfil us. In continuing to suffer the consequences of such futile efforts we begin to store deeper and deeper layers of resentment and disillusionment. We develop conflicting emotions that drive us deeper into the unconscious self. We begin to *contract*.

As we contract from life, we create an even larger barrier between ourselves and the abundant world we are connected to. Gradually, the contractions we create in our minds, our emotions and our energy fields manifest as restrictions in our very cells. Our energy bodies take on lower vibrations, resulting in restricted thoughts and an increasingly reduced level of awareness. It's as if the universe of consciousness that we are has been reduced to the size of a golf ball! And with such a small package, it is very difficult to be aware and open to life or to function at our optimum. In this reduced state, we close off from the natural flow and balance of life.

What was once a healthy circulation of universal energy in and through our being, connecting us with life as a whole, is eventually dramatically impaired. In such a constricted state, we also accumulate toxicity. Our whole energy field becomes dissonant. We live in a state of *dis*-ease. This produces a myriad of symptoms called 'illness'. With loss of emotional and physical wellbeing, our belief in lack is further validated.

## Symptom 3: Materialism

**Why has humanity made money its God?**

As we continue to live in a state of lack, our relationship with energy and resources becomes distorted. Our subconscious belief in lack becomes an even greater issue as we attempt to resolve our sense of conflict through material means. This underlies our struggles with money and the material world. *Every* struggle we have about 'abundance' is born out of the unconscious state of perceived separation.

Given you have lost touch with the real you (consciousness) and have become so identified with the body and mind, it makes sense that there is even greater clinging at the physical level. How many people do you know who feel truly content and at peace with life without the need to acquire more material possessions?

You may consider yourself abundant, yet it is still not enough, and you are compulsively driven to look for more material enjoyment in your life. Or, you may believe that money is evil, not at all spiritual, and therefore should not be used in any way related to helping others' spiritual development. This is impossible in the world we live in, because money is an intrinsic part of everything we do. Either way, both of these perceptions about money and resources are born out of a dualistic mental framework.

Whatever is seen as outside ourselves is perceived as either threatening or desirable. We either reject in order to protect ourselves, as in the case of spiritual/religious piety or fanaticism; or we seek to possess in order to feel more powerful, as in the case of capitalistic greed. Having deep-seated fears that drive the need to control and possess, humanity has found a very easy tool to use in this manipulative cycle: money! The extent of the power game with money is reflective of the depth of the fear-based need to control. Money has simply become the vehicle to control our material realm.

Living in this illusion, it is easy to believe that money is the solution to all our problems. Yet, ironically, the further we trudge down the material path looking for solutions, the further away we get from true security, belonging and fulfilment. As we continue to struggle with a distorted relationship with materialism, our underlying unconscious belief in lack continues to grow.

Symptom 4: Environmental imbalance

As our experiences of conflict and feelings of lack grow, so does our suffering. As our suffering grows we fall deeper into ignorance. Understanding of our true nature and our connection *with* the natural environment is lost. The gap we have fallen into seems to grow ever wider.

Our interconnectedness with nature becomes almost imperceptible due to our excessive focus on a conceptual separate ego at the gross physical level. Our *sensitivity* to nature is lost too, buried under our growing materialistic piles and ego pillars. We no longer feel or realise that all life *is* interconnected. We lose connection with the innate inner wisdom that knows the harmony that runs through our very being and all life.

Having taken on the belief that our needs are met at a material level, we struggle to control and manipulate the world around us. We even ignore the warning signs that our environment is buckling under the weight of our materialistic obsessions. We are perilously stranded, depleted of sensitivity to the natural world. We are unable to acknowledge our impact on this delicate ecosystem that is essential to all of life, and our dependence upon its wellbeing. This way of living clearly reflects deeply rooted fears that originate from our disconnection with ourselves and life as a unified field. It reveals our profound mistrust in ourselves and life. And it results in large-scale environmental destruction.

## Symptom 5: Collective disconnection and conflict

Struggling to gain power over nature and ourselves, we assert territorial and covetous measures of control, widening the rift between our human communities. Having lost our connection with life and our own innermost being, we collectively create a divisive world. Our system of living is the result of this: one that is primarily based on separation, exclusion and dictatorship, even in the guise of democracy.

For example, while we in developed countries live in veritable comfort, much of the world's population lives in poverty. In the year 2000, the richest 1% of adults owned 40% of global assets, and the richest 10% of adults owned 85% of global wealth. The bottom half of the world's adult population owned barely 1% of the global wealth.[1]

We struggle to feel a sense of purpose and are increasingly challenged by personal issues such as domestic violence, economic struggle or health crises. We are thwarted by disempowerment; we lack the virtues of self-responsibility, generosity, empathy and big-picture global thinking. We are sadly lacking in behaviours based in conscious awareness.

These issues all start at a smaller level. We have isolated ourselves to such an extent that we barely know our own community in which we live. How many of your neighbours do you know and interact with? How many of your friends participate in community events? When a young boy from Sierra Leone arrived in New York on a scholarship, he was

---

[1] J.B. Davies, et al., "World Distribution of Household Wealth," (World Institute for Development Economics Research, 2008).

shocked and confused when 'strangers' did not return his greetings. He was accustomed to the basic act of acknowledgment between all people. There once was a time when acknowledging each other, strangers and friends alike, was common practice. The loss of this connectivity leaves us at risk of misunderstandings and discord.

As a greater collective, we are still at war. We cannot agree on political or ideological policies that will support and unify us as one human family. In our delusion, we continue to believe that the violence of war will result in peace and freedom. Since war is created *in our minds*, humanity must learn to live in a place other than the mind. Since the home of peace is *in the heart*, we must learn to create from love. However, this will take great courage, discipline and awareness.

Our approach to dealing with conflicts is indeed very complex. We have not yet created a world of peace because individually and collectively we are not yet ready. The foundations are not yet fully in place and the building blocks are yet to become stronger. Each one of us individually comprises the necessary foundation, and the principles we apply through physical, mental, emotional and spiritual means are the building blocks we need to work with. Even whilst we appear far from the harmony we seek, we are this work in progress.

You will notice I have been highlighting a thread of unifying truth: All of our apparent issues spiral out of the central cause of disconnection within ourselves, the loss of awareness of the one True Self.

It is this state that progressively manifests symptoms of dysfunction, starting at the personal level and moving through to our family units, environment, communities, world and cosmos as a whole. However, awareness of this truth has the power to shed light on the very real hope we all hold in our hearts. It tells us that our hopes are not in vain, and that indeed we really *do* have all we need to regain a state of harmony within ourselves and with life.

## Symptom 6: Desire for peace and unity

Hope is not lost. The irony of our human problems is that they eventually lead us back to our true being, to freedom. When we struggle against the current of our true nature we create a great amount of conflict in our lives. The more conflict we create, the more we suffer. The more we suffer, the more pressure we feel and the more we box ourselves in. Eventually, the feeling of being trapped evokes a powerful desire to go beyond the confines of our suffering.

When suffering is intense enough, we start seeking... not in the usual places, but really longing for something deeper, something truly substantial. We long for truth, for peace and love, for freedom and unity. This longing leads us all on a quest of rediscovery. It leads us back to our hearts, to the essential Self. It leads us again to the light of conscious awareness. And so begins the journey of rediscovery, of the true nature of ourselves and life, and a return to oneness.

And there is much to discover.

**Humans were born to be aware of, to develop, and to understand consciousness. We want to know who and what we are.**

Our ability to turn our attention inward to consciousness is remarkable, and what we discover there is astonishing. In the moment we connect with this inner consciousness, we regain a sense of pure being. There is an immediate feeling of peace and perfection, a sense of reassurance that all is perfectly in place – all is just as it truly is.

The epiphany that 'all is just as it truly is' does not hide the suffering, the ruin, and the tragedy of things; and yet this epiphany is exactly what opens the way for us to trust in the power of creation, to know again that all things reach us and that, in fact, we are not helpless after all. We are all active participants in shaping this mysterious, wondrous world. *Everything* we do counts.

What we are ultimately looking for is beyond the mind and body as we know it. However, in order to open our being to the greater essence of our Self, of life, we must first begin by putting our immediate lives into order.

We must restore harmony and balance at our human level in order to create the space for our inner being to emerge. Through restoring balance we discover the deeper calm within. With balance comes a stillness in which we awaken again to pure consciousness and realise that *we* are who we've been waiting for. We are the answer to peace.

We each have within us the power of awareness, peace and love. Each of us is an instrument in the journey of awakening. And, as each one of us begins the journey, we reignite the light for all to see and know the truth.

Now I will end this chapter with a little story:

One evening an old Cherokee told his grandson about a battle that goes on inside people. "My son," he said, "the battle is between two 'wolves' that exist inside us all. The first is Evil, and it carries the energies of anger, envy, jealousy, sorrow, regret, greed, arrogance, self-pity, guilt, resentment, inferiority, deceit, false pride, superiority, and ego. The other wolf is Good, and it embodies the ways of joy, peace, love, hope, serenity, humility, kindness, benevolence, empathy, generosity, truth, compassion and faith."

The grandson thought about it for a minute and then asked his grandfather: "Which wolf wins?"

The old Cherokee replied, "The one you feed."

CHAPTER 2

# REUNITING WITH INNERMOST BEING

*There is but one cause of failure. And that is man's lack of faith in his true Self.* —William James.

When we understand that there is one underlying *root cause* of all conflict - our disconnection from our most conscious and unified Self - we can begin a remarkable journey of healing. The ability to live a life of awareness and harmony rests on the core principle of knowing our 'true Self'. For this to occur we need to be connected with our innermost being. Once we understand this, we can begin to rebuild a more conscious life. We begin to move beyond our fears of the unknown and into a revealing relationship with our existence. We can regain harmony in every aspect of our lives to ultimately reflect the beauty of our souls in each moment. And it all begins at the level of consciousness within our innermost being.

Until we establish an inner relationship, we remain trapped in a limited sense of who we are. Consider this profound statement by Einstein: "The true value of a human being can be found in the degree to which he has attained liberation from the self." This is a truth that reaches into the core of our human condition. Most people are bound by the construct they see as 'self'. Indeed, as long as we are caught up in the fears and conditions that we believe define us, we remain confined to them. Until we liberate ourselves from this constructed identity, we are unable to recognise the totality of Self that we really are. As a consequence, we always feel as if 'something' is missing. The real you is not present! As the musician Jim Morrison said, "The most important kind of freedom is to be what you really are."

We struggle to believe that *we ourselves* are the very source of the love, unity and peace we seek in our lives and the world around us. In our struggle, we limit our capacity to contribute in the most meaningful ways: with loving compassion, creative intelligence and soulful awareness. The process of liberation is the same for everyone. It is a release from our conditions and the illusion we live within. It is a shift from our fractured sense of self and life into wholeness again. It is a journey of awakening.

## Rediscovering our wholeness

As we continue to suffer from our sense of disconnection, our sense of dis-ease deepens. So does our questioning and searching. We travel far to explore the wonders of existence, searching our whole lives through for meaning, for that 'something' that seems to be missing. Yet rarely do we imagine that what we seek is *within* us. As Lillian Smith wrote, "No journey carries one far, unless, as it extends into the world around us, it goes an equal distance into the world within." If we turn our search within, we discover that the whole universe can be revealed in our very own being. In this 'universe' there is truly nothing missing, we are whole and complete. Once we establish a connection with our innermost being, we are able to have a relationship with life that is truly nourishing.

I remember experiencing a 'moment' of such satiation that I cried tears of bliss for days. In this state I knew the absolute connection between the core of 'me' and all things. I realised that there has never ever been a moment of lack; that I have always had everything, perfectly as truly needed, in balance with the whole. Indeed, *as I AM the whole,* there is never anything missing, for there is no thing outside of 'me'. This experience emerged from the depth of connection I had nurtured with my inner being throughout my whole life. Even as a child, there were so many moments of lucid connection with life that I really didn't know where I stopped and the stars began.

Moment by moment we are emerging from what is, born from this and dying into that, over and over until we can no longer precisely tell one from the other. The entirety of this is its wholeness, its liberation, its eternity. All of this IS us, *for* us.

It is only when our inner being is starved and we lose our sense of wholeness with life that we look to fill that sense of emptiness with more food, bigger flavours, more objects, bigger possessions. We fear death, and in the face of this, we fear life itself. We struggle to make transient things permanent. Of course, not only is this impossible, it is ludicrous! In doing this we fight against the stream of our true nature.

We are incredibly real, caught in a terribly false world. We fail to recognise how erroneous our thinking is, and that the mind is largely responsible for our fears. As the Japanese proverb says: "Fear is only as deep as the mind allows." Our minds are the elephant in the room. As long as we ignore this, life is one constant struggle.

In this state of struggle, there is nothing that can ever truly fill or fulfil us. We continue to project into the future, always looking for the next best thing. It seems as if nothing is ever enough. In continuing to suffer the consequences of such futile efforts, we begin to store deeper and deeper layers of resentment and disillusionment. Ironically, the more we extend ourselves outwardly, the more we *contract* from life. We create an even larger barrier between ourselves and the abundant world we are connected to. Over time the contractions we create in our minds, emotions and energy fields manifest as restrictions within our physical and cellular bodies. This produces a myriad of symptoms called 'illness'.

How this happens is a matter of vibration. When we look deeply enough, we discover that we, our bodies, our minds, all life forms, are vibrational. Everything is energy. Each thought has a vibration. These vibrations reverberate through the nervous system, affecting the vibratory rate of our cells and organs. When our thoughts are agitated and conflicted they create a discordant state in the body, which leads to more congestion. We literally become knotted up. So, simply put, all illness arises from contraction. And all contraction arises from our discordant state, at odds with our true Self.

When our thoughts are loving and creative, the vibration of harmony flows through our being, bringing us into harmony with the universe and realigning us with our true Self. It is love that unties our knots. It is love that brings us home to our whole being, revealing our most natural state.

**The most natural state of our being is *oneness*.**

Oneness always remains our true nature, however we can and do radically reduce our capacity to utilise the limitless energy of our being when we live in a contracted or dissonant state. And the further outside we look for answers, the further we travel away from the wholeness, the peace, and the conviction we desperately seek.

**The moment we begin to return to our innermost being is the moment we begin to return to wholeness. It is also the moment we begin to find truth again.**

By reconnecting with our inner being we are able to regain an open state. In this open state we generate clarity of observation. We are able to see, hear and understand how we have adopted behaviours that do not support or reflect the true nature of our being. As we begin to see consciously for ourselves, we begin to *experience* our true Self again. As we experience our true nature, we align with loving and creative thoughts, the vibrations that bring us back into a state of harmony. We regain our seat of power – the ability to respond to life in ways that are naturally nurturing and empowering.

It is, of course, a process. Having journeyed so far out of our centre, it can take some time to regain a deeply connected relationship with our inner conscious Self. And even when we do, there is still a journey through many stages to regain a balanced flow of consciousness and energy. So where do we start?

## SURRENDER

To surrender is to not 'know', to not attempt to define or control. It is the suspension of our conditions and beliefs. To be able to regain a true alignment with ourselves and with life, we must first be willing to accept a state of *not knowing*. This is the first step in untying the knot. It is our constructs of what *we think we know* that actually get in our way of experiencing what *we truly are*. We must momentarily suspend our identity, reconnect with our inner self that is rooted in purely *being*, and allow the experience of being 'no-self'. We must allow ourselves to rest deeply into 'what is', rather than what we think or expect things should be. And when we do, we must be willing to first sit in a space of 'non-outcome', and remain there for however long it takes to regain the centred connection needed for true insight and transformation.

In the grace of this space, we soon discover that 'not knowing' is not a dumbed-down state at all. Rather, remaining open and enquiring without presuming anything gives rise to a higher intelligence, a creative awareness that encounters circumstances as they are. In this fearless yet humble state, a more intelligent response becomes a real possibility.

Without surrender, our efforts to awaken, to enter stillness, will be tied to the identity that is striving to get somewhere. The effort becomes the barrier and misdirection. In this momentum, part of our being continues to focus its attention externally, with the deluded hope that circumstances will change. When we are able to stop and simply be present to what is here, now, we can gain access to our inner space ... a space of stillness and silence. Magically, the more silent we become, the more clearly we can hear; and the more centred we are, the more clearly we can see.

Only when we have a deep enough connection with the inner stillness and silence of 'no-self' can our journey of re-awakening and transformation truly begin. The inward journey allows us to reconnect with unconditioned Self, the one who is free of the false perceptions and expectations. In doing so we may begin to see with the clear light of consciousness again. And indeed, it will be as if veils have been lifted and the world is seen anew! When we see clearly, the whole world is radically revised by this seeing. The world's wholeness is regained within us. In this way, we begin to establish an open and connected state of flow with the universe again. We can begin to tune into reality again. The more we can cultivate this, the more we can unleash transformative and healing powers.

Most people are afraid of really letting go into this 'no-self', because the attachment to the identity of a separate self is so strong. But when we allow ourselves to surrender, we realise that there is actually *nothing* to let go of – there is only a *letting in* to 'what is'. This entry into 'what is' does not annihilate the 'me' that experience has shaped. It takes the veils off and reveals a being living and acting in the world through unique characteristics, each of us perfectly designed to fulfil every purpose in the world. When we open again to all that we truly are, we realise that each one of us is indeed indispensable.

The more we open, the more capable we are of making a real difference. We also find ourselves more able to tune in to our true Self and the world around us. This ability to be 'tuned in' heightens our awareness and is integral to our process of evolving into a more enlightened life.

## Tuning in

Paying attention with awareness is a very powerful thing. It is especially important for developing inner connection. It can be even more powerful when we focus and align our awareness with thoughts and words that *attune* our being.

As we develop our inner connection, we begin to embody more enlightened qualities. The more deeply centred we are, the more enlightened we are.

So what is enlightenment? In the most simplistic terms we either exist in an aware state or unaware state. One state, when we project outside ourselves, is un-enlightenment. The other state, when we are self-aware and present within, is enlightenment. The distinction is one of focus. If our focus is entirely on the outside, we lose ourselves, we sleep. We express the limited ego self. When we focus inside, we find our true Self, we awaken and reunite with enlightened self.

There are seven distinct qualities of enlightened being: Awareness (Consciousness), Love, Gratitude, Unity (Oneness), Energy, Presence and Embodied Love. As we attune to these qualities, we shift our whole vibration into alignment with our enlightened nature.

Over the following chapters I will introduce you to 'the seven attunements'.[2] These are core states of aware attention that facilitate a recalibration of your whole being into a state of loving oneness, presence and harmony. The attunements will assist you in gaining the correct focus to connect within and tune into the seven qualities of enlightened being.

The attunements work in a way that realigns you to the true nature of your being and of life. They act as powerful energy tuners, much like a tuning fork, that help you to exercise a clear, strong alignment with

---

2  In this book, you will be given the seven key statements for the attunements. For more on the attunements see: www.isira.com

consciousness, love, presence and oneness. They will tune you into the true state of *being*. As such, the attunements act to make your being more harmonious and conscious. Every time you attune, you strengthen and elevate your vibration. As you practice each of the attunements, you will increase your vibration of love. By aligning yourself with love, the fears you hold can begin to dissolve. As your fears dissolve, you will find yourself present to life as it truly is. You will abide gracefully in the ground of being.

To use the attunements most effectively, it is important to repeat them every day. I recommend three times a day – or at the least at the start and end of your day. In addition, it is also very effective to write the words out and place them where you will see them regularly. To use each attunement, take a few moments with your eyes closed, breathing into your heart centre and reflecting on the words. Hear the words in your being. Feel the vibration of the words. Feel the truth of the words. Then state the words clearly. You can do this silently in your heart or out loud. Repeat the attunement three times. Then continue to feel the state of your being aligned with the attunement for a few more minutes.

Working with the attunements and learning to focus internally will provide you with essential tools to establish greater peace. Remember, a strong inner connection is vital to wellbeing. It is our inner state that generates our whole experience of life, each other and the world.

Close your eyes and bring your focus to your inner being. Notice that behind your thoughts, your identity and the events of your life, there is always the presence that is truly 'you'. This 'you' is consciousness, not the thoughts. This is the source of the true Self. Notice this consciousness is aware. As you notice this, focus your attention clearly on the following statement (choose the one that resonates with you most powerfully.)

Attunement #1:

*I am consciousness.*     or     *I am awareness.*

The more you tune into consciousness, the more you will discover that everything you are and everything you seek arises from within you.

CHAPTER 3

# AS WITHIN, SO WITHOUT

*What can be gained by sailing to the moon if we are not able to cross the abyss that separates us from ourselves?* —Thomas Merton

As outlined in the previous chapters, our perceived separation is the root cause of all symptoms of dysfunction, including conflict with relationships, resources and nature. When we re-connect to Self, and live in a centred state, we also re-connect to others, to our material world and to nature. We heal the divide we felt between our inner world and the world around us. The degree of unity we feel within our own being is always reflected at a holistic level. What we experience is a product of our own perception. Our internal 'reality' is always mirrored in our external world: As within, so without.

## CONSCIOUS RELATING AND RELATIONSHIPS

From the moment we enter this world we are engaged in a constant array of relationships. From our parents, siblings and social circles to the suburbs we roam and the world we discover. Every single encounter presents us with an opportunity to relate. Whether we are aware of it or not we are shaped by, *and* shaping life through, every relationship we have.

Most significantly, all relating begins within us. The layers of beliefs and perceptions we accumulate determine how we relate with others and the world. Essentially, all is dependent on, and reflective of, the foundation of our *very own* being. Whether we relate through the mind or through pure awareness will have a marked effect on every relationship we have.

If you look closely you will see that your whole experience of life is relating. This is true of *every* single thing you feel, experience and encounter. Your whole life experience emerges out of *you*. There is only one person you will always be with, and that is you. Even when you are with others, you are still with yourself. When you wake up you are with yourself. When you answer the phone, turn on the TV or walk down the street, you are with yourself. The question is: What kind of person do you want to spend your time with? What kind of person do you want to see in the mirror at the end of the day? This is the most important question you can ask, because that person is yourself. It's your responsibility alone to be the person you want to be with. Wouldn't you want to spend your life with a person who is at peace within and without?

At the heart of our relationship frustrations we will always find the same cause. As long as our basis of 'self' is one that is unconscious, dislocated or externalised, every moment of relating with 'other', whether it be a partner, work or nature, will be based in conditioned perceptions and separation. It will be based in illusion and sooner or later will lead to frustration and disillusionment. This is because human nature seeks the experience of love and wholeness, and the experience and essence of love *is* wholeness. It is unity, not separation. When we feel dislocated we do not feel our true nature, which *is* love, which is *oneness*.

With the perception of duality, we experience a deep void in our being. This is why we place so many expectations on relationships. We are actually looking for our partners or another to fill a void within ourselves. We are centred in fear and the neediness that arises out of our unconscious relating to life and to ourselves.

These unresolved needs manifest in various ways. Perhaps one of the most obvious is sexual addiction. Does this mean there is anything wrong with sex? No, of course not. Actually, there is nothing *wrong* with anything. However, sex itself will never bring true fulfilment nor will the repression of our sexuality, as repression is certainly not a quality of wholeness or freedom either. The underlying conditioned beliefs we have about sex, including our fears and judgments that it is something wrong or bad, causes us to objectify it and actually lose presence during this most wonderful intimate experience. Flitting in and out of various thoughts instead of being wholly present in ourselves while in the act of love-making is not being truly in the here and now.

When we are anchored in self-love and in presence, sex is no longer a compulsive need. When we are deeply present and centred, making love becomes an encounter of even deeper, intensely shared beauty. But this beauty arises out of one's own wholeness and is mirrored in, with and through the other. In order to find love and oneness with another, to truly feel and see it, we must first have that experience within ourselves.

When we return to our innermost Self, we are capable of rediscovering our true essence which *is* oneness and love. In this presence we realise our own perfection. We realise we are a creation of love. Once we know this we are able to transcend the conditions of the mind, and as a result, our fears. We come into the fullness of ourselves, into conscious presence, and discover we are our *own* perfect partner. We realise that there is nothing missing from our very own being, and no one can ever take away the love that we are. This wholeness gives us the most extraordinary peace and strength. It gives us the capacity to love all things in every moment, all through realising the love of the true Self.

It is in our inner realm that we also re-encounter our Self as boundless, as energy, as *spatial* being. This spatial being is not constrained by time and space. It is not linear like the mind. Instead, it is multi-dimensional, encompassing *all* things in every moment, including what appears as duality! Through this we can truly experience oneness... and *love*. We can feel all things within our Self and our Self within all things.

When we see our Self in 'other', it is no longer possible to form a relationship based in fear. It is no longer an objectified encounter of competition, protection or possessiveness. It is a deeply encountered state of relating... *centred* in love, encompassed in oneness. This relating is pure and innocent. It is alive and flowing, centred only and forever in the now. This profound truth is conveyed in the ancient Vedic text, 'Isa Upanishad': "Who sees all beings in his own self, and his own self in all beings, loses all fear."

We are so anchored within our own being and *beingness* that we can truly be *with* another person, but no longer as a need. It *is* possible to grow in a relationship, but only when you are not losing yourself. When you have a deep connection with your own being you can have true relating, based in the consciousness of real love. It is no longer about trying to complete ourselves through another person, because we are complete within ourselves. Instead, it is about more love, deeper love, higher love. It is about elevating each other through bringing one's own consciousness into shared presence. And, it is no longer confined to the singular relationship. As we continue to experience the power of true love it multiplies and expands into the greatness of universal love and compassion.

Every moment of relating becomes a sacred encounter – an engaging, inspiring, nurturing, fulfilling event. We discover that our entire relationship with life can be one of depth and lightness, joy and wonder, purpose and meaning. We realise that indeed we brought ourselves here to engage in conscious communion, to participate in the ongoing relationship of all things. With conscious presence *every* moment of relating is an opportunity to express the loving Self and to feel and witness ourselves as love through the reflection and appearance of 'other'. This appearance is seen as a gift; a multi-dimensional mirror, to know our infinite Self in and through endless forms.

This is the true purpose of the experience of 'perceived' separation. With the perception of 'separation' comes the experience and expression of individuation. Through individuation we encounter the gift of life's infinite diversity. We encounter a field of context, giving us the settings through which we experience the wonderful array of our Self in its entirety. We also get to experience the wonder of 'uniting'. We get to participate – to see, feel, touch, hear, taste, smell and love life, our Self and all the 'selfs' – through an endless multitude of expressions and experiences.

As we slowly empty ourselves of thoughts that revolve around separation or independent, isolated being, we begin to open again. We rediscover that actually we are truly open. As Rumi so poetically wrote: "Why struggle to open a door between us when the whole wall is an illusion?" In this state of being sufficiently open and centred, we lose sight of the boundaries between our 'self' and the world around us. We discover that the smallest event tips us over and out and *in* to an overflowing state of empty fullness. This is the experience of enlightenment. Waking up is discovering ordinary humanness, worldliness, immersed in the radiant light of oneness. Here there is no distinction between 'self' and 'other'.

**Through a more unified state you may unveil the love that is always here and the opportunity it brings to encounter truly loving relating in every moment.**

The power of your attention – where you place your conscious awareness – is going to help you to establish a much deeper connection within your Self and to be present as love consciousness. Remember: everything is energy. Your whole experience is shaped either by fear or love. Remember the story of the two wolves? Which one are you feeding? It is very common for people to focus on negative thinking. Every time you criticise or focus on what is wrong, you bring your whole energy field down. In every single moment your thoughts are directing energy. *Energy flows where attention goes.*

The more you centre yourself in your own being, the more you centre yourself in consciousness. The more you are centred in consciousness, the more open and connected you are with life and with love. You literally become the conscious space of love. Imagine then if your whole life were seated in your true self as love. You – *love* – would be everywhere you are!

Attunement #2:

*I am LOVE.*

Take a few moments with your eyes closed, breathing into your heart centre and reflecting on the words. Then state the words clearly, silently in your heart or out loud, repeating the attunement three times. Continue to feel the state of your being aligned with the attunement for a few more minutes and endeavour to maintain this state throughout your day.

## Money, resources and spirituality

Our inner state also influences the way we perceive our physical world, in particular, our sense of lack. It gives rise to the many material challenges we encounter with energy, resources and value. 'Money' is perhaps the best representative of these. Money is a topic that most often hits an uncomfortable chord, especially when it comes to the arena of spirituality. Given we have adopted money as a fundamental tool in our lives, isn't it worth wondering why? In fact, money occupies us every day and is intrinsically woven into every experience we have. So, first of all, let's take an objective look at this thing we call money.

**Money, like all other 'things' we use in this world, is simply a tool.** Yes, money may take you wherever you wish, but it will not replace you as the director. Money is simply a tool through which we create and generate experiences. Metaphorically, the *tool* represents energy and value. We use money as a tool to measure and exchange energy, as well as to create and generate experiences. *What* we create or generate with money, however, is significantly determined and influenced by another intrinsic tool: **Beliefs.**

How many people you know have a healthy and well-balanced relationship to money? We might categorise one end of the spectrum as being greedy, materialistic, overly indulgent or miserly; and the other end of the spectrum as frivolous, lackadaisical, repudiating or ignorant of money's importance in today's society. How would you reflect on your own relationship with money? You may be one of those who do have a balanced attitude towards money, or perhaps one of the many who do not. Two interesting questions that can allow you to develop a more skilful approach towards money are: Why do these behaviours exist? And what can we do about them?

It is our beliefs that fundamentally underpin our behaviours. Our beliefs are tools we use every single moment, every single day, to flavour and shape what we create and experience. And, we use the tool of our *beliefs* to operate every other tool.

Depending on our beliefs, we will interpret and use the tools we are given in a variety of ways ranging from divisive, resentful and destructive, to creative, supportive and unifying. Money is our strongest representative tool. The way we use it is a measure of who we are and what we value. As Ayn Rand wrote, "Money is the barometer of a society's virtue," So if we accept it's okay to use the money tool for football, fashion and all things transient and frivolous, why are we so challenged to use money as a tool for spiritual growth that leads to more lasting fulfilment?

Given that money is the primary tool through which we measure value, exchange energy and create experiences, wouldn't we want to generate more life-supporting and spiritually uplifting experiences? Wouldn't we want to give abundant energy to the people and things that support our journey of enlivening and awakening? Don't we value these spiritual things deeply? Don't we want to change our behaviour for the better? For when we are uplifted in spirit, we want to give and love and behave compassionately towards each other and thus create a more harmonious world.

Bill Gates, one of the richest men on earth, admitted that one of the greatest gifts money gave him was a social conscience. Wouldn't we want to give and receive, gratefully, if it meant a thriving healthy planet and all that is committed to making the world a better place? Given that we all share the vision of a better world, understanding and being aware of our beliefs – particularly our beliefs around spirituality and money – could be one of the single most important matters to address in our lives.

So where can you begin? Firstly, recognise that *everything* you are using in this world is a tool. All 'things' are tools to generate and encounter experiences. Secondly, be very clear about the type of experiences you *want* to generate. Thirdly, assess your belief system. Does your belief system *support* a productive use of the tools that will help you manifest the experiences you *want* to create?

**How can you have a healthy relationship with money?**

You can re-establish your beliefs about money. Every destructive belief *can* be released. You were not born with beliefs. You picked them up... so you can change them or let them go. *You* are not a belief. A belief is merely a tool. It is up to you to choose which beliefs and tools you use and how you are going to use them. Be clear about your values. When you are clear about your values, you will feel a greater sense of empowerment with this tool called money, simply because it is a certificate that represents an exchange based on value.

Here are some practical steps towards a healthy relationship with money: Write down your feelings and beliefs about money and carefully look at each one. How does it really look? How does it feel? How does it influence, 'flavour' and shape the way you receive, use or give money? Now, write down the things and experiences you want in life. Recognise the relationship the 'money tool' has to manifesting these goals. Ask yourself how you feel about using money for this experience. What is the feeling and belief you are holding? Does it support you to receive or create this experience? Then ask yourself what is the best belief that *supports* a constructive relationship with money and the desired experience? Ask this question for *each* experience you want to generate. Adopt the *feeling* of the belief that best supports abundant manifestation with ease and grace.

The most powerful feeling you can adopt and use for a positive, abundant relationship with money is LOVE!

Remember, our entire experience of life can either be centred in love or in fear. Love is the true nature of all creation. Everything is created from, through and for love. Love is the vibration of our being as whole, as the infinite power of the universe. Fear is the opposite. Our whole human experience is about this. It is about us awakening from our illusions (fears) and rediscovering love. This means we will use our life experiences in two primary ways: to remember love (to receive love) and to create with love (to give love). Given that money is a tool, it makes sense that we can have a much more positive and abundant experience if we align it with love!

The second most powerful feeling you can adopt and use for a positive, abundant relationship with money is GRATITUDE!

In fact, if you want to feel truly content and satisfied in life, then gratitude is the key. It is actually impossible to feel lack when you are feeling gratitude. This is because gratitude puts you in the mindset of acknowledging what you *do* have. When you are in gratitude, you are focused on *having,* not on what is missing. This generates a strong subconscious energy association of fullness and wholeness. Once you start looking at the things you can give thanks for, you will discover an almost endless space is available in your heart for gratitude.

If you learn to see that money – as energy – can hold the 'flavour' of *love* and *gratitude,* you will have a journey of ease, grace and abundance. Everything you choose to generate and experience will be touched with love. Pay those bills? I *love* to! I am *grateful* for these commodities that make my life comfortable. Want to help the world be a better place? I *love* giving money to organisations that help make the world a better place! I am *grateful* for the work that others do and the opportunity I have to contribute to a better world. Want some spiritual advice and guidance? I *love* opening myself to conscious growth. I give *gratefully* for the spiritual support I receive.

So you see, money may have a history of corruption and limitations, but essentially it is not a problem; it is a tool. Nor are your beliefs a problem. They would only be a problem if you were stuck with them. But, you are not. It really is up to you to choose which tools you hold in your heart, your hands and your mind.

Exploring and transforming your beliefs about money can bring profound change into your life. But it is just the beginning. Understanding the power of beliefs is greatly significant to the journey of liberation. We will delve more deeply into the nature of mind, beliefs and transformation in the chapters to come.

Finding greater peace with money will inevitably lead you to feeling deeply at peace with *all* resources. You may even come to realise that *you* yourself are the greatest resource you have. Your strengths, talents and unique character traits are gold. Everything about you is designed to play a role in the evolution of life. And if you look closely, the inclination of nature – of life – is to flourish!

Attunement #3:

*I am GRATEFUL for this moment.*

Take a few moments with your eyes closed, breathing into your heart centre and reflecting on the words. Then state the words clearly, silently in your heart or out loud, repeating the attunement three times. Continue to feel the state of your being aligned with the attunement for a few more minutes. Endeavour to maintain a heart of gratitude throughout the day.

CHAPTER 4

# THE WORLD WE CREATE

*A human being is part of the whole, called by us 'universe', a part limited in time and space. He experiences himself, his thoughts and feelings, as something separated from the rest, a kind of optical delusion of his consciousness. This delusion is a kind of prison for us, restricting us to our personal desires and to affection for a few persons nearest to us. Our task must be to free ourselves from this prison by widening our circle of compassion to embrace all living creatures.* –Albert Einstein

Having considered the dynamic of material energy and resources, it naturally follows that we consider their source: the natural world that sustains us. Once we begin to understand that we are more than the individual – that indeed we are interconnected with *all* life - we begin to recognise the responsibility we all have towards our greater environment.

## THE PLANET WE CALL HOME

Our planet is home to billions of species, all of which play an integral role in the wellbeing of humanity and the ecosystem we are part of. This precious planet is the only home we have, and we must care for it wisely.

The environment is always reflective of our own state, individually and collectively, whether it be a state of wholeness and wellbeing or a state of fracturing and disease. Currently, our natural world reflects the extent of our individual and collective demise. Let's put things in perspective. The earth is 4.54 billion years old. Scaling to 45 years, humans have been here for less than a day, the industrial revolution began 1 minute ago, and in that time, we've destroyed more than half the world's forests. If we can throw any species onto the scrap heap, which we have done to many, we are effectively conceding that life itself is worthless. Our assent to the continuous ransacking of our world can be observed in the radical and perpetual rate at which we are replacing the natural world with material things. The result is that our grief and gradual autism as a species removes us from the story of the living world.

In this dark sleep, we have forgotten that life is a creation of love. *People* are born to be *loved*. *Things* are created to be *used*. But if we look closely at life today, we see *things* being loved and *people* being used. No wonder there is so much pain and sorrow! No wonder we have become so devoid of the spirit that makes us most human and most sensitively connected with life. In order to reverse the roller coaster of our collective destruction and regain environmental balance we *must* each, as individuals, return our efforts to awakening. That's right...

**Awakening is not simply a nice idea or a spiritual option. It is utterly essential to reverse the destruction we are causing – not only in our own lives, but also upon nature. It is essential for us to dig down into the real process of spiritually maturing.**

Without this, how shall we embrace our situation and respond effectively, rather than recoil in the face of planetary adversity? Will we take up this invitation before planetary emergency becomes planetary disaster? Will we risk stepping bravely forward with a vulnerable heart? Can we risk *not* doing so?

Isn't life demanding that we pay attention, that we recognise that the devastation of organic life on earth is the devastation of ourselves? Perhaps there is a great blessing hidden amidst the unfolding tragedies. Perhaps we are watching ourselves being torn apart only to come back to the realisation that we are one life, and that what happens to another is, in the great unfolding trail, happening to us.

Do we really need to continue debating whether climate change is real or whether we are causing it, when it is glaringly obvious we are responsible for ecological and environmental genocide? We are destroying the habitat of countless species every day. The evolution and collective fate of our human race is now inseparable from the evolution and fate of our planet, of every living creature. Never in human history have we been more clearly economically, politically and environmentally implicated as a species with a shared dilemma and common destiny.

So long as the environment is at risk, *we* are too. Our world is excruciatingly fractured and torn between so many different lines that the loving act of mending is not only long overdue, it seems beyond our reach. We have failed to recognise that it all began with the split in our own minds. It all stretches out from here, the cracks growing wider and deeper, in tandem with the spiralling collapse of ecology. The cavernous gulf between rich and poor, the judgments that qualify or divide us, and especially the disconnection we generate in our own minds, are the producers of immense suffering.

## Our shared experience

Collectively, we reflect a world of multi-layered conflicts. We are all universally impacted. Although we may not consciously realise it, the desire for collective harmony is inherent to each and every one of us. We all yearn for a world of greater peace and equanimity, yet given the state of the world today, most of these hopes appear distant to us. Despite this, the truth is that *our hopes are not futile*. Deep within each of us *is* the source of collective peace and harmony.

We must remember that the problems we face communally are all founded on the problems each person carries individually. The health or dysfunction of the individual is directly reflected in the health or dysfunction of the community. And the dysfunction of our human community is reflected in the collapse of our global ecology. Whether we are *prepared* to endure the consequences or not, we *are* already facing them. What we do to ourselves, we do to the whole. What we do to another, we do to ourselves. Whatever affects one directly, affects all indirectly.

It is impossible to live and act only for ourselves. Right now, someone, somewhere, is feeling the effects of something you have said or done. As Henry Melville described, "Ye cannot live for yourselves; thousands of fibers connect each and every one of us; and along those fibers, as sympathetic threads, our actions run as causes, and they come back to us as effects." Whatever we do in this great ocean of existence surely ripples through every other living thing. What is essential is our conviction in this truth. For with this conviction, we will take great care to consider every action.

In welcoming and re-engaging with our interconnectedness, we discover the answers in the very fabric of the life we are a part of. We *must* re-birth our relationship with life. It is only through a *relationship* that we can truly understand the plight of all living things.

Only when we welcome life *as it is* will we be welcomed back into the whole world, and will we see the world as whole again. So, the saying is true: It turns out the ones we have been waiting for are *us*. Rather than reason to despair, this is, in fact, great reason for hope. This is the very truth that says we *do* have a choice. We *do* have the ability to become the conscious stewards we were designed to be, for the healing of the planet begins with the healing of our painfully fractured 'self'. And that is in our own hands.

Mending our fractured 'self' begins inside each of us. It is only through reawakening to our innermost being that we can reawaken to our interconnectedness with all of life. Then everything we need to know is rediscovered. The journey of minding earth and mending the world all unfolds from here.

## Unity consciousness

Ultimately, although our conflicts cause us great suffering, this suffering eventually catalyses our deepest desire to return to harmony. In the face of our greatest adversity our desire for peace and unity becomes a voice that cannot be silenced. It propels us towards inevitable transformation. Until we take the path of awakening, we will continue to suffer. We suffer because we continue to project our false perceptions onto existence and each other. This creates a discord between our inner being and our outer experiences – even though existence is *not* separate. When we view life through an inwardly held map, the illusion is created that we *are* separate, and we encounter conflict – the two states do not match.

This is enormously significant to humanity because we seek consistency between our inner being – our hopes, desires, beliefs and perceptions – and our outer reality: how and what we experience and how reality *is*. This need for consistency drives and motivates every person on the planet. It is primary to our psychology. It drives all efforts to gain something, to remove something and to alter and adjust our experience. The degree to which we feel consistency reflects the degree of our happiness. The knowledge that all existence is the one *beingness*, the same stuff, is utterly central to this quest for consistency. As long as we view ourselves as something other to or separate from the All, *we will not experience consistency*. It is impossible to feel and know this consistency as long as we hold the view of 'otherness'.

When we reconcile this sense of division, we will experience true unity. We will *feel* consistency, and we will be at peace.

So this brings us back to the 'how', 'where', and 'what' questions, which in turn brings me back to the repeated message and direct experience of every awakened being:

**The 'how' is the NOW.**
**The 'where' is WITHIN.**
**The 'what' is BEINGNESS.**

When we are centred in the true Self, in the Now, and relaxed in 'beingness', we become presence itself. We are no longer the mind, the ego. We experience unity consciousness. We are alive, radiant, conscious loving. We are no longer seeking the 'how', 'where' or 'what', because we realise we already *are*. There are definite ways to encounter the power of this truth.

First of all, when the well-trained mind is focused on the level of perceived *objects*, it is difficult to shift that mind from the view of separation. To change this experience we must connect with the self that is *spatial*, the one that is not fixed in separate objects but is instead the whole field of life. This *one* is discovered in the aware Self. It is revealed when we are present. It is consciousness.

Remember the attunement: *I am consciousness*

As we deepen in awareness, we have an even greater desire to unite with our eternal Self. We begin to sense that what we truly are is transcendent of all we thought we were. Ironically, many teachings often appear to be saying we have to go *beyond* form. Yet, actually, conscious experience leads us to see the true, subtle nature of form as that which is all-connected energy. We come to realise that our whole being – consciousness and form – are not separate.

In this we realise our awakened Self is not actually transcendent as a *location*. It is not somewhere in the future or in some higher ascension realm. Our true Self is transcendent as a *state* – transcendent from our minds yet very much *immanent* in our beings, our cells, our manifestation, and in the living experience and expression of this very moment. The true Self is the perfection of *all* creation, *including* the duality experience. It is a truly united state. This is unity consciousness.

The essentials for engaging with one's true Self always remain the same as well. This Self, that which is aware beingness, cannot be encountered in or through the mind. We must enter more deeply into our hearts and attune to love. We must connect to pure consciousness, to pure awareness, as the true Self. We must relax and become a witness without judgments. We must transcend the mind and become conscious presence in the now.

Being centred in our Self as energy anchors us more consciously as the living, aware *experience* of the now, and as that which is boundless. This liberates us from the idea of a laborious task. Awareness does not come through effort or being serious. Yet the journey is a process of rediscovery, requiring diligence and patience. Indeed, the journey is one of commitment, a shift of attention and surrender to the mystery. It is also about applying ourselves and working diligently with the tools of awareness. The primary tool for awakening awareness is, of course, meditative practice.

Although meditation is not a method – it is a state – most people need a technique to help them rediscover their meditative self. Having become so lost in unconscious behaviours, very clear techniques can be immensely helpful in cultivating a direct experience and regaining conscious awareness. These techniques are helpful because they are scientific, and they save you from unnecessary wandering and groping. Without them, you can wander aimlessly for a very long time. With them, you can save much time and energy. Sometimes within minutes you can grow so much that you achieve transformation that may have taken lifetimes. If correct techniques are used, growth is accelerated.

The techniques I present in 'Part Two: Awakening YOU' are immensely powerful because they put you back in touch with your true essence. With them, it is utterly inevitable that you will grow. Many people will still think it all seems like too much effort. Yet considering it takes an enormous amount of energy to keep living an *inconsistent* life, this is an insane way to think! And it will certainly only lead to continued conflict and frustrations. Taking the time to centre yourself is well worth it. Not only will it bring you back to the true nature of your Self, it will reflect in the many blessings that come from living a unified life.

And for what purpose is one's life other than to realise the love, the peace and the liberation that really is one's true being? The purpose of awakening is not to transcend, but to realise the transcendent essence of oneself in order to bring its enlightened quality into immanent living... to bring love and unity, peace and awareness to the world. It is the harbinger of all we truly seek. It is a return to harmony.

The more connected *you* are to your inner being, the more readily you are able to feel truly connected with the world around you. Likewise, the more truly connected you are to the world around you, the more present you are, the more centred you are in your own being. In being centred, the wisdom comes. Awareness guides you. It's simply a matter of letting go of the conditions that prevent you from relaxing into what already *is*. It is a return to all that is true. It is truly the reunifying of your being with what you have always been, the entirety of existence. It is a reawakening to the truth that all is one. This opens the way for the healing of all things – within and without.

Later in this book we will explore various tools that powerfully aid this process of letting go, allowing the discovery of how profoundly connected each one of us is with the universe, how whole and perfect we are in each and every moment, and how capable we truly are.

As you attune to your inner being – consciousness – you are more capable of tuning in to the unified nature of life.

Attunement #4:

*All is ONE.*

Take some moments now to centre yourself and focus your attention on the connectedness of all life. As you do, breathe from your heart centre and feel how truly connected you are with everything. Now centre your attention in the statement: All is *one*. Repeat the attunement, stating the words clearly, silently in your heart or out loud three times. Try to maintain your awareness of connectedness throughout your day.

The more deeply you are connected within, the more clearly you will experience unity.

CHAPTER 5

# THE JOURNEY OF AWAKENING

*With an eye made quiet by the power of harmony... we see into the life of things.* —William Wordsworth

It is only when we heal the divide within ourselves that we will truly be able to heal the divide between each other, and in doing so, undertake the journey to the reunion and harmony we seek.

This brings us face to face with an inevitable truth: We are yet to pass through the passage of transformation, both individually and collectively. We are entering a transition of inevitable breakdown and major change in the world today; a time of unravelling, collapse, and ultimately, re-organisation and transformation. At this time, I cannot over-emphasise the relevance of *awakening*. Accordingly, the fundamental purpose of this book is to guide you in the process of awakening *you*. As the previous chapters have demonstrated, the spiralling symptoms of dysfunction we experience all point to an essential truth. If we don't wake up to our relationship with ourselves, with life, we won't be able to work together to find the real solutions.

Awakening and spiritual opening are not ascension into some imagined realm, nor withdrawal into a safe cave. Awakening is not a pulling away, but a deep engagement with every experience of life, with the wisdom of an embracing heart that holds no boundaries. It is a living state of unity with all things. The more you experience this unity the more you will awaken.

## So what is awakening?

Awakening has no exact definition. It is a *process* of shifting from the unconscious state of ego-driven identity to a conscious state of Self, one that *experiences* itself as the eternal awareness and oneness of all life. It is a state in which we transcend definition and consciously abide as pure being. Essentially, awakening is a return to consciously seeing, knowing, feeling and living in unity with the true nature of our Self and all life.

In the un-awake state, one lives within the mind and is driven by the ego. Life is primarily experienced through a constructed identity based on the perception of being separate from others, life, creation and source. You think you are an actual personality; a separate 'somebody' defined by your body and the events of your life. In this state it is the logical left-brain activity that is dominant, and so you remain caught in the analytical mind. Life is experienced in dualistic terms: up and down, right and wrong, you and I. Consequently, life is constantly defined and labelled. All of this is the construct of the ego.

**The ego is a veil between what you think you are and what you actually are.**

You live under the illusion of the mind, totally unaware that you are directed by a great big load of stories! Instead of seeing reality as it is, you are seeing through the layers of these stories, very much like looking through a collection of dirty lenses. Imagine watching your neighbour hanging out her laundered white sheets, wondering why they look so dirty. Then one day you decide to clean your windows, and - lo and behold - you realise her sheets are glistening white!

This is what it is like to be unconscious – to not be 'awake'. These dirty lenses influence you throughout your whole life and you don't even realise it. You play out the same stories over and over, wondering why nothing seems to change. These stories play out through subconscious and unconscious feedback loops. Hence your life feels like a constant swing between good and bad experiences, moments of pleasure and pain. Even worse, it may seem as if you have no control over it.

In this conflicting state, happiness is dependent on the circumstances and events of your life. Happiness and fulfilment always appear to be 'out there' somewhere or in something else. You live in the jumble of the mind's illusion, disconnected from the centred state of the *now*. Instead of being present to what *is*, you live in the mind's images, based in the past or future.

Awakening is an ongoing process that integrates over many stages. During this process you begin to re-engage in the here and now with exactly what *is*. When attention is centred in this way, clarity arises, allowing you to experience true presence. It creates a deep centring, a connection with your inner being. You then begin to experience direct states of awareness in which there is a remembering, a reconnection with knowing the true Self as eternal awareness and being.

Once you begin to see and feel the moment as it truly is, there is a connection to the consciousness of love. This love is a powerful energy. Its vibration begins to elevate your whole being – mind, body, emotion and spirit. Through the energy of love and direct experiences such as meditation, there is a direct effect on our physiology. A very real change takes place. The nervous system is balanced and the right brain becomes more active.[3] A gradual state of entrainment between the right and left hemispheres results in deeper and higher conscious activity, and one's whole being returns to a deeper state of harmony. The mind becomes very balanced, even still.

There is a deep centred-ness in the moment of the *now* and one enters a state free of the mind's stories and projections. What arises here is the direct *experience* and realisation that this Self is vastly beyond the body-mind of the 'individual'. This Self is infinite and at one with all things. This Self is both the One, which is undifferentiated, and the manifestation of every unique expression in the universe.

It is like a veil is lifted and life is seen in its full glory. All questions fall away, and along with that, the belief in a constructed identity. In this state a profound sense of liberation occurs. There is a realisation of the perfection of all things in all moments as the One Self. Happiness becomes a constant, a realisation that the Self is always freedom, peace and love. A deeply abiding state of harmony is revealed.

Essentially we become seated in our true Self, consciousness. We are

---

3  The references I make here regarding 'left' and 'right' brain activity are very generalised. There is no true polarity of brain activity. Rather, distinctions in brain behaviour are influenced by the individual's dominant mental identifications.

free of conditional attachments and aversions, no longer identified with thoughts and labels. We realise that 'I' am not my thoughts, 'I' am not the body, 'I' am not the identity or the roles I play, 'I' am not the events. Rather, 'I' am consciousness, boundless all-being, *with* thoughts, *with* the ever-changing body, events, roles and activities. As consciousness we realise that we have no beginning and no ending. We realise that we are not time or place, but rather that time and place appear within the experience we have through consciousness. It is *consciousness* that is always present.

If you look really closely at 'what' you are, you will discover that the only thing that has always been constant as 'you' is *awareness*. The body, the thoughts, beliefs, events, circumstances – all of these keep changing. Your body keeps changing. It is not the same body it was a year ago. How then can you actually be the body? Your personality keeps changing and evolving too. How then can you actually be the personality? The only thing remaining is awareness and the consciousness it arises from. This is the only constant 'you'. All else is ephemeral.

The nature of the world we experience is fluid. It is always changing, transforming, flowing from what appears to be one moment to the next. Yet, what appears to be based in time is always, only and forever happening in the now. This reveals that the 'I', as consciousness, is eternally present and contains all things. If we consider the insights from quantum physics that everything is energy and holographic in nature, then perhaps we can understand more clearly that everything *is* the play of consciousness. The more clearly we see this, the more 'awake' we become. We realise that what we thought to be real is more like a dream. We begin to awaken in the dream.

Awakening occurs in many ways and to varying degrees. It is quite common for people to experience 'satoris', moments of sudden or extended epiphany that return them to a feeling of unity with all. These can last from a split second to weeks, sometimes even months, before one subsides again into the thinking mind based in duality. This 'rise and fall' in and out of awareness can repeat itself many times, even over lifetimes, before there is a sustained integration in which there is no longer a shift from the state of ever-present awareness.

When we reach a saturated state of integration, we become the living, radiant, constant state of oneness, consciousness and *love*. We remain *aware*. We simply enter the being-ness of life itself, the play and process of consciousness in the ever-present *now*. This remembering or awakening of our true nature arises naturally the more we allow ourselves to connect with our innermost being. When we are connected in this way we are able to access our 'greater Self': pure consciousness, that which is powerful beyond measure.

In Buddhism this greater Self is described as 'anatta' or 'no-self' (no identity). While there is a sense of a 'self' inhabiting every sentient being, when we really look for it there is no individual, defined or fixed self to be found. In the space where we are left searching, this sense of individual self vanishes into something far more astonishing: a profound vastness of all-being. We return to our eternal Self that knows 'I' and 'universe' are one, and in this the very essence of our sentience, the sentience of *all* beings, is brought into light. Being aware and connected in this state is not only beautiful and liberating for us, it is also *the* vital tool to transform all of our apparent personal and collective issues.

## Why awakening?

Having explored the core symptoms of humanity's disconnection from spirit, we can see that every condition we encounter is intertwined with every other condition. We can see that the cause of *all* suffering and fear is our perceived disconnection. We also recognise that in every instance, no matter what type of problem we are facing, there is one certain solution: Regaining an awake or aware connection with our innermost being.

For aeons, however, this Self has most often been considered as something beyond, something other than the very living presence that is *us*. This Self has been seen as transcendent and therefore the elusive subject of debates and seeking. Yet, when we drop our concepts and projections, when we rest deeply in our own centre, when we are simply open conscious presence, we know that there is nothing but *beingness*. And this beingness is our living Self in this very moment. The entire universe is this field of beingness. It is present in this very moment, *as you read this*, and in every moment. We are never separate from it.

**There is no beyond. There is only here – the infinitely small, infinitely great and utterly demanding present.**

We, you, me, this body, this 'individual' human expression, are integral aspects of the all. Every molecule is oscillating in vibration with the entire universe. Today we are blessed with great scientific discoveries that back this up. Quantum physics tells us that every atom is emerging from space and that this space is a vast limitless 'ghost' of energy, something that cannot be called a nothing, yet that which is pre-form. Although it appears void it is certainly not lacking essence or substance. So actually every particle is made up of source, this essence that is pre-form. Not only that, but every particle has within it the potential of every possible state that can and does manifest in existence... in this very moment, in every moment. The microcosm *is* the macrocosm *is* the microcosm.

Remember these words: "As within, so without"? Well, these words apply at every level of existence. In other words, not only is your experience born out of your inner map of reality, existence is born out of *you*... out of the centre of your being. In fact there is no outside or inside. There is only all being, which is all centre. Whatever our body and soul are made of, whatever the universe is made of, we are made of the same stuff. Unless we can see this 'sameness' we will continue living on the perilous edge of divisiveness. Until we can expand our scope beyond egotistical concerns to celebrate with the trillions of lives on this earth and see ourselves alive in this seamless all-connected web, we are living on the brink of insanity. We are neither living in reality nor in harmony.

This is so pertinent, so immensely important, as a cue to *awakening* to all that we are. Why? Because we seek to be enlightened in order to feel whole again. We *seek* enlightenment to feel at peace – to feel unified within ourselves, with each other and with creation. What existence shows us, though, is that this is already the case. We actually are unified; we can never be anything but. We do, however, forget! 'Awakening' is the process of us waking up out of our unconsciousness and *remembering* the true nature of our being and all life. The journey of 'enlightenment' is about us coming home to this truth. It is about us *consciously responding* to life and embodying all of our most enlightened qualities. It is about us engaging with life as it really is.

## Is enlightenment desirable?

I raise this question because it seems evident that the idea of a rift between 'worldliness' and the 'spiritual journey' is still very much alive. Many people experience the same conflict, stemming from the notion it has to be one or the other.

Most people feel so deeply trapped in the worldly cycle that they can't help but recognise the suffering it causes them. This of course generates a very powerful desire to be free of this seemingly interminable cycle, causing us to 'seek' a solution, perhaps a spiritual one, and then the search for a spiritual path. Yet once faced with the 'conditions' of the spiritual path, an even greater fear arises, the fear that spiritual life demands we give up the 'worldly life'. Of course in this situation it is natural to be afraid. Questions arise: How can I survive without my job, without my success? Will my family and friends understand me, will I be judged and end up isolated, will I lose my grip on reality?

But these fears are largely based in our limited views, many of which are the remnants of indoctrinated 'spiritual' practices such as abstinence, renunciation, isolation, transcendence or ascension. Having been taught that worldliness is 'the root of all evil' we have overlooked the real thing of value: consciousness. It doesn't matter if you choose to be worldly or not. What matters is consciousness. The most valuable question is this: Are you conscious?

However, old stories die hard. We continue to be fed erroneous ideas. Of course these ideas cause enormous hesitation and resistance towards 'walking the path'. The idea of enlightenment seems suddenly much less desirable if you think it means you will lose everything in the worldly sense. We have become so afraid of the transformative process of anything truly spiritual, of awakening, that we have even deemed such things as signs of mental illness! How ironic when we are already stuck in so many delusions!

Yet if we look deeply into what enlightenment is, or the process of awakening, we may be radically surprised. Age-old stories around the journey of enlightenment have given it a bad rap. Of course it can look terrifying to face our dark conditions, because the enlightening path *does demand* this. It looks frightening to undergo the temporary chaos of releasing our internal madness. But the truth is we already hold this madness, and it will have to come out eventually. What is crazy is to hold on to it.

Still, we are desperate to get to the end goal, and we would rather take the leap as if by some magic rather than have to travel through the darkness. And, in the face of our conditions, the 'end goal' we seek seems so distant. It seems to be viewed as something beyond our human capacity. Maybe we believe it is reserved only for 'special' people like Jesus and Buddha. Yet what they both demonstrated was very real potential. They both taught from experience grounded in their own human journey. And they both encouraged us to recognise this very same potential in ourselves and in every other human.

The presence of consciousness in everyone is real. The nature of awareness within everyone is the same. The essence of love in all things is reality. Yet because we have forgotten these truths, as if we are lost in some deep prolonged amnesia, we doubt their power and presence within our very own being.

Yet life does what it does. As we deepen through love, as we encounter growth and more awareness, our individual consciousness expands and new realisations emerge. We realise that we have always had an inner calling. There has always been a yearning to know truth, to feel true freedom, to know pure love and oneness… to know that life *is* more than what we made it out to be.

But we have been taught a very damaging thing: that to step into greater awareness is arrogant, and it is reserved for a very select few. For fear of recrimination we shrink back from truth, from our very Self, from the greatness of the love we are. However, awareness is neither arrogant nor meek, greater nor lesser. It is real. It is what we are, what we always have been and always will be. Enlightenment is nothing more than our conscious return to this truth.

The greatness of awareness contains the courage to step beyond the confines of these old stories. The power of love contains the strength to stand alone, to break free of the mediocre mind and into the wholeness of Self. Arrogance, on the other hand, denies the Self and abdicates responsibility. Arrogance is humans destroying themselves, each other and life on this planet for the gratification of the ego. Arrogance is the masks we wear and the judgments we flaunt to assert power, create security or find a place of belonging.

We have also been taught that enlightenment is a zoned in or zoned out state where emotions no longer exist. However, the truth is the complete opposite. With enlightened presence we are neither suppressed nor distressed. Our emotions are neither blocked nor agitated. Emotional dysfunction belongs to the mind afraid to fully let go and let in. Emotional dysfunction is the man who is still trapped in the anger of the boy, the little girl who became the shrivelled woman afraid to laugh, sing and dance. Enlightenment is the full presence of our Self in each moment. It is the freedom of being and becoming in the perfection of all as it is. Enlightenment is free of every opinion that holds us in the falsehood of being lesser or greater. It is free of the illusion of separation and the boundaries we constructed out of dualistic delusion. Enlightenment is free of control and alive with what *is*.

Another erroneous idea is that enlightenment belongs to a different realm. This causes us to believe that we will disconnect from the real world. On the contrary, enlightenment anchors one even more deeply into life. It brings us fully into our centres, into the ground of being, into the very heart of reality. We become more present, not less. Enlightenment brings us into expanded awareness, and expanded awareness is the very thing that brings us success in every dimension of our lives. It reveals our true purpose and value. It opens us to creative intelligence, bringing new solutions and insights. It re-awakens us to the unity of all. It equips us with the power to respond consciously and with love. How could this not lead us to success? How could this do anything but improve our journey in this world?

Enlightenment is not about leaving life behind. It is about fully entering it. Once one is in the river of consciousness, one can't help but engage with even greater vitality, to continue this wonderful human journey with the clarity of awareness and a wide-open heart. This is why enlightenment is seen as a gem. It is the greatest treasure we can discover. Yes. Enlightenment *is* desirable.

There is no better time than now for awakening *you*.

## Awakening is *the* tool to overcome global breakdown

The Self contains the intelligence and power to answer every one of our questions, and the capacity to transform all that appears lost and broken. Yet unless *we* ourselves experience this all-connected Self, we continue to doubt this basic truth. This is not just a wondrous metaphysical concept. This great Self is the very intelligence that is informing every function of existence. This field is in fact a living hologram revealing itself through every part, including the mind.

This Self – or 'no-self' – is behind all creation. It precedes the choices we make and the actions that follow. It is the moral seat and compass of every soul, permeating our existence in ways that enable us to be ethically transformed through its infinite wisdom and grace. It is the intricate ecological intelligence of creation, of the earth; that which has shaped our whole existence and drawn each of us into being. This provides us with true insight into how *every* action shapes and is interconnected with the whole. It gives us a very different perspective of our place and purpose, our ethical duty and our creative power in each moment.

Whilst it is the great aware Self that naturally manifests in ethical actions, we struggle without it. Regardless of this, the human body and energy system provide hardwired feedback regarding morality and skillful, or not so skillful, living.

Have you noticed that when you feel stressed or tired you are prone to feel angry and say hurtful things? Conversely, have you noticed that when you are in an optimistic mood you tend to feel energetic, happy and healthy, and that your mood has a positive impact on the people around you? The body is able to tell us very directly and immediately what is 'right' or 'wrong'. If we are sensitive, we can attune to this in the moment and recalibrate. If we are less sensitive, we tend to end up getting a bigger whack over the head from life to draw our attention to it!

We are actually incredibly powerful and creative beings – and *the way we think* plays a critical role in the world we create and experience. Yet despite this immense power that abides in each of us, we largely seem lost, trapped in the surface of our material world. When we place greater belief in the feeling of separate identities, we blindly continue to fight with ourselves and with each other. We look for answers outside ourselves, which are really just projections of our own conditioned and painfully limited minds. When we look only with the eye that sees objects, we don't absorb life as a whole ecology, an interconnected field. It remains impossible to cultivate true self-empowerment, empathy and the will to act for the betterment of the whole.

Encountering our greater Self changes all of this. With a *heartfelt* connection to Self, we shift from being confined and self-centred to being far more aware of all life. We become *allocentric* in spirit.[4] Our view of past and future is brought into a whole new dimension. We are able to see that all along the universe has shown us nothing but the power of inclusion. No part of it is possible without the rest of the whole.

Thich Nat Han expressed this beautifully when he wrote: "Apple, seed, mosquito, breeze, mountain peak and distant starry galaxies... each one, the face of the whole."

As we look into the face of creation and see into the unfolding of earth, we begin to listen to *her* story again. We become acutely aware of the far-reaching and irreversible impact of each and every one of us through every choice we make, in every single moment. With eyes wide open to this, we also begin to glimpse the real possibility of human peace and freedom. As Dr Seuss wrote, "You'll miss the best things if you keep your eyes shut."

Through the power and awareness of this great Self, we become a big-picture thinker and doer. We become *macro* aware, capable of imparting this wisdom at the *micro* level. Every action is seen in relation to the whole; motivated by profound gratitude and respect for all that we are and have, in the now and for all time. We become the open, engaging presence of inclusiveness. Is this not *love*?

With connected awareness, every action arises from our innermost centre; from our soul that *knows* how truly precious and connected all of life is. We become the most conscious expression of ourselves and recognise the immense significance of our own individual role in relation to the whole. For it is when we live from our soul that we know and reflect the natural purpose and harmony of all existence.

---

[4] Focused as the 'all' instead of focused on the ego.

Part Two

# AWAKENING YOU

In this section you will take the journey into transformation and gain a much deeper understanding of your true nature, as well as the potential you have to live a life of love and harmony. Through an interactive process you will awaken your own innate power – the YOU that is love consciousness. In unifying more deeply with love and consciousness, you will discover for yourself how to create a life, and a world, of love and harmony.

In essence, this section provides a concise and integrated step-by-step model for conscious insight, self-transformation and awakening. First, you will learn how to nurture your being holistically and prepare yourself for transformation. Then, you will discover the power of conscious habits and learn how to put greater awareness into action in your own life. I will share with you the same methods and habits that every enlightened person knows and understands – methods that have contributed to greater harmony in many people's lives. When applied, these methods will help you cultivate your own *direct experience*, which is essential for authentic awakening.

CHAPTER 6

# THE MICROCOSM AND THE MACROCOSM

*Health is the proper relationship between microcosm, which is man, and the macrocosm, which is the universe. Disease is a disruption of this relationship.* —Dr. Yeshe Donden, physician to the Dalai Lama

To restore balance in our lives, it is helpful to understand the primary aspects of our being: spirit, mind, emotion and body. Each is integral to our wholeness. Each in itself has a particular nature which, when honoured and nurtured consciously, creates a state of balance and harmony through our whole being. *Holistic* wellbeing, which takes into consideration every aspect of who we are, is an important facet in the human journey towards greater harmony, integration and enlightened being.

As we consider these aspects, we discover the unique qualities that make us human and drive our human experience. Fundamental to each are natural laws, quintessential needs that when met become the measure of our wellness and enlightenment; or when denied drive our dysfunctional and unconscious motion through life.

Our spirits, minds, emotions and bodies are instruments. The way we align and tune them will determine how harmonious our lives will be. Everything comes from, and is, the creation of spirit. It is spirit that vibrates as different levels of consciousness, from the macrocosmic, immeasurable presence of infinite life to the infinitesimal realm of the microcosm, immanent life.[5] These energies all draw down, condensing into and through our human experience.

It is through our souls that we manifest the mind, which generates the emotions, which determines our physical experience, the state of our bodies and our life circumstances. Of course, ultimately we cannot say one comes before the other because all levels are of the same being, simultaneously co-existing. However, as a human we primarily experience life as something sequential, as well as through the dynamics of cause and effect.

This is why it is not enough to assume that we can take on a spiritual mindset and focus purely on the ethereal or metaphysical level of spirit in order to attain a state of wholeness and harmony. Each level of our being has its own nature and 'laws' of cause and effect. As we delve deeper into spirit, and how and why everything rests on us re-awakening to the truth of ourselves, it is helpful to understand the 'needs' of each aspect of our human nature as manifesting through spirit, emotion, mind and body.

## NURTURING SPIRIT

To begin with, let's explore the nature of this thing we call 'spirit'. Somewhere deeper than the surface of our thoughts and the events of our lives lays the ineffable essence of all life. This essence seems impossible to explain yet is something that can be sensed and 'understood' in the light of consciousness. It is an inherent knowing that there is a life force that we have come from, that carries us through each moment and which will carry us beyond this world. Some may call this the soul. Yet 'soul' is but a river compared to the endless ocean of spirit.

It is when we look inward that we begin to discover the soul and our individual spiritual expression. The more deeply we sense this subtle element of our being the more we discover the subtle element hidden within all things. We begin to recognise the innermost essence and spirit of original being.

Our soul is like a ray of the sun. Paradoxically, this 'ray' that appears distinctly individual is *simultaneously* the connection to the 'sun', the

---
5  Immanent is defined as 'existing or operating within; inherent.'

whole of spirit, the omnipotent essence *and* the *source* of all-being. Although the rays appear individual and distinct, they can never be separated from the sun itself.

'Spirit' is the pure conscious energy of all existence, which is always here, in the very source of our own microcosmic being. When we are deeply connected with this essence, we are capable of attaining the state and awareness of the omnipotent eternal being. We are able to feel united as the microcosm and the macrocosm. We sense and see the very same spiritual essence in every drop and every particle as one great oceanic field.

The central need of our human spirit is stillness and silence. To experience the essence of our eternal Self, we need time to rest into pure awareness and encounter the spaciousness of 'simply being'. This stillness isn't only something we encounter through formal meditation. When was the last time you simply laid on the grass and gazed up at the trees and the clouds? Can you remember how it feels to be immersed in nature, to be so deeply engaged with life that your spirit is alight and your heart is truly content? This is what we feel when our spirit is nurtured.

Without this we lose the openness to see and feel our own connection with the innermost essence of all things. When we do have this connection, we are able to live deeply centred in the *now*... where the essence of our Self, and all of life, truly is. When we are present, we are aware that our Self is in the centre of all things and every moment; free of time, attachments and aversions. As spirit we know the synergy of existence, the formless presence of pure consciousness in which all exists, ever-changing and flowing, transforming the world of form and experience. We know that we are already the liberated Self, and we become the living encounter of this truth.

## Nurturing the Mind

In exploring the nature of the mind, let us first consider consciousness. Consciousness is the source of intelligent awareness and creative potential. It is that which precedes, yet is the very essence of, all form. Consciousness is simultaneously that which is immeasurable and endless, yet always the essence and expression of the now. It is also the manifestation of every possible frequency arising within itself, from the most expansive to the most contracted.

Our minds are an example of the contracted end of consciousness. Being confined by definitions, images and concepts, the mind conveys perceptions that appear to be finite in nature. As such, what is seen and experienced through the mind is profoundly limited, superficial, linear and dualistic.

In the individual, the collective definitions or beliefs that make up the identity or ego may be considered the microcosm of mind. At a larger scale, we discover the collective mind of humanity, an example of the macrocosm of mind.

At the collective level, we see that there is no 'individual' fear, anger, hurt, hope or desire. These expressions, thoughts and feelings are whole energies in and of themselves, belonging to a universal mind. Each of us can 'tune into' any of these given aspects of the mind, and in doing so the experience is personalised through our own position and circumstances in life.

As we take the journey away from the confinement of the unconscious mind, we develop more conscious awareness, which leads to 'witnessing' awareness, which further opens our consciousness and brings us back into expansive 'pure' consciousness. Pure consciousness is the ultimate macrocosm of 'mind', that which is transcendent of mental construct.

Every mind needs balance, and although there are many biological factors involved in maintaining this balance, it is still greatly overlooked that our connection to spirit has a significant impact on our mental health. A nurtured spirit helps to maintain a balanced mind. When we are mentally balanced, our minds are wonderful tools, able to do the job they were designed to do, to serve us as we interact with life. It is now well documented that spiritual connection and meditative practices strengthen and improve the balance and function of the brain. Our connection with spirit keeps the function of our minds well lubricated, clear and vital.

To maintain connection with spirit the mind needs a great amount of stillness and silence. Therefore meditation is *the* most central tool for the mind to maintain appropriate balance. Meditation also has a direct and proven effect on the balance of brain activity, literally creating harmony between left and right brain hemispheres and stimulating more expansive and integrated states of (higher) consciousness.

Time to 'day dream' is also vital for the mind to re-balance and integrate life's experiences in the healthiest context. Daydreaming naturally supports and nurtures right-brain activity, the creative aspect of the mind, and is proven to play a significant role in information retention and assimilation and the inspiration of new ideas.

Exercise, fresh air, connection with nature and changes in environment all provide vital, healthy stimulation for the mind. Creative stimulation ensures a balancing with the right brain. The mind also needs appropriate oxygenation and nutrients. Without the oxygenation gained from correct and balanced deep breathing, the mind becomes sluggish and dysfunctional. Typically the left-brain becomes dominant, resulting in the many mental health disorders that are increasingly prevalent in our society.

## Balancing emotions

One of the common definitions for emotions is 'energy in motion'. I'd like to expand on that. This energy in 'motion' arises as a result of us sensing and expressing. Therefore emotions are the moving energies of our being and through which ultimately life as a whole is being sensed and expressed. If we look deeply into what we are, we discover nothing but energy. Consciousness is energy. Mind is energy. Form is energy.

The energy associated with thoughts and experiences is at the very core of our human nature. Why? Because each thought has its own type of pattern or vibration. For example, anger has a distinct vibration compared to kindness. Although there are vast arrays of energy vibrations in consciousness, the average human remains quite confined to a narrow spectrum of emotions born out of 'dualistic' perceptions. In other words, polarised feelings between 'good' and 'bad'. This is the microcosm of emotion.

However, as we extend our awareness further, we recognise how deeply sensitive we are. We are sensing beings. The moment another person walks into the room we can sense their mood. This indicates how interconnected we actually are at the feeling level, and is an example of the macrocosm of the emotional level. We are, every single one of us, intimately connected to each other. And, indeed, we are all energy. In fact, what we are feeling is generated through our 'attunement' to the collective field of energies of the one life we are all a part of.

**Literally, we are 'transceivers' – transmitters and receivers of energy.**

Most of this exchange is happening at a level we are not even aware of. Our emotions are a good gauge of which energies we have identified with most, which energies we are holding on to in our nervous system and which energies stimulate us most.

The central need of emotion is expression, the most important being from the soul. When we lose our connection with inner being, our feelings become trapped in the confined and superficial layers of the ego. We begin to develop an emotional body that is constructed of various energies relating to the beliefs we have collected throughout life, beliefs that are distant from our authentic self.

These energies are created largely through the conflicting vibrations we feel, arising from the contradictions we experience as we encounter people and circumstances that are disconnected from the true nature of Self. Consequently, we develop dysfunctional mechanisms to cope with the disparity we feel, which in turn only lead to more conflicting emotions. We are also taught to suppress emotions, which results in unhealthy accumulation of distorted and trapped energies.

Our inner being always feels and 'knows' what is true and authentic. Yet, from the very beginning we have been confronted with a world of mindsets that have lost touch with this deeper abiding truth. This is the very foundation of conflicting energy that all emotions are built on, leading to layers of distorted emotions. This also indicates how important a healthy and balanced mind is. Without a healthy and balanced mind we create deeper layers of unconscious behaviours and emotions. We travel further away from our authentic selves.

When we are able to express ourselves authentically, all energies we encounter flow freely and are assimilated and integrated in a healthy and conscious manner. Whatever energies are not expressed in this way become suppressed. Whatever is supressed eventually becomes distorted, perverted, dysfunctional and destructive. These energies become so deeply buried and so painful that a person does anything they can to avoid truly *feeling* his or her emotions.

As a result most people are trying to mentally solve or understand their emotions, when actually what is really needed is simply the energetic expression, the mobilisation of the feelings through breath, sound and movement. This leads to a completion, rather than a deeper validation, of energies (and the stories associated with them) that tie us to the past.

Ultimately, our emotional being needs space to be expressed authentically. In our most natural and healthy emotional state, we express freely, with conscious consideration *and* spontaneity. It is vital that we find a way to simply express our innermost feelings, not those which are bound in dysfunctional and distorted views about ourselves and life,[6] but rather those which express the beauty and harmony flowing through the soul of one's being and all things.

These feelings are exquisitely unique. No one else can ever express the true emotion of another. As Oscar Wilde said, "Be yourself; everyone else is taken." By expressing the uniqueness of your own soul, you bring the gift of yourself into the world and fulfil the true potential and beauty of your emotional being.

## Nurturing the body

First, let's explore what we mean by 'the body'.

Consciousness as energy is vibrating at different frequencies and with distinct patterns of energy. It is the presence of these energies that reveals our manifest world, what we see and experience as physical. At the sub-atomic level, particles dance in a vast field of 'formless' being. In fact, our so-called physical world is actually 99.84378 % space, or close to that! Reality is not reality as we think it to be! As Einstein famously stated, "Reality is merely an illusion, albeit a very persistent one."

At the deepest level, there are no particles. *There is no form*. Existence is more like a holographic field. Within this field all potential forms are present. From a non-particle state, waves of energy interact. At a point of interference where like vibrations cross, the wave suddenly takes on the

---

[6] These feelings do need to be expressed, too, but this is best done via breath, sound and movement (as described above) rather than by 'unleashing' them unconsciously on others. Some useful techniques are explained further on in the book.

appearance of a particle. This 'particle' is both non-form and appearing as form. Furthermore, our perception influences the form.[7] Each particle contains the expression of every other particle until it adopts a more 'fixed' state. This is very much like a hologram. If you slice any piece out of a holographic image it will still contain the *whole* image.

In the play of vibrating quantum particles, alchemy occurs. Energies combine and coalesce to draw different frequencies together into greater complexity, giving rise to the appearance of particles, from atoms to single-cell life and expanding into multi-cellular, multi-dimensional existence. As these patterns appear to adopt states, the formless nature of energy takes on that which appears as distinct form. Like a vortex in a river, our bodies vibrate at a distinct frequency, giving the appearance of something individual even though we are really one great continuum; a 'rivering' of energies.

At the smallest scale, these energies appear as distinct particles. At the largest scale, these particles vibrate in synchronicity, creating what appears as 'bodies'. In this way we see the cells of the human body as the microcosm, and the whole human organism as the macrocosm. On the other hand, in relation to the rest of life, the individual human is the microcosm, whilst the whole of earth, the galaxies and the cosmos are the macrocosm.

So, at every stage and within every aspect of our being, there is always a direct relationship between the microcosm and the macrocosm.

Understanding this is crucial to our process of regaining balance and harmony, not just at a personal level, but also at a collective level. As evidenced by quantum physics, each and every 'particle' is entangled with every other particle. *And*, each particle is inextricably the expression of the whole. We literally are the microcosm *and* the macrocosm.

**Essentially, our 'awakening' or enlightenment is not an isolated experience for the benefit of the individual. It is a process of the whole, for the evolution and wellbeing of the whole.**

Let's now explore the needs of the body.

The central need of the body is harmony. At the physical level, the body is always striving to maintain a state of equilibrium, as reflected

---

[7] If you are curious about this, search for information on 'Schrödinger's Cat'

in certain dynamic states of the body such as core temperature and pH balance. The observed human temperature range is 33.2–38.2°C (92–101°F) with 37°C being the commonly agreed average. The body's acidity and alkalinity levels vary depending on health, diet and environmental factors. In general a pH of between 6.5 and 7.5 is considered to reflect the best balance.

There are many functions of the body, all operating at known levels of balance. Disease can be gauged according to the body's (im)balance in relation to its chemistry, enzymes, minerals, fluids, temperature, oxygenation and pH. When we stray too far from balance in any of these core elements, the body immediately descends into a state of stress, creating a trail of destructive states that lead to various health issues.

Holistic health sciences such as Ayurveda and Traditional Chinese Medicine have an extensive understanding of the body's constitution(s) and what is required to maintain optimum health and wellbeing at the physical level. In principle, there are simple basics at the core of good physical health including good diet, rest, exercise and regular interaction with nature.

At the deepest core of our bodies' wellbeing is the wellbeing of our spirit. When a person experiences a sense of disconnection from his or her spirit, there is a loss of awareness. With loss of awareness, many misperceptions and limited identifications are developed, becoming the driving force behind imbalanced actions. And, significantly, a person loses sensitive awareness of the body's signals, signals that are constant cues of our deeper cellular intelligence. In a healthy, aware and connected state, a person is conscious of these signals and capable of responding to the body's needs. Without this awareness, a person makes *un*conscious choices, choices that ultimately move us away from a healthy and balanced lifestyle.

## Balancing the needs of our being

Happiness naturally arises in our lives when we feel a fundamental balance between the physical, mental, emotional and spiritual aspects of our being. When we attend to the basic needs of each of these, it is much easier to find a sense of wellbeing. We are much more likely to find that we somehow feel happier, rather than feeling conflicted and constantly trying to get to the next happy moment. As Thomas Merton said, "Happiness is not a matter of intensity but of balance, order, rhythm and harmony."

While different needs can be experienced at the same time, a certain need tends to dominate at any given time. In his 'hierarchy of needs', psychologist Abraham Maslow described these needs and the order in which they should be met.[8]

At the primary level are physiological needs such as breathing, food, water and sleep. These stem from the basic human requirements for survival and should be met first. When these basic needs are satisfied, the need for safety and security takes precedence. Once a person feels safe and secure, the focus moves to interpersonal needs such as friendship, love and intimacy. Humans need to feel a sense of belonging and acceptance within social groups at all levels, from intimate family groups to wider social connections. In some cases, the need for belonging can override physiological or security needs. The next level of need is esteem. This includes the need to feel accepted, valued and respected by others, as well as the desire for self-respect, mastery and freedom.

These four levels are what Maslow called 'deficiency needs'. If these needs are not met, the individual will suffer physically or at the very least feel anxious and stressed. Deficiency needs must be met before humans will be motivated to focus on the highest level or apex of Maslow's hierarchy: self-actualisation. This is the need to realise one's full potential. How this is perceived will vary depending on individual desires, passions and perceived purpose in life. Ultimately, however, humanity shares one common purpose: to love, to evolve and to serve the whole. In this sense, self-actualisation becomes *Self*-actualisation.

Whether consciously or unconsciously, all of these fundamental needs motivate us in varying ways. We must always be aware of the balance between all levels of our needs, not just at an individual level but also collectively. Without this our hopes for peace and wellbeing on earth seem distant. However, this knowledge does give us great hope.

Indeed we do have the knowledge, the resources and the capacity to

---

8  Abraham Maslow, *Motivation and Personality* (New York: Harper and Row, 1987), Ed.3

establish balance at each of these levels. For example, the United Nations estimates that for less than half the amount spent by the US on the war in Iraq we could provide clean water, adequate diets, sanitation services and basic education for every person on the planet.[9]

As a greater number of people step into the 'apex' of Self-actualisation, a tipping point will occur, enabling a cascading effect of compassion and care so that the basic needs of *all* living beings may be met.

YOU are essential in this shift.

---

9   John Perkins, *Confessions of an Economic Hitman* (San Francisco: Berrett Koehler Publishers, 2004).

CHAPTER 7

# PREPARING FOR TRANSFORMATION

> *If you want to become whole, let yourself be partial. If you want to become straight, let yourself be crooked. If you want to become full, let yourself be empty. If you want to be reborn, let yourself die. If you want to be given everything, give everything up.* — Lao-tzu

The peace we seek in our lives and in the world is a call for true revolution. There can't be any large-scale revolution until there's a personal revolution. That has to happen inside first.

At first, our quest for this peace seems to highlight how lost we feel and how alienated we have become. That spark of awareness tends to throw us into a painful paradox. It tells us that life is meant to be truly magical and that we recognise the divinity within us. But it also tells us that things have become terribly distorted. The more awareness we gain, the more we see our conditions. This awareness leads us to a realisation, one that is both frightening and exciting, that we must undergo radical change in order to become all that we truly can be. We must enter the great passage of transformation. We must learn how to go within.

## PREPARING FOR MEDITATION

Meditation is the practice that most clearly facilitates our inward journey. It opens us to the space in which true transformation can happen. But it doesn't always come easily. I often hear how people feel frustrated with their efforts to meditate. This is usually because they haven't learned how to create the right conditions. In order to be more conscious or attain a meditative state, two primary 'conditions' are necessary: an ability to relax, and space.

The ability to relax is utterly essential because meditation is about being centred. It's about being still yet flowing, surrendered, open and aware. So if the body is disturbed it will be very difficult to find stillness. Likewise, if the mind is very disturbed it will be difficult to find inner calm. It is for this reason that 'catharsis' is essential as a preparation before creating the space to meditate. In fact, catharsis *creates* the space that allows you to discover a deeper stillness within. Once there is enough spaciousness, meditation comes easily.

## Clearing the way

If there is too much clutter in the mind there will be too much attachment. If there is clinging in the mind, it will never allow you to settle in your being. This clinging keeps you interested in something you are not: thoughts, stored energy, emotions, beliefs and agitations. When there is no more clinging there is nowhere to go. You suddenly become aware of where you truly are, in the here and now. Then relaxation happens of its own accord.

So never try to begin the journey back into your true self by *starting* with sitting meditation. For as long as you are storing agitations there will be clinging in the mind. The body may sit still but there will be no true relaxation or stillness in your being. Actually, something worse happens. The agitations become suppressed as they have no way to move, to escape. The more you try to just sit, the more disturbances you will feel. You will only become aware of the crazy mind, as well as more frustrated, more agitated or more depressed. So first you must allow the craziness to move, to be expressed and released.

Catharsis mobilises whatever has been suppressed. If you shake and move, dance and stomp, sing, cry and scream wildly, something will really change. All of the madness will begin to move. All of the madness can be thrown out of your being. This is a very different type of releasing compared to therapies that want your mind to be involved in the show.

Most therapies reinforce the ego – the story that you are these terrible feelings and thoughts and that somehow you are a product of all the emotional baggage you carry.

If you can just allow your body and mind to shake and your spirit to cry out wildly, then gradually, simply by the motion of energy and expression, whatever has been suppressed will be set free. Whatever you are suppressing simply needs to be expressed. And, whatever is suppressed will eventually come out. If you do not consciously allow yourself this release it will break out of you in destructive and unconscious ways. Or it will create havoc internally, perhaps manifesting as a life-threatening illness. It is not a matter of *if* things will become more disturbing, it is a matter of when. It makes so much more sense to take conscious charge of releasing these distorted energies.

Most people have been suppressing so much that could have easily been released and left behind if it weren't for society's stifling rules. With more conscious education and more aware parenting we could have very different lives. With an understanding of the workings of our minds and souls, we could have been given the freedom to express, release and integrate emotions and to mature through a continual flow of our energies.

For example, when a child is angry, the parent tells him to stop, often angrily. Every time the child is told to stop being angry, the child suppresses the anger. The child also stores a conflicting message: 'I am told anger is not good or okay, but anger is controlling me'. The child sees the world is full of contradictions. Gradually and repeatedly, what were transient feelings and energies become trapped and accumulate. Something that was momentary becomes permanent. Soon the child learns to not act angry, while inside anger is always present. Which of course leads the child to either internalise anger or bust out with it whenever he or she is overwhelmed. Anger can only continue if it is suppressed. When it is not suppressed it takes on a new form and it gradually brings new awareness. It catalyses change and the emotions mature.

It is not just the emotion of anger that has been suppressed and accumulated. With so many suppressed feelings and desires – greed, jealousy, grief, fear, sexuality, shame, happiness, power, and creativity – a deep-seated madness is developed. This madness is within you. It is not because that's how creation truly is, it is not because it is who you are, it is because of a collection of unresolved energies, it is because of suppression. So if you begin with sitting meditation you will just adopt another form of suppression.

During programs I take people through a cathartic practice called 'unveiling'. It creates the opportunity for whatever energies are inside to be expressed, not at an object or for a reason but simply to allow the energies to be mobilised, expressed and released. Always, after great noise and turmoil, each person drops into a deeper space of stillness and silence. People feel more relaxed after one hour of wildness than they have felt in their whole lives.

And really, this experience is very much like life itself. There is all this noise and chaos going on at the surface, on the periphery. But deep within it, at the centre of it, is something so still and silent, something that cannot be disturbed, something that is always present. That something is who we truly are. Everything else is simply a transient flow of energies being expressed and experienced. It is only when we take on the periphery, the commotion, as if it is fixed and real, as if we *are* it that we lose touch with who we truly are, and it appears that we have lost our inner calm.

Therefore, releasing and cleansing is an effective first step. With catharsis, something beautiful can begin to flower within you again, something free, alive, natural and flowing. You will have a different quality to your being. You will discover your authentic self. And when all of the madness has been released, and you fall again into your centre, you will feel like a child again... pure, present, innocent, curious, open and filled with awe and enthusiasm for the life that you are, for the life that is.

### Dynamic catharsis

There are many ways you can practice dynamic release. No matter which you adopt, I always recommend that you start by connecting with the breath. Let your breathing become deep and full, perhaps even fast and powerful, like you are breathing yourself into a storm. You also might like to put on music that connects you with a feeling of power or wild release.

Once you feel you are connecting to the breath, simply begin moving. Let your body move wildly, however it wants to. Do not be timid or tame. Let your body shake and shudder completely. Let every part of the body throw itself into wildness. Dance, spin, stomp, clench your fists, let yourself scream, cry, rant, heave, pant, laugh... simply let go. Endeavour to keep up the commotion for at least half an hour. Forty-five minutes is a good period to aim for because you are more likely to release something deeper.

By giving yourself enough time something else will begin to happen: it will no longer be you that is thinking or doing the moving. The moving will happen itself. Whatever has been held, buried deep inside, will unleash itself. You may find the body simply winds itself out or you might want to put on a timer. When the time is up simply stop still, whatever you are doing, whether standing, sitting or lying down. Simply be present. Be aware. Watch. Experience. After a few minutes, sit or lie down and simply allow yourself to be in the space... as if everything has died to the moment.

You may remain like this for 15 minutes or half an hour; or you might find you drop into deep meditation, even for an hour. Gradually you may come out of the meditation again, and as you do, open your eyes very gently and slowly. Be fully engaged, aware of the experience. Be the seeing, feeling, listening that is simply you in the now.

Through this practice you will discover that the world appears new, as if you are seeing for the first time. Something will feel fresh. You will feel a deep calm. Make it your intention to stay present and aware of this inner calm even as you go about the rest of your day.

## ESSENTIAL ATTITUDES

As you continue your journey of transformation you will discover many challenges, because that is what comes with change! When we understand the nature of transformation we discover particular attitudes that either heighten our sense of turmoil or ease us into and through the process. There are seven essential attitudes that help us find more grace. They are: love, playfulness, patience, diligence, acceptance, not seeking results and non-attachment to the experience. Once we understand these attitudes we can even begin to see our process as fascinating and adventurous. Then the process we face is seen for what it is, a passage to the freedom we seek.

## Love

Love is the highest vibration we can experience as a human. It is the great harmoniser, the unifier. Whenever we bring our thoughts into love we are instantly brought into a greater degree of presence. This energy literally transforms us. It elevates our whole being – body, mind, emotion and spirit. Even if you struggle to feel unconditional love for yourself, by aligning your thoughts with love and making it your intention, you already connect with the energy that will reveal the perfection of yourself and life. Love will show you the way.

## Playfulness

One of the most important things that can be dropped as we prepare for transformation is seriousness. When suppressed energies are released, not only are we freed of a lot of baggage, but also a sense of humour begins to surface. We begin to see the unreal nature of what we have taken so seriously to be ourselves, and a new sense of playfulness emerges. People often mistakenly think the spiritual path or process is a serious one. But as I always say: sincere, yes, but serious, no. The spiritual path is about freeing yourself of all seriousness. The ego has given you enough of that! It is a journey of rediscovering that life itself is playful. For a truly meditative person life is an adventure, a wonder, a dance.

## Patience

Awakening does not come with a 'go home' ticket, nor does it come in a jar of instant coffee. So don't be in a hurry. You may crave awakening, you may be hungry for it, but it is important that you can accept waiting... patiently. The more deeply you surrender to the waiting, the sooner the awakening comes. Humanity forgets that everything natural takes time, just as a seed takes time to sprout, to grow, to blossom. You must work to plant the seed, but then you must leave it to nature. You may water it and tend to it, but still you must be patient and leave it to nature. When it is ready it will blossom.

With hunger there is yearning, but not struggle or force. With impatience there is struggle and force, and true yearning is lost. Awakening cannot be forced; it is encountered through surrender, not struggle. Everything essential is born from God's waiting room.

## Diligence

Although patience and surrender are required, so too is diligence. Many weeds may grow around a young sapling, and it takes diligence to keep them from strangling it. Likewise it takes diligence to keep one's attention aligned with truth. Do not let recurring thoughts from the ego continue to take root.

## Acceptance

Ironically though, as diligent as one may be, the process of developing more conscious awareness will shed light on how much 'unawareness' is occurring. It is vital this is accepted to begin with. Non-awareness simply is. It is part of the human experience and part of the journey, like being awake and going to sleep. Sleep provides renewal. So too does non-awareness. You may momentarily feel great awareness, only to feel it has submerged again into non-awareness. This is not a problem. From non-awareness awareness will also rise again.

Life is the way it is. Why does the water boil at 100°C, not 99°C? Because it does! It is simply a natural phenomenon, just like it is the nature of the mind to have thoughts, just as it is the nature of the body to feel tired at the end of the day, just as it is the nature of some people to have blue eyes instead of brown.

Interestingly, our judgmental mind is more accepting of nature than *human* nature. For example, we accept that it is the nature of the wind to blow, it is the nature of the sun to be hot and the nature of the volcano to erupt. We are much less accepting of the fact that it is also human nature to blow hot and cold. We struggle to accept that someone may be conditioned to get angry when they miss a train or explode when everything is simply too overwhelming. We may think that punching the wall and dropping a few 'F-bombs' is an overreaction, yet it is an inevitable consequence of a person's lifetime of conditioning, their genetic composition and the type of day they have had. There is no need to judge them – just watch and accept. Likewise, when you find yourself in reaction, allow yourself enough space to understand this too is a consequence of your conditioning, and give thanks that you have enough awareness to come to accept it!

It also helps to understand that every experience occurs in a field of context. This means we will always experience what appears as opposites through the flux of life. We will always encounter the ups and downs and the light and dark of life. Like waves rising and falling in the ocean, our life is given momentum. This is just the rhythm of life. Like a star resting in deep inky space, it's the darkness that allows it to shine. So it is in your life. The stage is set in each moment for you to be the experience of all you have come to discover, express, realise and fulfil. Simply allow each moment to be its own expression. So next time you find yourself in a rage, really look at it, experience your own human storm, and remember… this too shall pass.

## Do not look for results

The ego is always looking for results. The mind is driven to serve the ego's result-oriented attitude. However, awareness itself is not a result. Awareness is that which is always being. It always is, always has been and always will be. It is already its own result. True freedom comes when we are able to let go of the need for results and can instead celebrate each moment as it is.

## Do not be attached to experiences

The ego is also looking for experiences to validate its identity. Too easily spiritual seekers become trapped in the lure the ego has set, becoming addicted to the experiences that meditative being may give. However, these are still surface fluctuations. The feeling of peace or bliss may be wonderful but it is not the awakened One. Awareness is not a feeling, experience or a state. Awareness just IS. The real you *is* awareness. Although it is beautiful to cultivate more aware experiences, if we become attached to them or mistake them to be enlightenment, we still remain caught in the conditional realm of the ego.

When you can surrender all experiences, including even the most beautiful ones, there is no longer a someone or a something remaining. There is only being. As a Zen master once said: "When I heard the bell ring, suddenly there was no 'I' and no 'bell', just the ringing." Once this is attained, there is a true state of self-realisation; there is true bliss, unconditional being. From this the real essence of life can flow through us in every moment, unhindered, liberated.

There once was a student who desperately wanted to achieve enlightenment. He listened to everything the master taught, and with great serious effort applied himself to meditation every day. But after many months he still had no results. So he went to the master for advice. "Master", he said, "I try so hard, but still I feel frustration... all I feel is agitation." The Master gazed at him with a serene face and replied, "Ah my son, this shall pass."

The student took this as a message – perhaps the results were soon to come. With renewed hope he continued to sit. And to his wonder, in the following week he discovered himself in a great field of bliss. Everything took on a glow, as if lit up by a great presence of love, peace and joy. Feeling so excited and overjoyed he went to his Master to share his happiness. "Master, master... thank you! You gave me hope and now it is as if everything is alight!" The Master gazed at him with a serene face and replied... "Ah my son, this too shall pass."

Just like the master, serenity comes when we embrace and flow with all as it is. *Life* is the master. Deep calm is always present within each and every moment. Deep calm is present in the roar of the river, the cry of a bird, the volcanic eruption. Deep calm is always here, but it is only when we flow with the river, whether it is turbulent or calm, that we know it. Awareness too is always here. And it is when we engage with this greater aware self that we can flow with life this way.

Then we discover what the Zen masters call 'wu-wei'. This is one of the most important Taoist teachings, which sometimes translates as 'non-doing' or 'non-action'. But really it is more of a paradox; it is the 'action' of 'non-action'. Wu-wei refers to the nature of life as it is, and the practice of relaxing into this. It invites us to align our actions effortlessly with the ebb and flow of the elemental cycles of the natural world. It is 'going with the flow' that is characterized by great ease and wakefulness. In this state, without even trying, we're able to respond perfectly to whatever situations arise.

This is the very nature of awareness. It is simply being, knowing, responding. If you find a scorpion in your hand, you will naturally let it go. Awareness will see you quickly but gently place the scorpion on the ground with compassion and walk away. However, if the scorpion runs towards a small baby with its tail raised, ready to strike, awareness may see you stamp very hard on the scorpion. The mind does not enter to cogitate on the right thing to do: "I believe in non-violence so I don't want to hurt the scorpion, but a raised tail is usually a sign of aggression… Hmmm, what a dilemma…" With awareness there is simply a natural, intelligent, effortless response. The same is true when you realise you are holding onto beliefs that do not help you. Awareness does not need rules or teachers or beliefs. Awareness already contains wisdom, intelligence and love.

Even Christopher Robin from Winnie-the-Pooh had this wu-wei worked out.

"What I like doing best is Nothing."

"How do you do Nothing?" asked Pooh after he had wondered for a long time. "Well, it's when people call out at you just as you're going off to do it, 'What are you going to do, Christopher Robin?' and you say, 'Oh, Nothing,' and then you go and do it. It means just going along, listening to all the things you can't hear, and not bothering."

"Oh!" said Pooh.

## The Conscious Habits

**Peace and liberation are found not by rearranging the circumstances of your life, but by realising who you are at the deepest level.**

However, here is the paradox: Although everything is perfect as it is, we are so deeply entangled in unconscious beliefs and habits that a process *is* required for us to open and relax again, to become wu-wei. In order to do this, it is important we *do* re-arrange our habits.

It is through habits that we continue to live a life that is largely entangled and unconscious. Because our fears and beliefs are habitual, we need tools that are able to bring about a shift and create a new experience. Most people continue to blame life, as if the world is the problem when actually the only 'problem' is a lack of awareness. This is a truth that is stacked with potential. It means we really are not bound by 'problems' in the way we have been imagining. It means we all have the ability to elevate our lives.

Whilst the nature of deep-seated unconscious habits can make this look like a difficult task, the good news is this: There are definite habits we can adopt that realign us with our most authentic, aware, present and flowing Self.

In the following chapters I will outline the seven 'conscious habits': *Breathing, Meditation, Being Centred, Flowing with Energy, Witnessing, Self-Reflection and Being in the Now.* You will discover how easily you can adapt to these habits and how they will make your conscious experience of true Self a greater reality.

Each chapter will give you a depth of understanding about the most important behaviours and practices that will aid you in living a conscious life. Once you understand these core behaviours you will discover how easily they become a natural part of your daily living, enabling you to create a more sustainable quality of true presence in your life. In fact, you will recognise that the behaviours underlying the 'conscious habits' are a natural part of your being. These habits are available to all of us. They are found in the very fabric of our ordinary humanness. And, as we apply ourselves to more conscious habits, we discover we are much more than we thought we were.

We truly are powerful in ways we never dreamed of. What lies within us is nothing less than astonishing. Indeed, we are capable of living lives of great peace, wellness, love and purpose. We are capable of bringing our true Self into the world, and in doing so, creating harmony and peace for the world as a whole.

CHAPTER 8

# BREATHING

### Conscious Habit I

*I know of no more encouraging fact than the unquestionable ability of man to elevate his life by conscious endeavor.*
— *Henry David Thoreau*

Correct breathing has been at the centre of every liberated person's conscious habits. It is the very foundation from which all awareness, balance, healing, transformation and awakening emerges. As we deepen in awareness with our breathing we elevate our consciousness. Mastering our breath opens us to greater and greater presence. Remember, there is no rush... the process of awakening is a journey.

### Why breathing?

Breathing is something we all have the ability to master. We all breathe. Correct breathing is important for many reasons. To begin with, breathing is constant, always flowing in the here and now. As such, it aids in anchoring us more deeply into the living presence of the now. This is where true freedom is realised and where reality may be experienced directly as it is, free of the ego or unconscious habits that disturb our connection with the pure nature of existence.

Try losing yourself in consciously flowing with your own breath as it rises and falls, and you will enter a different state of being. Keep it up for a while and the very sense of your being shifts significantly. Breath is a source of life. It maintains our life force and revitalizes our life energy. Consequently it contains the power of transformation. This applies at a physiological level as well as at emotional and spiritual levels. Breathing is integral to the balance, flow and transition of all energy within our body/mind/spirit.

Furthermore, breath has no opinions! Breath has no thought form, so when we are centred in it, thinking slows down. Breathing is purely a flow of energy and therefore enormously significant as a tool for us to go beyond the conditioned mind. When we centre in our breath, we rest into awareness rather than occupying thoughts. Breath draws us into the silent realm. It enables us to let go and to let in.

The more we rest into breathing, the more deeply our physiology changes into a rhythm that matches the vibration of deep awareness and open-heart presence. This is incredibly significant, because it's all about the energy. Try losing yourself for a while in the lightness of just watching your breath flowing in and out, and you will discover that the very nature of the moment changes quality. The sense of time, form and boundaries slide into edgeless, seamless being. You discover there is great roominess in your being after all.

Our ability to live life consciously, with power or joy, is dependent on the energy we are vibrating and the degree of openness we rest in. When we are vibrating in the energy of the mind we are confined and incapable of living our greatest qualities or experiencing our liberated nature. When we are vibrating in the energy of deep, open life force we are capable of things beyond our imagination. As we exercise more conscious breathing we can have the true experience and realisation of absolute oneness. Furthermore, we can develop the way to tap into universal consciousness and unleash potent creative energy. We can unveil intelligence we never dreamed of and cultivate a life that is not only successful but also based in enlightened consciousness and freedom.

Breath is the interface between our formless, expansive, eternal Self and our individual self as the living expression of energy. This is a very important key, helping us to develop a more conscious understanding of life as form (manifest levels) and formlessness (consciousness, thought and pure awareness). The more we merge with the breath, the more we can be present to and realise our formless Self; that which is eternal, infinite, ceaseless, life flow.

Breath, which is drawn from space, the formless dimension, carries within it life force that contributes, directs, channels and manifests energy at the level of form. Scientists are now finding that most of the universe consists not only of dark matter, but of dark energy, something they struggle to explain or comprehend. Yet it has been known by various masters and geniuses throughout history that this so called 'dark energy' is the very essence and energy of the entire universe. It is this energy that is the conductor and connector of all things. Breath, and what we breathe, is very much like this. It appears vacuous yet it contains elemental life. It connects the microcosm and the macrocosm.

The more deeply we explore this the more we gain an aware experience of the true nature of our being and the universe. We are drawn into the source from which we have come. We release ourselves from the confined illusion of our reality being something fixed. We realise that in actuality all form is transient and without any true substance yet never ceases or vanishes. We encounter the deepest level of truth: *Rupa eva shunyam, shunyam eva rupa*.[10] Form is emptiness and emptiness is form.

Physiologically speaking, breath is the pivotal gauge of all awakening practices, and integral to all transformation and integration. It is the pivotal point at which we shift to a different state. Why? Because breathing literally adjusts our physiology and brainwave patterns. Specific breathing techniques provide the right environment of brainwave activity and nervous response to see and feel from a deeper and more expanded state of awareness. Breathing has the power to alter every state of our being, corresponding directly with our different states of consciousness, and is integral to the release of mental, emotional and physical toxicity.

Essentially, breathing is a rhythmic activity. Normally a person at rest takes around 16 to 17 breaths a minute. The rate is higher in infants and in states of excitation, and less during sleep and in states of depression. The depth of the respiratory wave also varies with emotional states. When you are in your mind, in your ego identity, your breathing is shallow and

---

10 A Sanskrit verse to describe the non-dualistic nature of form and formlessness – they are the one same being.

erratic. When you are in your 'stories' and unconscious feedback loops, what happens to your breath? It becomes constricted, erratic and very shallow. You even hold on to it. Breathing becomes shallow when we are frightened or anxious. It deepens with relaxation, pleasure and sleep.

Unconscious thoughts and habits build up as energy in the body and come to characterise our physical and emotional nature. The body is a storehouse of the patterns of energy we occupy in each moment. And, remember, what you dwell on in the mind grows in your experience. *Which wolf are you feeding?*

Generally speaking, the left part of our brain is basically our filing system. Like a computer database, information is stored and utilised as we interact with life. Due to habit most people follow the same developed mental and emotional pathways over and over again. Essentially, most people have been operating with a lot of unconscious thoughts and habits for a long time, simply running on default.

The body's cellular field has been built up around the patterns of stored thoughts and habits held at the unconscious level, including our breathing. To most people, shallow, erratic breathing feels normal and natural. In fact, the task of breathing more deeply or in specific rhythms can create a feeling of great discomfort, sometimes feeling unnatural or like effort. This can seem contradictory to the intention of 'just allowing'.

However, we must understand that we are experiencing the bodymind *as it is*, in a developed pattern. If you, at this level, are already in a pattern of limitation and conflict and you apply the notion of simply 'letting it be'… what is going to happen, what's going to continue? The same pattern!

It's important to understand that there is a required balance between surrender (or letting be) and the determination to transform. Application of dynamic activity is required in order *to move beyond* habituated patterns and states. This is essential to raise your energy field and shift to a different vibration, and to unleash the experience of your true, liberated self. It's also why a 'teacher' is so relevant. The teacher will 'expect' (without attachment!) a whole lot more of you than you expect of yourself, because they see and know your greater potential.

For true progress it is important to apply habits known to be successful, in other words, the same habits adopted by people who have demonstrated mastery and liberation. Remember, new habits do take time to be established. It is well worth spending time improving breathing skills before hoping to gain deeper meditative states, because it is the breath itself that will open the door to the space of deeper awareness.

Remember that breathing is completely natural and really very simple, yet it is also incredibly powerful. When you get your breathing right it does the work for you! Really, you won't need to try very hard to enter into deeper meditative states once you master your breathing. The following techniques are quite simple, yet very effective.

## Deep diaphragm breathing

This is a good place to start because it will help you to relax and go deeper with your breathing. Make sure you are seated comfortably with the spine upright.

Close your eyes and take three deep full breaths, in through your nose and out through your mouth. Attune to your body. Relax your shoulders; feel them drop away from your ears. Relax the face, feel the jaw soften, the eyes softly closed, the mouth relaxed. Let the tongue rest at the roof of the mouth behind the front teeth. Now feel your chest and run your fingers down the middle of your rib cage. Feel the sternum and then touch the hollow beneath the sternum. Feel your breath expanding through your rib cage, flowing like soothing light. Feel it softening your chest until you feel your whole diaphragm relax.

Centre your awareness in the diaphragm and bring your attention to your breath. Feel it rising and falling gently. As you breathe in, the abdomen expands – like a balloon filling up with air. As you breathe out, the abdomen empties. Keep your attention relaxed and centred in this way with gentle breathing for a few minutes.

When you feel you are softening and relaxing more, let your breathing deepen, but not forcefully. As you breathe deeply, feel your diaphragm and abdomen expand. Relax as you let yourself rest deeper and deeper into the energy and flow of the breath itself. Feel its lightness and ease. Notice tension melting away as you simply let yourself rest into the softness of your breath. Gradually expand the space of your breathing until you can feel yourself breathing through your whole chest, abdomen and through the back. After 15 minutes, or when you feel deeply calm and nourished by the breathing, take a deep breath into your whole body, stretch and open your eyes. Endeavour to maintain deep aware breathing throughout the rest of your day.

## Nose-tip breathing

This method is essential to develop powers of concentration, which aids in mastery over the mind – one of the most important things to achieve along the path to liberated being. Without it, most people remain a slave to the mind and its unconscious habits.

Again, centre and relax as outlined above. Bring your attention to the tip of your nose and focus your awareness on the breath as it flows in and out. Simply keep your awareness centred at the tip of your nose as you breathe deeply in a gentle and slow rhythm. If you notice your mind has wandered, simply bring your attention back to the tip of your nose and the flow of breath again. The goal is to be able to maintain aware breathing at the tip of the nose for 15 continuous minutes. Keep a small clock close by to gauge your practice. If you notice a distraction simply note the time and begin your focus again, each time having the goal to maintain the focus at the tip of the nose for 15 minutes.

Don't be disheartened by the degree of distraction that can occur when you first start this practice. When I first started, I was shocked to find that I would be wandering off in some other direction every 30 seconds! I wondered if I would ever achieve the 15 minute goal, but with consistent practice and focus I achieved it, and along with it an incredible feeling of elation. Not only that, I noticed how powerfully it translated into every other area of my life. My ability to focus and stay clear increased dramatically. This practice also has the benefit of slowing down mental activity whilst sharpening mental clarity.

## Alpha breathing

Next you may consider a foundational practice of breathing, one that supports and leads further into other breathing and meditative abilities. I particularly emphasise the use of a technique I call 'alpha breathing', based on a flow of breathing in to the count of four and out to the count of six. I discovered this when I was very young.

I used to pay very close attention to my energy states, especially before going to sleep. As I watched I was able to literally feel and see the body fall asleep whilst 'I' was still awake. In this state I discovered a very particular breathing rhythm that naturally takes over as body-mind consciousness moves into the most relaxed phase on the edge of sleep, and which corresponds with the alpha brain wave state and meditation.

Alpha breathing is so effective because it creates a very easy and fast shift into deeper brain wave activity of alpha and theta, both frequencies that correspond with meditative being. These frequencies quickly shift and release agitation, leading to a state of calm without much effort involved.

Habits held at the unconscious level, including depth and rate of breathing, have particular vibrations and frequencies. Given that your field is already holding various unconscious patterns it is very important to clear and transform this. The reason most unconscious habits and energies are stored in a way that still affects you is because you haven't yet mastered the art of letting go. The mind is an instrument that holds onto things, it boxes things and stores them. You hold onto your emotions, your beliefs, your past. You hold on to that which is not truly real.

Breathing, on the other hand, particularly in specific rhythms such as alpha breathing, catalyzes an emptying out. This is very important because you must start clearing out accumulated energy for a greater power and consciousness to be able to flow through you and for this to be integrated. It is also vital that we have a clear space in our being if we want to experience our true nature as that which it really is... as oneness, love, infinite power, awareness and freedom.

When you breathe deeply enough, at the correct capacity, whatever is blocked will begin to be dislodged. Whatever is tight and contracted will be stretched. When you breathe out with a longer, slower rhythm, the debris of blocked energy can be emptied out more fully.

Do you notice times in your day where you really have to go "Aaaahhhhh!" and take a big sigh? Why? Because you are not in the conscious habit of emptying or releasing stored energy from your field. The spontaneous sigh is an unconscious response to that need. Imagine then how much more is stored and blocked that is not being dealt with, that needs to be released consciously.

What would happen if you didn't take a proper poop every day? Your body would be pretty full of crap! In fact it would become so toxic you would most likely die. Likewise, your energy field is doing the same thing. Your breathing is one of the most important mechanisms for releasing waste, that which is no longer of purpose to your moment of now. Breathing helps you to consciously clear unnecessary emotional baggage, and alpha breathing is one of the most effective methods for this purpose.

Why the odd count? The usual pattern of breath corresponding with the busy mind is shallow, contracted and erratic. Likewise, the energy is shallow and contracted in the cells, nervous system and aura. This means there is a lot of toxic accumulation. A slower out-breath creates a deeper release pattern, allowing stored and blocked energy to be released from the system. This rhythm also works on slowing down the mental vibration, and in turn our physiology, taking us into a deeper current of calm awareness. It also stimulates the parasympathetic nervous system, which activates renewal and creates an open state of mind.

In an active mental state we most typically operate with beta brain waves. The alpha breathing rhythm slows the brain waves down to alpha and theta frequencies, both associated with witnessing awareness and meditative abilities. At this level we also begin to create entrainment, a balance between left and right brain activity.

With more regular practice this breathing rhythm also creates a total shift into a much higher calibration: gamma brain wave. This state unleashes extraordinary levels of creative inspiration, insights and states of satori.[11] The gamma state also corresponds with saturated feelings of compassion and bliss.

After mastering this rhythm for some time you might want to extend the rate of the breathing rhythm. I worked my way up to a deeper, slower rhythm of breathing in to eight and out to thirteen. Alternatively, if you find you have a very shallow breathing capacity you can start with a

---

[11] Encounters of the pure conscious realm which usually ignite profound epiphanies, recollection of the eternal Self and states of 'God-awareness'

shorter rhythm of in three and out five. Once you establish a very deep state of clear conscious presence your breath will naturally adjust itself, usually into a very steady, even rhythm.

I do not recommend an even counting rhythm of breathing as the basis to get to a deeper level. 'Even breathing' rhythms tend to hold us at the level we are generally occupying and inhibit the ability to go much deeper. Generally it will take a lot longer to get to a deeper state of awareness by starting with even rhythm breathing.

## Practicing alpha breathing

Begin with sitting in a comfortable and balanced position. The spine must be upright for the *prana* (breath/energy) to flow clearly. Start with your attention at the tip of the nose to bring your full concentration into the breath. Feel the breath flowing in and out through the nose.

Now, consciously keep your attention aligned with the flow of breath as you breathe in through the nose to the count of four and out through the nose to the count of six. It is important there is no tension in your breathing and no pause between the in and out breath. Just let it flow in and out, like a wave coming in to the shore and drawing back out to the ocean.

Once you feel the rhythm is established you no longer need to focus on counting. Simply let yourself rest into the rhythm and flow of the rising and falling breath. Continue this way until you feel deeply relaxed. Let it be your intention that you become completely at one with the breath. With each breath allow yourself to rest deeper and deeper until you feel at rest in the depths of your lower abdomen, as if you are breathing from a deep ocean.

I recommend a minimum of thirty minutes in order to establish a true physiological shift into deeper states of calm. It is natural that you can achieve a state of calm meditation very quickly with this breathing method, however, the real benefits are revealed when you are able to hold a more sustained state. I cannot over-emphasise how powerful the alpha breathing method is as a tool and habit for enlightened being.

The teaching of breathing is so essential because it connects us with our own process. Oftentimes we are so caught up in the idea of peace or enlightenment that we overlook the fact that it is hiding, waiting for us to take up the dance in our very own being. The following is a wonderful Zen story that reminds us how fundamental breathing is, not just for our enlightening, but to the very life we are. It is only when we embrace this that we can truly wake up.

One day a student goes to the Master and tells him, "I'm getting really bored with just feeling my breath coming in and going out all the time. Don't you have a meditation that is more exciting?" The Zen Master replied, "Yes. You are now ready for a greater teaching. Follow me." With that, the Master led the student into a courtyard where there was a large barrel of water. "Gaze into the barrel," said the Master.

As the student leaned over and looked in, the Zen Master suddenly pushed the student's head into the water. The Master was quite strong, and he was able to hold the student under the water for quite a while, even though the student struggled desperately. Finally, the Master let the student come up for air, and as the student gasped the Master asked, "So... is *that* breath boring?"

Breathing is one of those things in life that we can call 'nothing special'. However, when we purposely pay attention to the breath, it becomes something *very* special. When we devote attention to the breath, we are capable of being truly devoted to life, to our being. Only then might we discover that the very thing we seek has hidden itself in the most obvious place...

CHAPTER 9

# MEDITATION

CONSCIOUS HABIT 2

*Meditation is the dissolution of thoughts in Eternal awareness or Pure consciousness without objectification, knowing without thinking, merging finitude in infinity.* —Voltaire

Meditation in the truest sense is a state of being rather than an exercise. It is the state of being centred and aware. In this state consciousness remains clear, uninterrupted by any mental activity or egoic identity. However this state is not something readily experienced or acquired by most people. Due to a great amount of conditioning, it usually unfolds only after a process of re-orienting our attention and physiology.

Given that meditation is a state of consciousness, it is also a way of life. Practices or techniques that cultivate a meditative state must become an integral part of daily living. Unless such activities become our most essential habits, the results remain elusive. Most of our life experiences are built upon habit. It takes practice and repetition before a new behaviour is fully adopted or integrated into our lives.

'Meditation' translates as 'a cessation of the thought process'. This describes a state of consciousness whereby the mind is free of scattered thoughts. As we enter deeper meditation, our prior occupation with thoughts and ego identity begins to dissolve. A greater distancing of mental identifications arises until there is no longer any belief in the mental construct as being something substantial or real. This itself is the state of liberation: *a cessation of identification with the mind.*

However, enlightenment involves a deeper passage of integration with boundless consciousness, giving rise to states of oneness, not merely as satoris but rather as ongoing embodied states of being.

## The science of meditation

In recent years there has been a great amount of scientific research into the effects and benefits of meditation. In particular, the field of neurology has uncovered some distinct and direct links between meditation, brain wave activity and behavioural states.

Various studies measuring brain wave activity of meditation practitioners have found that meditative states have a direct correlation to brain wave activity.[12] In particular, alpha, theta and gamma activity becomes heightened and prolonged through regular practice. Each of these brain wave states is associated with relaxation, peace, resilience, cognitive re-appraisal (changing negative impressions into neutral or positive ones), emotional balance, deeper awareness and creative capacity. The previous chapter touched on some of these states in the description of 'alpha breathing'.

Like all energy waves, brain waves have a frequency, measured in cycles per second or hertz (Hz). A lower hertz represents a slower wave. Brain waves are categorized by their frequency. In general there are five main brain waves known to science: alpha, beta, theta, delta and gamma.

Beta brain waves, measured at 13-40 Hz, are the state of our normal waking consciousness. Nearly all forms of action, thinking, and problem solving are done with a beta brain wave. Most people spend the majority of their waking lives in a beta state, a defensive and reactive state in which the mind is often in the fight-flight mode. Consequently, they experience heightened degrees of agitation or stress and often find it very difficult to 'switch off' or address conflict and challenges effectively.

Alpha brain waves, measured at 7-13 Hz, are the brain state of relaxation and meditation, occurring predominantly during wakeful relaxation with closed eyes. Given the alpha wave's connection with relaxed mental

---

[12] Brain waves, electrical activity in the brain, can be measured by a device known as an electroencephalogram (EEG).

states, we can understand the direct relationship with meditation. The alpha state is also associated with creativity and receptive 'super-learning', where the brain learns at a faster and deeper level than it does in beta. In fact it is very easy to absorb and store information when in a relaxed alpha state. More serotonin is released, aiding in regulation of learning, moods and restfulness. Most meditation and healing methods utilise an alpha brain wave for relaxation, transformation and attaining deeper states of awareness.

Theta brain waves, measured at 4-7 Hz, are the brain state of REM sleep,[13] hypnosis, lucid dreaming, and the barely conscious state just before sleeping and just after waking. Theta is the border between the conscious and the subconscious world, so by learning to use a conscious, waking theta brain wave, we can access and influence the powerful subconscious part of ourselves that is normally inaccessible to our waking minds. This is a significant factor behind the powerful effect of hypnosis, and the primary reason it works for conditions most people find difficult to resolve through their own conscious means.

While in the theta state, the mind is capable of deep and profound learning, healing, transformation (such as cognitive re-appraisal) and growth. In this state, the parasympathetic nervous system response is more stable and the ability to overcome bias may be greatly improved.[14] This is also the brain wave in which our minds can connect to the 'divine' or super-conscious Self to access greater insights and transcendental states.

Delta brain waves, measured at less than 4 Hz, are primarily known as the brain state of deep sleep and unconsciousness. However, this state also corresponds with some of the deepest meditation states such as *nirvikalpa-samadhi*, a state of pure awareness in which identification with an 'I' has dissolved, and there is no mind; there is only infinite peace and bliss.

Gamma brain waves, measured at 40+ Hz, are the brain state of 'whole-brain' activity,[15] super-learning, higher perception (epiphany) and integration of sensory input. This particular brain wave is predominant

---
13  REM stands for 'rapid eye movement'. Dreams generally occur in this stage of sleep.
14  See research papers by Michael Frank, et al, for The National Institute for Mental Health, USA.
15  'Whole brain activity' refers to high levels of integrated learning and activity between left and right brain hemispheres.

with compassionate meditation practices, such as meditating on love and wellness for all beings. It also occurs with seasoned meditation practitioners when meditation is mastered and becomes a more enduring state. Gamma brain waves also correspond with physiological or neurological shock, such as during a car accident, when time seems to slow down. In a high gamma state a person is able to respond in ways that seem paranormal.

Ultimately, science is much closer to understanding the real value of meditation, mindfulness and compassion. So if it is logic you need to be able to take the next step, then you are well supported. There is plenty of scientific data to back up the powerful benefits of meditation!

## The benefits of meditation

Aside from the ultimate goal of liberation and enlightenment, meditation can bring us a variety of great benefits along the way, all of which lead to a more liberated life. Following are some of the benefits that daily meditation provides.

### Stress reduction and resilience

Meditation helps in reducing stress and also increases our resilience to stressful circumstances, by teaching us to switch off from and rise above the worries that can plague us through the day. Spending 15 minutes quieting the mind and focusing on the present moment makes us more relaxed and effective decision makers. Meditation techniques adjust our physiology in ways that directly reduce stress. Slowing down brain wave activity and adjusting brain chemistry increases serotonin levels, positively influencing mood and behaviour, and switches on endorphins, easing the nervous system and improving healing responses.[16]

In fact it is proven that meditation stimulates the parasympathetic nervous system, creating significant positive physiological and emotional changes. Stress, on the other hand, activates the sympathetic nervous system and triggers an ongoing flow of cortisol into the blood stream,[17] diminishing immune system function and inhibiting neurogenesis.[18]

---

[16] Endorphins are the hormones that give us nice feelings, like euphoria or the glow of being in love.
[17] Cortisol is a steroid hormone that is released in response to stress.
[18] Neurogenesis refers to the growth of new neural tissue.

Chronic stress causes the body to adopt a defensive mode and also results in perceptual, cognitive and emotional impairment. To change this we must be able to stimulate the parasympathetic nervous system, which allows for renewal.

By activating the parasympathetic nervous system through meditation, you feel warmer, your blood pressure and pulse rate drop, and your breathing slows down and gets deeper. You also engage your immune system to its fullest capability. Your body rebuilds itself neurologically and you become healthier and more open to new ideas, emotions, people and situations (especially if they are different). You also become more open to learning, adaptation and change.

### Health benefits

There is a growing awareness of the link between our state of mind and physical health. Numerous studies have shown that meditation produces great health benefits. Many of these benefits are related to the decrease in stress that occurs through meditation. It is also well understood that many, if not all, physical ailments are symptoms of inner turmoil.

Meditation can give us peace of mind and change our physiologies, which prevents and cures many stress-related ailments. For example, with lower levels of stress and anxiety, the probability of psychological disorders and heart disease diminishes significantly. Meditation has also been shown to relieve pain associated with certain illnesses and to improve immune response. With a well-established habit of daily meditation, even terminal illnesses have been totally cured.

### Mastery of thoughts

The Buddha was asked, "What have you gained from Meditation?" He replied, "Nothing."

"However", Buddha said, "let me tell you what I lost: anger, anxiety, depression, insecurity, fear of old age and death."

Humankind has conquered space, Mount Everest and numerous other challenges, but are we able to conquer our own minds? How often do you find yourself victim to your own negative thoughts? Some people feel it is impossible to control their thoughts. The art of meditation teaches that it is not only possible to control our thoughts, but to learn to transcend them completely. Through meditation we can bring our unruly minds under control. By mastering our own minds we immediately attain a new level of empowerment. Not only does this liberate us from feelings of failure or inability, it brings peace of mind and enables us to achieve our greatest potential.

The Dalai Lama was once asked why he didn't feel angry that China had taken his country from his people. He replied, "They might have taken our home, but why would I let them take my mind too?"

## Concentration

Be it in work, sport or music, concentration is essential to fulfil our potential. There is a great power in one-pointed concentration. Our energy becomes focussed and harnessed rather than dissipated. With concentration we can do more in less time, and do it more efficiently and with better results.

Through meditation we gradually improve our powers of concentration, which can be used positively in every area of our lives. Increased brain wave coherence is also developed. Greater communication between the two brain hemispheres increases one's perceptual ability and motor performance, supports the growth of higher intelligence, and slows down mental aging.

## Non-attachment

When we live in the mind it is easy to get distracted by small irritations. For example, we may find it intolerable to be kept waiting in a line, or the small misdemeanour of another person upsets us. The solution is not to avoid these minor problems, because life will always present these, but *to expand our ability to be unperturbed by life's conditions.*

The most effective solution is to develop non-attachment and keep things in perspective. Meditation supports us to detach ourselves from insignificant yet irritating thoughts. This non-attachment is not indifference; it is just that we are able to maintain equanimity in the midst of life's inevitable turbulence. It is also the ability to recognise that the conditions themselves have been less of a disturbance than the way our minds have reacted.

With this recognition comes a deeper sense of freedom (non-attachment) and peace. We feel liberated from our frustrations about circumstantial factors that were really just a product of our minds' conditions. Hence, meditation is said to give us the power of freedom. To be in the middle of a storm, or the middle of a chaotic city, and still feel peace is a profound gift that is available to each of us. We just need to create the habit of meditation in our lives.

### Spontaneity and creativity

When we live in the thinking mind, we are usually preoccupied with the past or future. When we spend our energy regurgitating the past or worrying about the future, we inhibit our natural spontaneity and creativity. We may feel we lack creativity or spontaneity, but if we can learn to silence the mind, we discover that we have far more potential than we currently realise or have ever known. To access this source of inspiration, we just need to quiet the mind.

Some of our greatest inventors and scientists were able to make important discoveries when they could absorb themselves in their work to the exclusion of all else. Most of our greatest potential lies dormant, not because it is lacking, but because it has not been accessed. By helping us live in the current moment, meditation enables us to unlock this creative potential. Liberation and enlightenment are not just about transcending life as we have known it or re-awakening to our 'God-Self', they are very much about living our highest qualities and potential... fully... here.

### Happiness and peace of mind

Is there anybody who does not, in some way, seek happiness? Meditation takes us to the source of happiness, which is to be found in our own peace of mind. If we have no peace of mind and are constantly plagued by negative thoughts, happiness will remain elusive no matter how outwardly successful we are. It is perhaps hard to imagine that happiness can occur from the simple act of being. However, if we can meditate with a still mind, we will discover an unexpected source of happiness within our own being.

**Meditation shows us that happiness is not dependent on outer circumstances but on our inner attitude.**

## Discovering the purpose of life

Although many people do feel a sense of fulfilment or success in their lives, most would recognise that underneath the surface of life is a deeper yearning, as if something 'more' is missing. If you recognise this yearning, if you feel empty inside, if you aspire to know more about the nature of existence, life and yourself, then meditation can be a great ally. Usually we look for meaning in life through external events and other people. Yet all of these things remain subjective and subject to change, and therefore leave us feeling unsure and insecure.

Meditation shows us that we can gain a greater understanding of life through knowing *who we truly are*. Through meditation we gain a new perspective on life, untainted by our own egoistic perspective. We also transcend our fears, which for the most part are unsubstantiated and pointless. By gaining a more awakened awareness about the true nature of life and ourselves, we attain a greater sense of power, freedom and release from our own imaginary limitations. If we enter the meditative state often enough, we walk through the doorway of the mind to find the true answers to the deeper questions such as "Who or *what* am I?"

## Silence

Think of meditation and most people think of silencing the mind. Whilst this is true to a certain degree, the goal of silencing the mind can become an obstacle in itself. This is largely due to a misperception that all thinking must cease and that meditation is a state in which all is completely absent of noise. This tends to lean people towards a great effort, driving themselves mad by thinking, "Stop thinking, stop thinking!" It is madness because there is a constant fight against the nature of the mind. Instead of creating calm, it keeps the mind very busy!

Yes, it is true that with correct meditation techniques the mind becomes calmer and quieter, and the quieter the mind is, the more clearly we can experience the true nature of our being and life. Yet the silence occurs not because we eradicate something. It occurs because we let go of the fight. We give up the *identification* with thoughts. We no longer resist whatever is occurring within us or around us. This means that thoughts can come and go, sounds can come and go; yet we are simply present and aware without the interruption of conjecture.

In fact, if we really look at what silence is, we discover it is a quality of wholeness. Just like white is the sum totality of all colours; silence is the sum totality of all sounds. White is the unified essence of every colour. Silence is the unified essence of all sounds. It is the dimension of being in which there is no longer distinction. So to encounter this dimension we need to be willing to allow all sounds to simply be as they are. When we allow our minds to simply be as they are, something incredibly surprising happens… the mind becomes silent.

## Beginning a meditation practice

The benefits of meditation are real, but mediation requires perseverance. It is a mistake to expect all these benefits in the first few attempts; the mind takes time to tame. Also, it is difficult to explain all the benefits of meditation, because meditation involves a state of consciousness and being that is beyond words and concepts. As the author Herman Hesse famously said, "Knowledge can be communicated, but not wisdom. One can find it, live it, do wonders through it, but one cannot communicate and teach it."

Indeed, meditation paves the way for our own inherent wisdom to be realised. To appreciate the benefits of meditation it is essential to meditate yourself, to make it a habit, a way of life. You can use the attunements as well as various other methods I describe throughout the book to practice daily meditation. You may find one method more appealing than another. What matters is that it helps you centre into a place of quiet awareness and that you aim for half an hour. Any less than this and you will not really create enough space to enter a good meditative state. As a start, I most strongly recommend the nose-tip breathing or alpha breathing practices described in the previous chapter.

Meditation fosters qualities that increase composure and the ability to act in considered and constructive ways. Gradually a stable, more balanced personality is developed and greater purity of character is acquired. But the most significant benefit is the feeling of greater liberation and empowerment. This is where the deeper value of meditation lies. It leads us to that which is within, to the truth, awareness and love, which is transcendent of the conditioned life we live.

CHAPTER 10

# BEING CENTRED

CONSCIOUS HABIT 3

*You believe happiness to be derived from the place in which once you have been happy, but in truth it is centred in ourselves.* —Franz Schubert

If we are centred in our being, allowing ourselves to experience life from a centred state, we experience two things. Firstly, we experience our own true, authentic nature, which is peaceful, unattached, curious, present and aware. These qualities constitute the natural state of happiness, which is unconditional and remains undisturbed by circumstances. Secondly, we experience the true nature of what is occurring and embrace it for what it is, free of attachment or aversion. We are able to see and experience the fullness, the beauty and the wholeness of life in the ever-present moment, flowing freely. We are free of judgments and therefore encounter life as perfect, simply as it is.

The combination of these two unconditional states, our inner orientation and our response to outer circumstances, results in a unified state. This gives rise to a more constant feeling of true happiness, even bliss. It is the consistency we have been seeking. By being centred within our being, within the moment, we are even able to live in a 'permanent' state of happiness. Inner connection enables us to maintain and cultivate some of the most desirable attributes in our lives. By being more centred we can:

- Develop and maintain deeper awareness of our being *and* the world around us.
- Stay connected with our authentic self and purpose, and with life as a whole.
- Think and act with composure and equipoise.
- Stay attuned to a deeper source of wisdom and operate with heightened intuition.
- Be present as love consciousness.
- Stay more deeply present in the *now* and enjoy each moment.
- Lose interest in judgments, dramatising, worrying and over-interpreting life or others.
- Allow things to simply unfold rather than resist or manipulate.
- Access higher creative energy and intelligence.
- Sustain a state of peace and happiness, irrespective of circumstances.
- Maintain a state of harmony – physically, mentally, emotionally and spiritually.
- Feel true contentment and smile more

Naturally, the more we embody these attributes, the more we experience our enlightened Self.

## INNER CONNECTION

For many people the notion of sitting still and simply being seems pointless, boring and un-productive. However *the degree to which we have an inner connection dramatically reflects the degree of our happiness*, effectiveness and fulfilment in all areas of our lives. It is in simply 'being' – sitting still and resting into our inward silent space – that we develop a deeper inner connection.

When you lose touch with inner stillness, you lose touch with yourself. When you lose touch with yourself, you lose yourself in the world... you wander aimlessly, looking for a place to belong, to feel safe, to call home. When you are not in your centre, it's as if the light is off. You live in a perpetual world of fog and darkness. In fact, you come to fear the very thing that will liberate you – the light of consciousness.

As Plato said, "We can easily forgive a child who is afraid of the dark; the real tragedy of life is when men are afraid of the light." Does this mean we can ask the darkness to disappear? No. But we can ask the light to appear. Darkness will always be... *and*... we can turn on the light.

**The truth is, the only way to see beyond your darkness is to be set alight by your inner sun.**

And for this to happen you need to be in your centre, connected with your innermost being. Every emotional disorder we have, every 'problem' we have with life, originates from being *disconnected* from our innermost being, and consequently (seemingly) disconnected from source, Self and all of life. Of course we are never actually disconnected. We can't be, because we are forever connected. All of life is always *one*. However we can lose our *aware* connection. We also lose our 'operating' connection. In other words, we no longer live and act from the centre of our being but rather from the mind and its layers of conditions. And the mind is very noisy indeed. It makes it difficult for us to hear the deeper wisdom that speaks to us from our souls.

Identification with your mind creates a dense screen of images, definitions, labels, and judgments that block all true relating. This screen comes between the real you and yourself, between you and others, between you and nature, between you and creation. It creates the illusion that there is you and a completely external separate 'other'. It causes you to live in a perpetually disconnected state. You then forget the essential, eternal truth that, underneath all physical appearances of separate forms, you are one with all that is. *You are* that *one* that is.

It is when your consciousness is directed outward that mind and world arise – as you perceive it to be. By mistakenly thinking everything valuable is found outside of ourselves, we lose touch with the true essence of our being. In fact we lose touch with *truth*. Once we take the journey, we come to see that truth is not something outside to be discovered; it is something inside to be realised.

When you are not in your centre, when you are unaware of your inner essence, in the end misery is always created. It's as simple as that. When you don't know who or what you are, your true nature, you create a mind-made identity. You cling to that fearful and needy impostor. It becomes a substitute for your beautiful divine being. Protecting and enhancing that false sense of self then becomes a primary motivating force.

Humanity lives in a self-imposed prison where nothing is ever enough, yet ironically, we consider ourselves to be superior and all-important. Through our false sense of self-importance we believe we must control and engineer things to create ever more improved outcomes. Yet all around us life is in perfect balance in every moment – in being and becoming. Nature is not driven to control or produce anything better than itself through distorted efforts and *doingness*.

As the Taoist master Chuang-tzu said, "Each thing minds its business and all grow up out of inaction... Heaven and earth do nothing and there is nothing that is not done." This is that Taoist thing called wu-wei again. Nature *is* this. It is not controlling, not manipulating, not forcing, not scheming; yet it is not in resignation, nor is it sitting around on its hands. It is centred in being and becoming.

When we are no longer centred in the natural order of life's unfolding, we struggle against nothing but our own delusions. This leads us to such an unconscious state that we ignore the warning signs that our lives and our world are tipping radically out of balance. Of course this produces consequences for the environment. We abuse it and we fight each other over it. Our problems spill out from our own nucleus into the wider arena of fractured communities and, ultimately, a world of dangerous imbalance.

Our fear grows to the extent that the true nature of existence is obscured and we seek to explain it or control it, not just in a personal sense but as a collective; for example, through science or religion. Eventually our pain and suffering lead us back to a more personal, soulful quest – a desire to reconnect again with truth, with life as it truly is, and with our own being as we truly are.

This quest ultimately leads us to turn inward again, to our centres. It is a humbling journey. Inevitably we must admit that the mind that expects to fully understand the universe will fail. Our minds cannot trace a link between ordinary existence and the numinous depth of the whole. None of this can be realised through reasoning but only through curious open wonder and the willingness to die into the unknown.

Having conscious access to the formless realm is truly liberating. It is life – the life that is you and every other thing – in its undifferentiated state, prior to its emergence into diversity and what appears as multiplicity. It is a realm of deep silence, stillness and peace, but also of joy, wonder and intense aliveness.

Whenever you are present at your innermost centre, you become more transparent to the pure consciousness – the light – that emanates from this Source. You realise that this light, this consciousness, is not separate from who you are but is *your very essence*. The more we abide in this presence, the more centred we are, the more readily we become the living grace of wu-wei.

## ALL SOLUTIONS ARE WITHIN

**When you change the way you see things, the things you see are changed.**

Given that most of our problems appear related to our external circumstances, it seems very natural to look for external solutions. However, this usually results in feelings of confusion and limitation. This is because most people do not realise that everything we are experiencing externally comes from our inner realms. Or, this is realised only as a concept, and not as a consciously embodied truth.

Our 'problems' are due to our internal response. For example if we are angry with a 'bad' driver, the anger is coming from our reaction to that driver, not really the driver himself. Everything we encounter is the result of everything we have put attention into at the inner level of our being. A 'problem' is a sign that we need to create a new outcome or a new way of looking at the situation. As Einstein suggested, no problem is solved on the same level it was created.

Even when we think a problem is related to our external circumstance, a simple internal change in *attitude* or view can transform the 'problem'. When the problem is because of attitude, it signals we need to shift to a higher level of understanding. This leads us from the outer setting to our innermost being, and, ultimately, to our most direct connection with the highest level of the universe – *divine intelligence* (the source of all solutions) and *love* (the great harmoniser and unifier).

Furthermore, that which we see and experience externally is so small, transient and finite. Science has shown that our perceived physical world is not even 0.1% of existence. It is the *space* of existence that accounts for everything, well... 99.84378% (or close to it!) of the universe. The physical world is actually drawn from the unseen. It is in this space that all things come and go, all things are drawn from this and return to this, all from centre! This infinite space contains every possible thing. Therefore, every possible formula and solution for our 'problems' is in the space of our being. If we quiet our minds and look within, we connect with this space.

Here, once again, we encounter pure awareness and divine intelligence. When we understand this, it makes good sense to stop looking at our very limited physical, external field for answers and start looking within! When we do, we tap into the infinite source that is connected to everything in existence. Why would we limit ourselves to anything less?!

With inner connection we are able to resolve and liberate ourselves from every known condition. We attain healing, peace, balance and ultimately... enlightenment.

**Cultivating more enlightened qualities depends entirely on the ability to connect with that enlightened source in our own being.**

This is not something present in some people and not in others. The enlightened essence is in every single one of us. *The enlightened essence is YOU* – the only thing that distinguishes an enlightened person from one who is 'not' is that the enlightened person is *awake* to his or her essence and has integrated that aware state into every level of their being. Such a person lives consciously from the centre and source of their being, in a state of oneness with all, whilst continuing to experience life.

**Being centred is *central* to the enlightened state.**

The beauty of this is that every person has the ability to be centred. Of course many people do not feel this is true, simply because they are conditioned to operate through the mind and fixate on the body or external events. When this has become the 'norm', it can seem as if more enlightened qualities are unattainable or simply fantasy. This 'norm' however is not our true nature. It is something learned through *habit*.

Before we focused so much importance on the mind, we were already naturally connected with everything. As an infant, before taking on and storing mental conditions, we live in an 'oceanic' state. In this state we experience connectedness with all things, *and* we live from the centre of our being. We are acutely sensitive and connected to every energy within us and around us and already know its inherent nature. This knowing, however, is at an innate level rather than at a conscious or cognisant level.

The child is surrounded by the habits of the adult world, taking on the influences, the generalisations about life and, consequently, the polarisations. The state of being and experiencing simply 'what is' is replaced with a conditional model. A 'map' of reality is gradually developed and stored in the unconscious self, which divides everything in life into 'good' and 'bad', 'right' and 'wrong'. Mechanisms are learned and established as the conditioned environment and behaviours become habituated for the child. Gradually, these mechanisms cause the child to focus more and more on the external world and to shut down to the authentic self from which he or she was born and lived.

The good news is that our most pure and authentic essence is never lost. In the same fashion we 'learned' limiting beliefs and behaviours, we can just as readily 'unlearn' them, and learn to reconnect to the authenticity of our being and life. Regaining our authentic presence, however, can be quite a process. After many years (and lifetimes) of built up habits and identifications, it can seem like one will never get back to that pure and liberated essence. However, with meditative technique and correct breathing habits, this can be rediscovered very quickly and easily. Then the 'work' is in making meditation and breathing *daily habits* in order to regain a deeper and more integrated centring of being.

## Centring practices

There are definite ways of awakening our inner centre again and gaining a deeper connection with it. The most important meditative practice for this involves an energy centre in the abdomen referred to as the *tan tien*.

In Taoism, tan tien (or dan *tian*; tandan) is also known as the Hara (life force) or sometimes the 'Field of Elixir' or the 'Sea of Chi'. It is located about three finger widths below the navel and two finger widths internally into the body. It is the seat of personal power and one of the most important energy centres (chakras) for someone on the spiritual path. Life force is stored in the tan tien centre just like in a battery. If a person is in an unbalanced state this centre will collect a lot of stress, so it is vital it is strengthened and rebalanced. When attention is centred in tan tien, the thinking process slows down. Thoughts and emotional charges associated with the persona gradually dissolve without conflict. This is why the tan tien centre is a vital key to authentic meditation and centred power. Here, we are able to attain a state of mastery over thoughts and emotions.

Tan tien is a reservoir of chi (vital energy) and is often likened to the ocean. From the tan tien, chi flows out to the body, rejuvenating it with life-force. Chi then returns to the tan tien, reinforcing its power. Hence it is important to learn how to clear toxic energy, rebalance our energy centres and retain vital energy. This helps us to remain centred even whilst we are in more disturbing or challenging environments.

Anchoring in tan tien also plays an important role in aiding our ability to read and understand the different energies that are flowing through us, or the environment we are in. This in turn strengthens and heightens our intuition, our 'gut awareness',[19] so that we are able to stay clearly centred in our own energy as we interact with life rather than being pulled into other energies around us. Furthermore, we are able to begin rebuilding reserves of greater source energy, the type of energy that provides us with higher levels of stamina and extra-sensory powers. Rather than energy from deeper states of meditation simply dissipating, we begin to store and harness it for further integration and awakening.

Acting from tan tien is related to the state of samadhi, a state in which identification with mental activity and the ego is transcended. During prolonged periods of absorption in samadhi states I became very aware of a distinct sense of fullness and power in this centre, as if I were rooted down and anchored by the entire universe, and there was no power that could move or disturb me. This is what it means to be anchored in the ground of one's being.

So the ability for us to anchor attention and energy in tan tien is vital to maintain centred awareness and be very centred in our own body field. This is very important because in truth we are not supposed to be trying to get away from the body or our world. Really, we want to

---

[19] Notice the physical link of this term 'gut awareness' to tan tien.

abide in the world, *consciously* at peace, in order to manifest our greatest potential – living in love, joy, true power and oneness.

Here is a simple way to start.

### Sitting in tan tien

Use the diaphragm breathing from Chapter 8 and then relax into the alpha breathing rhythm. Breathe for a few minutes until you start to feel clear and calm. Bring your full attention to your inner being, feel the inner space within you. Attune to this as energy.

Now attune to the energy of spirit, the universe flowing from above you in through your head and into the tan tien. Then feel the power of earth energy, flowing from earth's core, up through the soles of your feet, through your legs, your base chakra and up into the tan tien. As you concentrate on your breath, feel these energies continue to flow into your being, anchoring you into tan tien.

Now take your attention deeper into the tan tien centre. Imagine it as a ball of glowing warm energy. Let yourself tune into this as you continue breathing deeply. With each breath feel the energy centre fill up as you breathe in, and with the out-breath feel the energy expand and flow out to your whole body. Continue breathing this way, letting yourself rest deeper and deeper into the flow of energy.

After 15-20 minutes let your attention simply settle into the core of the tan tien. Feel as if your whole being is rooted here. Gently affirm to yourself "I am here." As this centred presence, simply continue to breathe deeply and maintain awareness. Just allow yourself to be wakefully present, experiencing the moment and the energies of yourself as they are, all from this innermost centre.

When you feel it is time to resume other activities, take another deep full breath into the tan tien and re-affirm "I am here." Feel the energy flowing from the tan tien through the rest of your body. Feel the connection with the universe and the earth. Feel yourself anchored in your centre. Take another breath into your body, gently stretch and slowly open your eyes.

When you initially start this practice, you will most likely feel as if nothing much is happening, as if the energy is quite neutral. One of the virtues of resting in the tan tien centre is that it *is* a neutral sensation, especially at first, and that there are no particular feelings there to reject or crave. However, with more practice and strengthened focus, the energy centre will definitely begin to feel palpably warm and powerful as you restore more vital energy.

Of course there are other important and vital energy centres that all play a role in your awakening. But to begin with, tan tien will enable you to establish inner connectedness, balance and meditative awareness quite easily and powerfully. In fact, some enlightened masters spent their whole lives focusing on this one centre alone. As a result of the centring and balancing, they attained a powerfully liberated state.

## Standing tan tien

To deepen the experience of tan tien I also recommend a standing tan tien practice. This helps all energies to centre and anchor in our being.

First stand with your feet shoulder-width apart and take three deep full breaths, in through your nose and out through your mouth. Align the three points of your crown, your tan tien and your base chakra. Feel the column of energy that runs through you from spirit above, through your central channel and down into earth's core. Feel this channel to be at least the same diameter as your head.

Raise your arms in front of your upper chest in a hugging posture, just like you are hugging a tree. The elbows should be relaxed and align to the level just under the armpits. The pinky finger curls inwards towards the heart and the thumbs raise upwards.

Now slow the breath down. Feel the breath softening and deepening as you let all the energy flow from above into the tan tien and all the energy from earth's core rise up into the tan tien. As you breathe, feel your tan tien centre being filled. Feel the infinite power of spirit and earth anchoring you. Imagine yourself to be deeply rooted and powerful like a tree.

After the hugging duration (start with a minimum of three minutes) slowly lower the palms to rest out in front of the tan tien, still in a hugging pose (again for three minutes). Feel the energy centre pulsing and radiating with energy. Then, taking a deep breath in, bring the palms (left over right) to the abdomen. Gently rotate the hands around the abdomen anti-clockwise. Feel the warmth of the energy centre and the deep peace of being anchored and centred as you breathe out gently, slowly and deeply.

Then open the palms, extending arms out to the side of the body. Breathing in again, draw the palms upward until over the head, bringing the palms together in prayer and drawing the hands down to the heart. As you breathe out, feel yourself centred, light and flowing with energy as you give thanks. This completes the exercise.

Start by holding this posture (the first stage of hugging) for at least three minutes. Each day you may increase your standing practice by a minute until you develop enough power to stand and hold this pose for 10-15 minutes. As you increase the duration you may also begin to relax the knees, the shoulders and the back more, entering into a more curved stance as if you are holding a ball of energy. For the stage of hugging in front of the tan tien, three minutes remains sufficient.

You will find this practice enormously energising, strengthening, uplifting and grounding. The ability to maintain a deeper state of presence is developed naturally through this practice. Remember, being centred is central to the enlightened state. It is well worth your while taking the time to master practices like the ones outlined, as they will definitely aid your ability to regain and sustain a more centred state of being. Eventually you will come to a moment where you just stop and see you are already the place you have been seeking… you *are* centre.

Now I will leave you with a Zen story.

One day a young Buddhist, while on his journey home, came to the banks of a wide river. Staring hopelessly at the great obstacle in front of him, he pondered for hours as to how he would cross such a wide barrier. Just as he was about to give up his pursuit, he saw a great teacher on the other side of the river. The young Buddhist yelled over to the teacher, "Oh wise one, can you tell me how to get to the other side of this river?" The teacher pondered for a moment, looked up and down the river, and yelled back, "My son, you *are* on the other side."

CHAPTER 11

# FLOWING WITH ENERGY

CONSCIOUS HABIT 4

*If you want to find the secrets of the universe, think in terms of energy, frequency and vibration.* —Nikola Tesla

Everything we are and everything we experience is energy. *All* of life is energy. This is the nature of consciousness; that which appears as a play of form and formlessness.

As such, consciousness is manifesting itself as an all-encompassing, infinite spectrum of energy frequencies – from source, the microcosm, to the most expansive omnipotent field of all-being, the macrocosm. It is the absolute zero, the formless, the absolute all, that which is pre-manifestation. Yet it is also the many, the form, that which is creating and created. All of this is *one* being, co-existing simultaneously as that which appears to be sequential in time, yet that which is forever the eternal instant, the now.

What we are, what we perceive and register, is not even a speck of a speck of a speck of this vast play of energy we are a part of! At the deepest and innermost source of our being, we are, and always remain, the very presence of omnipotent being – that which is never born, never dies and is eternally present. This, our Self, which is pure consciousness, is the one giving rise to the manifestation of our 'individual' self.

This individual self is an incredibly small expression of energy, yet is also a conduit, and a manifestation of the infinite energy of the universe.

It is important then to recognise that this body/mind we perceive is not actually an object with boundaries, but rather a field of energy that is both concentrated in frequency and pattern *and* open, flowing and interconnected with every other energy in the universe.

## Practicing energy awareness

As Einstein explained, "What we have called 'matter' is energy, whose vibration has been so lowered as to be perceptible to the senses. There is no matter."

When you experience your being and all life as *energy*, you begin to truly *feel* oneness. There are definite ways to regain an aware connection with yourself and life at the energy level. First of all, shift your attention from object and identification (thought-based perception) to energy awareness (feeling-based consciousness). Try these simple meditative steps:

Slow your breath into a deep, steady rhythm and place your attention in its flow. Slowly let your attention move into the energy that is flowing internally. Bring your awareness fully into the inner space of energy. Simply observe and experience this as a field of energy. Let your awareness expand with the energy. Where does it start? Does it have a boundary? What is it connected to?

Simply experience the flowing boundless nature of energy and awareness, letting yourself rest deeper and deeper into the unified field of energy. Breathe into the innermost source of this energy and acknowledge its presence. Simply witness and experience whatever occurs. Give thanks for the re-connection you feel with the boundless presence that is yourself and all life... oneness.

If you practice this daily, you will find a growing connection with your inner being and with yourself as energy. It will naturally follow that you will feel a deeper sense of oneness with all life. Bringing your attention to life as energy is powerfully revealing. It will help you make sense of yourself, the world and how everything really is connected. Understanding this is just the beginning. The more we understand this, the more we liberate ourselves from the confined realms of our minds' illusions and misperceptions.

No energy can ever be bound or remain static. *All* energy is constantly in flow. This is reflected in the nature of life's ever-changing display. And given that our minds are but a small spectrum of energy, it follows that *we*, as energy, can never be truly bound to the mind, which is energy! When we realise this, it is much easier to flow with the transient nature of life. It becomes a curious thing then to encounter the constant transforming nature of the world around us, and it is much easier to relax when we know that each moment will pass and carry us on, always in the flow of the universe. It serves us well not only to understand the nature of ourselves as energy, but also to be more 'in tune' with it.

This is the basis of the fifth attunement (presented at the end of this chapter): *All is energy. I am energy, connected with all.*

In the previous chapter I introduced the understanding of the tan tien, which is integral to our ability to be centred. It is also integral to restoring harmony and balance to all energy that flows in and through us. Further to this are all the energy channels and chakras, through which distinct currents of energy operate and flow to form the various expressions that make us human. However, the first or most common level at which we know and experience energy is through our senses. Unfortunately, in most cases, our senses have been overloaded, and due to lifestyle we have become 'desensitised'. So, before we even begin to develop awareness of more subtle energies, it is important to bring balance and awareness back into our basic five senses.

## Awareness through the senses

As a child I was the opposite of desensitised. I was so present and 'awake' that I was aware with every sense of my being! It was later, as a young adult, that I realised the direct relationship between being aware and being grounded with the senses, and that this can be put to use as a specific tool.

It is good not to underestimate the power of awareness waiting in our senses, which are usually taken for granted. The teacher Gurdjieff knew the truth when he said, "It is only by grounding our awareness in the living sensation of our bodies that the 'I Am', our real presence, can awaken." In fact it works in reverse as well. When you cultivate more awareness you can't but be more present with your senses!

Deepening our awareness with the five senses helps us to be more centred in the now. Significantly, this is because each of our sensory experiences *is* happening in the *now*! It is also how we understand ourselves and the universe as energy. Learning how to re-engage with life more deeply through our senses is a great gift. It is also clearly the embodied state that a truly enlightened person occupies.

The other blessing that arises when we are more centred in our senses is the silence of the mind! Our mind becomes profoundly quiet, calm and positioned in its correct role, simply serving our (higher) being and our interaction with life in each moment.

There is a wonderful analogy about this: 'The emperor, the general and the soldier'. The emperor is *consciousness,* the general is the *mind* and the soldier is the *body*. In most people's cases, the mind, being a dictator type, has staged a coup over the emperor, and the emperor's true power has been abdicated to the ego. This leaves the soldier – the body – in a state of conflict, struggling with the mixed messages of an inherent connection to the deeper truth of the emperor, whilst being controlled by the power-hungry general!

A great way to bypass this stranglehold of the mind is to go directly to the senses, simply with aware attention. And guess what, the mind actually goes along willingly because the mind is hungry for the sensations of life! In fact, the mind is also incredibly curious. It is this curiosity that can be utilised when you practice returning awareness to your senses.

With curiosity, you can more readily be present with the senses, no matter what the senses are registering! And with curiosity comes the ability to engage with the flow of what the senses are registering, rather than flipping back into the analysing mind. In this way you can become the experience of 'active being'. This *being* is an aware state of flowing, dynamic, shifting energy. Life and the self are then experienced as a 'rivering' of energy rather than as fixed and defined objects and events.

Then there is *feeling*, rather than the object that was touched; *seeing*, rather than the perception of what was seen; *listening*, rather than what was heard or defined as a story; *tasting*, rather than an object to consume; and *smelling*, rather than the containment of aroma. Each of these experiences becomes one that is deep, rich, flowing, boundless and interconnected. You'll notice that each sense ends with 'ing'... hence I call our experience one of 'rivering'. It is also worth noting that we are human be-*ings*. *Life is a verb, not a noun.* Life is energy... it is *happening*. It is not actually a series of fixed objects or events.

Through this type of experience-*ing*, there may be true realisation of the nature of our being and the universe as energy. This is because truth is a living energy, not a concept. Realisation does not occur in the mind or concept itself. *Experience* is needed for us to have true realisation. And indeed, our senses are the gateway to our experience!

When a child was given the task of naming the 'Seven Wonders of the World', she struggled to finish her paper before the end of the class. When she finally handed it up, she changed the way her teacher thought forever. On her page was her list: "to See, to Hear, to Touch, to Taste, to Feel, to Laugh, to Love."

Imagine how you would have lived your life if you had been taught this from the beginning! Instead we have gradually come to believe that we need multiple distractions in our lives, that if we experience what is really happening, things will no longer be okay and that the wonder is somewhere 'out there'.

When we are not given the space to stay present to our experience, we begin to lose touch with our authentic Self. After years of distractions, we become very disengaged from present moment awareness. By practicing the following you can recreate a very strong connection with present moment awareness. Over time you will also develop a state of authentic *Self* awareness: feeling, seeing and sensing what simply is, as it is, rather than feeling, seeing and sensing through the layers of the ego's filters. The practice involves 'anchoring' one's point of attention and awareness towards life within one central sensory state.

I experimented with this as a specific technique after I had been in prolonged states of samadhi. Anchoring one's attention in the senses is perhaps the most powerful way to attain a sustained state of presence and flow in the now.

I recommend that you start with the first sense-awareness, and work with it over a period of two to four weeks, until you can sustain this state of attention for longer periods and naturally re-centre yourself into sense-awareness during other activities. The best order to work through awakening sensory attention is as follows:

1. Physical – body: touching, physical feeling awareness
2. Sight – eyes: looking, seeing, observing awareness
3. Sound – ears: hearing, listening awareness
4. Taste – tongue: tasting awareness
5. Smell – nose: smelling awareness
6. Energy – subtle body: vibrational (non-distinct) feeling awareness
7. Conscious presence: witnessing, pure conscious awareness.

Of course, pure conscious awareness is not a sensory state, yet ironically our ability to be centred in the first six senses enables us to become so still and present that we are able to rest easily in a state of pure witnessing. When you feel you have mastered the ability to anchor with each of these senses, you can make a routine practice that will keep deepening your development and integrating the states of aware attention further.

I took up the practice of anchoring into a single sense state per day. For example; Monday: touching and feeling; Tuesday: seeing; Wednesday: listening; and so on, following the order above. This order is significant because it leads you from the gross level to the subtlest level of senses. If you do not have the ability to hold your attention at the grossest level, which is the level we are most identified with, how do you think you will be able to hold attention at the most subtle level?!

So, don't be in a rush. If you truly want to develop your being – to embrace all that you are – start where you are. There is no point dreaming of flying to the moon, then wasting time jumping up and down on the spot. We have to build our way from the ground up, developing a greater ability to go beyond our usual realm of occupation, creating the vehicle to launch ourselves into a higher state of awareness and experience.

## Transformational energy

Once we are more deeply centred in energy awareness through our senses, we open the way for a deeper process of transformation to unfold. When we are centred in energy, it naturally follows that our energies begin to balance and we occupy a more authentic state. We also begin to naturally rest in a state of presence. We begin to truly live from the 'ground of being'. The key then is to be more constantly connected with your inner body, to feel it at all times. This will rapidly, and deeply, transform your life. The more consciousness you direct to the inner body, the higher its vibrational frequency becomes.

Additional to this is a freeing up of contracted energies and conditioned habits we have adopted over many years. Usually, most people experience their lives through the layers of these conditions. These patterns of energy are stored in the unconscious field, the subconscious mind and the nervous system. These stored energies are responsible for the way we misinterpret life and continue to react to it. Consequently, most people are living in a perpetual feedback loop, unable to see and experience life as it truly is.

It is important to wake up and mobilise these deeply stored energies – *not* with mental effort or emotional stories, but rather with dynamic and cathartic energy practices. In this way stored and blocked energies begin to move and are able to flow through our natural energy systems uninhibited. When moving and allowed to flow without resistance, these energies carry a new level of awareness. Through the process of setting these stored energies into motion, insight naturally follows.

Unfortunately, most people go about a process of transformation in reverse. They struggle with the mind, analysing and agonising over memories, in an effort to gain answers so as to be able to let go. Actually this has the opposite effect. It continues to send the same energies through the nervous system and into the subconscious where the stories are only re-validated and gain greater strength, creating even deeper layers of the same energies. This pattern results in deeply rooted blocks that seem impossible to shift. It can also easily become a practice (therapy) of indulgence. Many people become addicted to this version of drama without even realising it.

Further to the cathartic practice explained in Chapter 7, there are definite ways for us to mobilise these deeply stored energies, leading to a clear transformation. The first practice is breathing. Yes… we come back again to the power of breath! If we are breathing deeply and efficiently, it is impossible to continue on the same track with blocked energies.

Deep efficient breathing is what mobilises all energy in our body. Our breathing is the fanning mechanism to keep energy flowing.

I already outlined the powerful benefits of alpha breathing in Chapter 8. Now you might consider using a deeper, dynamic practice that helps open your energy centres, clear blocks, and moves and awakens energy throughout your whole being. This is a practice I call Shakti Shake.

### Shakti Shake

In this practice, the deeper reserve of universal energy, shakti, is awoken and utilised. This becomes the most powerful practice when combined with *prana-yama*, energetic breathing methods.

Again, adopt the standing pose with feet shoulder-width apart. Make sure the spine is balanced and the body is centred. Start with alpha breathing, building the strength and pace; then drop into deep rhythmic breathing, still breathing from the abdomen. As you breathe in, lift the arms up and raise the body by lifting your heels from the floor. With the out-breath, swing the arms back down and let the heels drop back to the floor with a light thud. Gradually move into a swinging motion, letting your movements gain speed and momentum, like the action of a piston.

After 5-10 minutes of this, the body will be full of energy. Let yourself simply drop into a shuddering rhythm, letting the body shake like a milkshake, perhaps still up and down, or the body might take on a swaying or jiggling motion. It is important to let yourself stay in the momentum, letting the body take over. Simply let the body do whatever the body needs to do. You might find the feet start stamping, the hands shaking fists, or the body twirling and spinning. There might be tears, grunting, screaming or laughing. Whatever happens, simply let it be. The more you surrender, the deeper the energy will flow and release.

You should try to maintain the shaking momentum for at least 10-15 minutes. If shaking continues longer than this, simply allow it to follow its natural course. When the shaking has subsided, lie down and simply breathe from your tan tien centre as you maintain wakeful awareness. Simply be present as you observe and experience yourself as a state of alive, flowing energy. If you genuinely want deep transformation, I recommend this as a daily practice. These practices, as well as cathartic

unveiling (Chapter 7) enable deep layers of stored emotions to be released and allow you to:
- Feel more 'anchored' in conscious awareness whilst being very present in the body.
- Create a fast, powerful and effective release of built up tension and stress.
- Work with breath and body movement to stimulate a deep process of transformation without mental analysis.
- Awaken deep reserves of source energy to regenerate life force quickly and easily
- Integrate and stabilise energy in the primary energy centres.

Using these techniques regularly will allow you to develop the *habit* of releasing energy and letting energy flow consciously, leading you to states of deeper harmony.

Attunement #5

*I am ENERGY… connected with all.*

Take a few moments to tune into the energy of your body and the energy that surrounds you. Notice your senses as they register the different vibrations of life happening within you and around you, then repeat the attunement three times. Endeavour to remain aware of the energy and vibrations that flow within you and around you throughout the day.

CHAPTER 12

# WITNESSING

Conscious Habit 5

*Until you make the unconscious conscious it will direct your life and you will call it fate.* —Carl G. Jung

One of the most consistent tendencies of liberated people is the ability to 'witness', to simply watch what is happening with curiosity and unattached awareness. Witnessing is integral to our conscious shift from the unconscious aspects of our self. With witnessing we can overcome resistance, release the power we have given to our conditioned 'map', strengthen the practice of self-reflection, and expand into deeper states of pure awareness. It is then that we see truth, because pure awareness *is* truth. Awakening is inevitable. However the awakening of our being from unconscious conditions into a more conscious state is a considerable process.

The journey of awakening consciousness involves specific steps or stages. In the first stage of human consciousness, most people are ninety-nine percent unconscious. When a person begins to use the one percent of conscious cognition, the state of a more conscious mind develops. As you become more conscious you gradually bring light to all that has been unconscious. The cognitive mind begins to expand through the act of being more conscious, or simply by paying attention. This naturally gives rise to a state of *witnessing*, simply watching thoughts and feelings without identifying with them. Witnessing expands into awareness and, ultimately, into that which is transcendent. As such, witnessing is the *bridge* between a less conscious state and conscious awareness, and it is integral to the journey of awakening.

## The journey of awakening

Consciousness is a spectrum of frequencies, from that which is most contracted to that which is all-expansive. The human journey *is* one of consciousness: From unaware existence manifesting through the experience of matter, towards awareness and pure consciousness – that which is the eternal formless Self. Between what we call 'matter' and the Divine, the difference is always the level or frequency of consciousness.

Matter, such as at the mineral level, is the state of consciousness that is unaware. Matter is not unconscious; it is simply unaware and at the lowest frequency of consciousness. The plant and animal kingdoms are at the next vibration or frequency. Plants are conscious, but not cognitively 'self' conscious. Animals have a degree of 'self' consciousness yet primarily operate instinctually with the surrounding environment. Human existence is cognitively conscious, or 'self' aware, and humans have evolved to interact with and manipulate the environment in complex ways. The human experience is very much a mind phenomenon.

When you become conscious of your own *consciousness*, it begins to increase and unconsciousness will go on decreasing. This is the process of blossoming human consciousness. So becoming aware opens the way for great alchemy. The more awareness you develop, the more you will find your life changing for the better in every possible dimension.

**Throughout the human experience we journey through seven primary stages:**

1. **The unconscious – sleeping mind:** The narrowest spectrum of consciousness, characterised by a lack of awareness, gross perception and identification, physical survival, hierarchy, ego, fear, competition, greed and fighting.
2. **The unconscious and subconscious – dreaming mind:** A very confined spectrum of consciousness characterised by the perception of duality, conditional behaviour, reactivity, fear, self-need, lack of trust, judgement, attachment, deception, aversion and ego-centred relating.

3. **The conscious – cognitive waking state:** At this level the spectrum of consciousness moves between contraction and expansion, sharing many characteristics from the previous level whilst also encompassing reason, thoughtfulness, creativity, perfectionism, transformation, growth, courage, surrender and soul connecting.
4. **The conscious – awakening awareness:** An expanding conscious spectrum, characterised by self-reflection and awareness, witnessing, recognition of interconnectedness and qualities of love, acceptance, humility, truth, authenticity, clear vision, gratitude, trust, mindfulness, creativity, moral integrity, compassion, forgiveness and generosity.
5. **Conscious awareness – aware presence:** An all-open spectrum of consciousness. All of the former states have been processed and integrated into consistent aware being. Egoless being, still expressing and embodied as individual, yet aware of *one* Self (allocentric). Qualities include unconditional love, selfless service, unconditional being and divine will in action.
6. **Divine consciousness – pure consciousness:** This state is unbound, 'empty-full', all-being, oneness, transcendent and immanent, limitless. At the greatest stage of evolution a person can enter this level of consciousness during prolonged periods of samadhi.[20]
7. **Unity consciousness – pure conscious dissolution:** The indescribable return to source. During higher states of samadhi, various yogis and masters have encountered this dissolution in which the fully enlightened nature of Self becomes an absolute.[21]

As we journey through the levels of consciousness, it is common to experience characteristics from two or three different levels at once. Most of humanity is still at the lowest stage, in unconscious (unaware) activity, which is the primary state of most minds. However, no single person is entirely unconscious. It is the presence of the very small degree of consciousness that sparks the journey of awakening.

When a person first begins to develop their conscious mind, they become acutely aware of the unconscious aspects of the self – the ego.

---

20  At this stage an individual may complete with their incarnation or settle into full conscious presence (stage 5) in service.
21  Following this, such an individual may complete their incarnation or continue in service (stage 5).

This often causes them to feel 'worse' than they did previously, but it is simply the effect of becoming more aware of what was already there. During this stage, the subconscious mind is still very much responsible for driving one's experience. The thoughts, beliefs and identifications are operating mostly on default.

Without you even realising it, the subconscious mind is constantly interpreting each situation and correspondingly generating a response or, most often, a 're-action'. As you develop more conscious cognition, this becomes painfully frustrating because you are deeply aware of your unconscious behaviours yet feel as if you have no control over them.

Gradually the power and nature of being conscious leads you more readily to a witnessing state, a state which you can intentionally put to use. You can begin to pause when an unconscious belief has been triggered, and the more you pause, the easier it is to prevent compulsive, unconscious behaviour. Witnessing also allows you to be less attached to thoughts and identification, yet there is still a relationship between subject and object. Although there is greater stillness in the mind, there is still the presence of the individual doing the act of witnessing – the perception of the 'I'.

As witnessing becomes more established, there is a greater sense of distancing from the mind. You no longer identify with the mind or analyse the thoughts and feelings that appear to be your 'self'. Instead there is simply the act of witnessing, a state of watching thoughts and feelings, like passing images or phenomena on a movie screen. But there is still a 'someone' watching the movie.

Gradually a state of disassociation develops. You begin to feel a sense of distancing from the thoughts and feelings, and the ego's tendency towards identification begins to soften and dissolve. Through the act of witnessing, the (mis)perception of *being* the thoughts begins to dissolve into the state of being a presence of awareness. You begin to feel and realise that you are something far greater than, and beyond, the thoughts or ego.

Through witnessing the practiced mind helps access a calmer, steadier sense of self that is more at ease, even in challenging situations, because it realises that, ultimately, 'I am not my thoughts and feelings.' When you land in the realisation that *the awareness* of anger is not *angry*, the awareness of struggle is not *struggling*, and the awareness of fear is not *fearful*, then something great in you is freed up.

Witnessing is the bridge that takes us gently and surely from the tangled mind into a freer state of being. In this state of expanded awareness, there is luminosity and a clarity of consciousness that is transcendent of the thoughts. Here one realises it is impossible to find any enduring pain or fear. Instead what we discover is the freedom, the love and the power of our being.

In this state there is no longer identification with the mind; there is no unconsciousness and no corresponding cognitive activity. There is simply awareness. The perception of 'this and that' – the duality that corresponds with the mind – dissolves into a crystalised state of pure awareness. You transcend a 'self' who is aware and enter pure (or super) consciousness.

Awareness is absolutely devoid of any subjectivity or objectivity. There is no one who is witnessing in awareness; there is no thing being witnessed. It is a unified state in which a subject and object are no longer related. They are dissolved. They are merged as one. In pure awareness there is no 'person' who is aware, and nothing is being attended to. Awareness itself is non-doing – *wu-wei* – it is the presence of pure conscious being.

**Awareness equals whole consciousness.**

Awareness has become the totality, and the mind itself is now absorbed into awareness. So, as the mind has been completely absorbed, beyond fragmentation, there is transcendence of the mind. It is only through making a complete state of conscious mind that we go beyond mind, and pure awareness becomes possible.

**Consciousness is a quality of the mind, which leads to a totality of mind. Awareness is the transcendence of mind; it is beyond the mind.**

The mind is very much the 'me', the ego identity, and always operates within the field of context. It is always conscious of something, and there is always 'someone' who is conscious. So consciousness is part and parcel of the mind, and mind, as such, is the source of all duality, of all divisions, whether they are between subject and object, activity or inactivity, consciousness or unconsciousness.

Every type of mental activity is dualistic in nature. This is the very source of every perceived fear, problem and suffering in the human experience. Through the perception of duality, a person lives in a state of illusion: the belief of separation from source and from others. Awareness is non-dual, so awareness reveals the state of no mind. Freed from the mind, you are freed from the illusion of separation and experience the true nature of life... you are liberated. You become the experience of wholeness and oneness.

**Conscious awareness is the 'final' verge of spiritual progress... from conscious awareness there is nowhere else to go but into the all that *is*.**

Through awareness you can achieve the realisation of all that is already achieved, all that has ever been, is and ever will be – you awaken to pure consciousness. This is the enlightening of the human.

## Witnessing as a bridge to awareness

In witnessing, a duality still exists between subject and object, and there is still the presence of a doer. But, through witnessing, greater conscious awareness is possible because it is a conscious act; it is an act, but conscious. Conversely, you can do something and be unconscious (unaware). Most people's ordinary activity is unconscious activity, but if you become conscious in it, it becomes witnessing. So witnessing becomes the tool to shift from ordinary unconscious identifications that operate at the subconscious level, to becoming more consciously present and expanding into awareness. Our ability to expand into awareness is integral to being a more enlightened person.

**Witnessing is both a function of the more conscious mind and a method (the bridge) toward awareness.**

Witnessing is not awareness, but compared to ordinary unconscious activity it is a higher function of the mind, so it is possible to say such a person is 'more aware'. Cognition has become conscious; unconsciousness is now illumined by consciousness. However, there is greater expansion and change yet to occur. That is, the usual cognitive activity of mind has yet to rest into the stillness and inactivity of pure awareness.

So the journey of awakening consciousness involves a process of moving through specific steps or stages. It is almost impossible to shift immediately from unconscious states into awareness,[22] so a method in between is integral and corresponds with a more natural process and order of conscious expansion, like going from first to second to third gear. If one begins with witnessing – conscious activity – then the shift becomes easier. Witnessing naturally flows into the deeper state of pure awareness.

There is a very close relationship between 'being' conscious and witnessing, though they are not exactly the same thing. If you begin to be conscious of your actions, conscious of your moment-to-moment happenings, conscious of everything that surrounds you, then you naturally begin to witness. Actually, the real 'practice' then is in being conscious – being conscious is the *method*. This is why developing the power of concentration is so relevant and important.[23] The ability to concentrate goes hand in hand with being able to pay attention. Being conscious is an act of enduring attention. Witnessing naturally follows as a result of being conscious. Witnessing becomes your state.

In the stage of conscious awareness, you lose the 'witness' and only *seeing* remains. You lose the doer, you lose the subjectivity, you lose the egocentric consciousness. Eventually the 'one' who is left is purely the seer. Then pure consciousness remains, without the ego.

## Mastering witnessing

By choosing a few moments of stillness, and by slowing down the pace of thoughts with breathing, the next conscious skill is to be able to mentally step aside and, with great curiosity, watch yourself simply have the feeling or behaviour. You might say to yourself, "Huh... look at the mind thinking.... Hmmm... now the body is feeling... Oh... what an interesting series of stories... fascinating!"

Typically when we sit down to meditate, all of the uncomfortable stories and feelings become more evident, because we are finally being present! Usually the first response is to want to resist again. However, with

---

[22] It is possible but arduous, requiring extraordinary commitment and focus, and even so, there will still be an interim witnessing state, even if that state is very brief or so powerful that the person drops into deeper awareness.

[23] See the practice of nose-tip breathing in Chapter 8 to develop the power of concentration.

witnessing we can get to the deeper place within our being that is free of *all* conditions. In Buddhism this practice is referred to as Shamatha or mindfulness-meditation, and in Zen practice, Vipassana.

The act of stepping aside to watch helps create conscious awareness because it keeps you from indulging in the feelings or behaviours, and/or your mental analysis of them. It actually makes it much more difficult to continue suffering. This watching needs to be done, however, without attachment to the outcome. You must objectively and curiously watch what is happening, not in order to change anything, but just to notice what is happening. The ability to step aside and watch yourself feeling and acting is an acquired skill and takes time and practice to develop, but it will totally change your life.

Meditation naturally develops your ability to become the witness. Over time your mind can watch its flow of thoughts and feelings with unidentified, undisturbed interest. In this observing flow state, one becomes aware of the pattern of the thoughts and feelings, as well as their insubstantial forming and dissolving. With practice, a more tolerant and flexible relationship with your mind just 'as it is' can open – in moments slowly, in other moments suddenly – into a wider, receptive state of mind that is less confined or disturbed by the content of thoughts.

This conscious state wants nothing and has no borders. It is a vibrant state of rest. It is deeper than joy and fuller than contentment. All that 'is' feels wholly alive, unified, present and unconcerned with 'better' or 'worse', 'right' or 'wrong', 'this' or 'that'. Curiously, it is this engaged, lovingly dispassionate state of mind that is most receptive, ready and able to bring forth useful and creative responses to any event or challenging situation.

**Witnessing helps us become better at being human.**

Being the witness, the observer, has been a part of meditative practice for centuries, but *why* it is so valuable is not often explained in basic terms. This is a deceptively simple instruction that has tremendous power. Although witnessing is ultimately the key to liberation, it is first and foremost a key to release suffering.

**All suffering arises from resistance.**

If you are experiencing any discomfort in your life in general, it's because somewhere, on some level, there is resistance.

**So if resistance is the problem, witnessing is the solution.**

First of all, remember that the discomfort is not necessary. It is only there because of resistance. It is not there because of the situation, because of other people, or because life is unfair. It is there because you don't feel safe changing and you are resisting the change, or because you are resisting someone or something being the way it is. Witnessing is a definite way to release yourself from resistance and the suffering associated with it. By stepping back and just watching whatever is happening, with no agenda for what does or does not happen, the resistance disappears. And, the process of change can happen without suffering.

The experience of awareness and our encounter of life also becomes one filled with wonder. Whatever flows into our awareness can be its own gift when allowed to be exactly what it is. This in turn draws us more deeply into what we truly are. The inherent peace that abides in all things in every moment is revealed.

Remember, you can only continue self-destructive feelings and behaviours if you do them unconsciously, without awareness. All personal transformation techniques that *work* bring consciousness to that which has been held unconsciously. Most of us have very elaborate ego strategies designed to keep us unaware, but there is a very simple way to defeat them: with witnessing! Try this witnessing technique:

Close your eyes and take three deep full breaths in through the nose and out through the mouth. Now focus on the following attunements: *I am consciousness, I am here*. Contemplate deeply with these attunements, and then use either alpha or nose-tip breathing for a few minutes to centre yourself and deepen into awareness.

Now simply begin to pay very watchful attention. Be present as the watcher of your mind. Be curious. There is no need to judge or analyse the thoughts or feelings that arise. If you find you have wandered off into thoughts, just bring your attention back to watchfulness. Breathe more deeply into your body as you continue to witness. If you wander off again, repeat the attunements: *I am consciousness, I am here*. Maintain a watchful state for at least 20 minutes. You can also continue this practice throughout your day.

Be the observer of your thoughts, emotions and reactions in various situations. Be just as interested in your reactions as the situation or person that causes you to react. Don't judge or analyse what you observe. Also, notice how often your attention is in the past or the future. Watch the thoughts, feel the emotions, observe the reactions. Do not make a personal problem out of them. Simply be an observer. You will then feel something more powerful than any of those things that you observe: the still, observing presence itself behind the content of your mind. You will begin to feel the silent calm rising up from your inner being. You will feel the freedom of love, the One that is okay with everything as it is.

If you step back the next time you are feeling any kind of discomfort, and consciously acknowledge what is happening, you can instantly apply the power of witnessing. Simply observe yourself. Maybe make a small comment..."Well... here I am, feeling angry", or whatever it is you are feeling, and then just notice yourself being angry, without trying to stop it or change it, without any agenda for what should or should not happen. Any feeling you have will be a sensation in your body, so just notice where in your body you feel it. Notice if it stays the same or changes, if it stays in one place or moves around. Become genuinely curious about it. Continue to watch very closely as you feel. Pretend you are a scientist, an inner explorer, and here you are finally seeing the landscape of your ego! See how carefully and curiously you can watch.

Whatever uncomfortable feelings you are having, you've probably been having them repeatedly for a long time. Usually most people are too busy trying to make the feelings stop – or blaming them on someone else, or analysing them, or being unconscious about them – to actually be a witness to them. Yet in truth, *you cannot be stuck in your suffering very effectively if a part of you is watching.* If you are curious and watching, resistance falls away.

Curiosity is a state in direct contrast to resistance. Once you are successfully watching, it becomes very obvious that you could make a different choice about how to respond to whatever is happening. On the other hand, if you are watching with an agenda to stop the feeling, you're not really watching. To be the witness, there must be no agenda other than to watch and be curious. Curiosity may at first seem like an airy ideal, but don't underestimate its power. As James Stephens, an Irish novelist and poet, wrote, "Curiosity will conquer fear even more than bravery will."

Many years ago, a young woman I had been counselling called me in an extremely disturbed state. "I feel like I'm going insane!" she cried. "I can't see any point to my life any more... I think I want to kill myself... what do I do?" The first thing I told her to do was to breathe deeply and slowly. I asked her to connect to the calm flow of her breath, then go and lie down and pay very close attention to the energies and feelings that were flowing in her body. I told her simply to watch any thoughts or images that were playing in her mind. "Just watch them... be very curious, as if you are really trying to see and experience the mystery of thoughts and feelings going on inside of you." I asked her to just lie there and be the witness for half an hour and then call me back so we could reflect on what she had noticed.

She did call me back, but not that day. It was two days later. She sheepishly admitted that there really was nothing wrong at all and that, much to her amazement, after only ten minutes of 'witnessing' she had a sudden epiphany: that *none of what she was feeling or thinking was even real*. All of the terror she was feeling simply vanished, and she was left in a state of deep calm in which she felt she was something much bigger than her body, her life or her thoughts.

Because she followed my suggestion and was simply trying to observe what was happening, she didn't fall back into the state of resistance. Her agenda was not to make her fears or feelings go away but just to notice what was happening. If you do the same thing you'll get the same result, but only if you are watching with genuine curiosity. You cannot be trying to make the feeling change. You must really just be the witness.

The good news is that your feelings are your feelings alone. No one else can witness them, and, given they *are* your feelings, *you* can witness them. Once you become the witness and you truly bring curiosity to them, they can have no more power over you, simply because the truth is this: Who you really are, is not the thoughts or feelings. *You are pure consciousness.*

One of the wonderful things that happens for people who meditate regularly is that this 'watcher' becomes more and more prominent, easier to summon when needed, and soon becomes a constant companion. This is the real turning point in what masters and yogis call awakening. It is from here that a person develops greater consciousness and expanded awareness.

This is why making the practice of witnessing a habit is so valuable. From this point, expanded awareness grows even greater to include an increased sense of connection with the rest of the universe. But it begins with the simple ability to reserve a small part of you that just watches yourself and whatever is happening with detachment and curiosity.

Actually, this witnessing act is like a gateway into the real Self, the one that is simply awareness. Everything else, the identity and perceived idea of reality, is just a creation of your mind. All activity of identifying, thinking, analysing, blaming and suffering is just your mind distracting you from the real you. This is what meditation has always been about: to quiet the mind, so as to get past it and reunite with our real Self.

The principle of resistance applies to everything in your life. In any situation where you are uncomfortable, no matter what it is, you are resisting. To the degree you do that, you suffer. If you can step aside and watch yourself have whatever reaction you are having, you will find that there are other choices about how to respond, at which point you can pick the one you would like to have, rather than being unconsciously driven every time you are stimulated in a certain way. This mindful state allows you to respond with greater choice – to take charge of your destiny – rather than always feeling at the hands of fate. This is the beginning of self-mastery. It all starts with our ability to master the mind, which leads us to the ultimate liberation.

People with 'higher consciousness' or 'enlightened awareness' are those who have mastered this principle of witnessing. It does take practice and some willpower because the habit of resisting is deeply ingrained. It has been a significant part of the unconscious default setting for some time. The Dalai Lama once said, "If you have willpower then you can change anything."

After some practice, witnessing will become an effortless part of you, your own personal conscious companion to lead you through and beyond any 'challenging' situation or conflict you encounter. And, of course, remember that daily meditation is the most effective way to foster and strengthen this very essential part of you.

Chapter 13

# SELF-REFLECTION

## Conscious Habit 6

*The ultimate value of life depends upon awareness and the power of contemplation rather than upon mere survival.*
—Aristotle

Self-reflection and self-inquiry are integral to our process of change for the better. For this reason, I have dedicated two chapters to this subject.

For peace to prevail, for us to return to harmony, it is essential we understand how the very thinking that shapes our reality confines us. Release from a conflicted and destructive mindset lies in knowing we are not yet seeing beyond our confines but that we are indeed capable of it. This transformative process is not only essential for our personal comfort, but for the collective wellbeing of humanity and all beings on earth.

We have all dreamed of the perfect life, yet we fail to recognise that life, in its own natural state, *is* perfect. As Buddha declared, "When you realise how perfect everything is you will tilt your head back and laugh at the sky." I did just that. And I laughed non-stop for five days – not just giggles, but tear-streaming, soul-jiggling laughter!

Yes, it does happen… because that realisation is who we are at the very core of our being, every single one of us. And when we are at rest with our innermost being this realisation is inevitable. It is not a matter of 'if' we get it... it is a matter of 'when'.

But it does require our presence. It requires us to enter the dimension of our being that is free of distorted, conditioned perceptions, and to make the shift from what we *think* we are to what *is*. It is only then that we can see everything in its infinite truth. We all yearn for this truth so deeply that some of us have even created an imaginary utopian dream of heaven or nirvana. Yet, as one great Zen master once said, "Nirvana is exactly what is happening, minus our opinions about it."

Every human has four endowments: self-awareness, conscience, independent will and creative imagination. These are the ultimate source of human freedom. They give us the power to choose, to respond and to change. Self-reflection becomes a significant tool when it comes to putting these endowments into action.

Initially many people get the acts of self-reflection and self-criticism mixed up. This is why the understanding of witnessing is so valuable. Witnessing has a neutral quality. This means there is a distancing from emotions tied to the beliefs we have collected. We are able to see that all beliefs, perceptions and even values, whether negative or positive, are simply tools we use to interact with life.

We see that these tools can be more or less effective in creating the life we want, and we are able to observe our own experience with greater acceptance. Essentially we can choose which tools to continue using. If you don't make the time to work on creating the life you want, you will eventually have no choice but to spend a *lot* of time dealing with the life you *don't* want. The bottom line is this: A negative mind will never give you a positive life.

Oftentimes the need to change our beliefs and behaviours seems like an impossible task. It seems like our problems are insurmountable. But the truth is, the size of your problems is nothing compared with your ability to solve them. Don't overestimate your problems and underestimate yourself.

Self-reflection will give you the space and clarity you need to connect with deeper awareness. You will see what you have been operating with, what no longer serves you, and what will serve you more effectively. It will also open you to new insights that you may never have imagined.

Self-reflection puts you in a more powerful position of self-awareness. The more you apply self-reflection, the more awareness you develop. Without this you remain caught in the automatic feedback loops of unconscious identifications. To move beyond this cycle and into a passage of genuine renewal, self-awareness is essential.

## SELF-AWARENESS AND THE POWER OF BELIEFS

Opinions begin to shape us from the very beginning of our lives. Based on our early interactions with our families, teachers and others, we all develop generalisations about who we are and what our relationship to the rest of the world will be. These generalisations – a collection of stories, beliefs and identifications – form the basis of our own sense of personality and our way of interpreting the world around us.

Becoming aware of our beliefs is essential in our development for greater self-awareness. It is because most of these beliefs run at the 'unseen' level that they tend to block us from true self-awareness. We don't even realise who or what we truly are, let alone how we seem to create conflicting experiences. Until we bring greater awareness to them, our beliefs continue to hold great power in our lives.

We don't 'knowingly' choose these beliefs. We absorb them from our environment, mostly when we are too young to know any better. And we continue to absorb information throughout our whole lives. Our subconscious mind is constantly tuned in and listening to everything around us. The subconscious mind has no discriminating powers, it simply stores whatever information we come across as a given.

Gradually, this information creates our 'map' of reality. Against this map, our minds screen the information we receive. We accept the *familiar*, whether it's healthy or harmful, and *reject* the unfamiliar, whether it's beneficial or not. Although this may seem counter-intuitive, it is unfortunately the way our subconscious self tends to work.

All of these underlying beliefs become core components of the way we see other people, the world, and ourselves. Some of these beliefs give us outcomes and experiences we want, while others create outcomes and experiences we don't want. In the world of thought, like attracts like. This is how people get stuck in routines or ruts. Understanding this, and mobilising our own power to actively respond to this, is critically important to our perception of happiness.

The brain is bombarded with so much data all the time – 10 million bits of information per second – that in order to maintain sanity and function effectively, we only process a small fraction of incoming data, about 40 bits per second. And, whatever our brains access is dictated by filters, stored information about our values, beliefs and memories. This is referred to as the 'conditioned self'.

Human beings have a powerful need for consistency between what they *believe* to be true and what really *is* true. Unfortunately, most people would rather be right than be happy. This means that regardless of how erroneous your perception of things really is or how much your beliefs result in misery, you will arrange to be right about them by creating situations that seem to confirm what you believe is true.

This is further compounded by the fact that many beliefs you might have about yourself, such as being 'bad', 'unworthy' or 'unlovable', are too painful or shameful to hold in your conscious awareness. Consequently they are repressed into your unconscious mind, where they are buried out of sight but still affect you. Because of this, they are unavailable for conscious examination and transformation. The other thing we do with our repressed parts is to project them onto others. This results in extreme emotional reactions to others who exhibit the characteristics we believe are 'bad' or unacceptable in ourselves.

In many ways, emotional healing involves 'unlearning', transforming and releasing these old beliefs and sometimes making new, healthier ones. In essence, the mind does not only believe things that are good for us. In fact, the mind is completely neutral and will take on whatever it's exposed to – good, bad or ugly. This means that with more conscious tools we are able to work with our minds to great benefit.

The mind is a goal-seeking mechanism, and a very powerful one. Your mind can make whatever it allows into it – and *believes* – come true in your life. As Abraham Lincoln said, "Most people are about as happy as they make up their mind to be." Many people who have had significant negative emotional experiences tend to focus on what they *don't* want. However the universe doesn't see or hear 'don't want'. Your mind and the energy of the universe simply respond to the image or feeling you hold of yourself. So when you notice yourself focusing on what you do not want, *change the focus to what you do want.*

Beliefs come true because we need consistency between what we believe (inwardly) and what we experience outwardly, and we will do anything to create this consistency. For most people this dynamic is happening at a very unconscious level, in four primary ways as follows.

1. **Energy attraction and interaction:** We get attracted to people and situations that contain the energy of our beliefs, which of course confirms that the belief is true. For instance, you believe no one will ever really love you, which causes you to be drawn to people who will leave you. Yet what is simply happening is the law of attraction: Energy (internal beliefs) attracts like energy (external events).

2. **Owning the belief and giving its meaning power:** We 'pretend' that the belief is true even if it isn't. We walk around with lenses coloured by our beliefs and project that meaning onto whatever happens. This confirms in the mind that the belief is true.

3. **Behaving in ways that drive people to act in the way we feared they would:** For example, we fear that people will leave us, and because of that fear, we act in a way that eventually causes the person to leave. This again creates the confirmation in the mind that the belief is true.

4. **The limiting beliefs literally become a 'mind trap':** This means that our beliefs all conflict with each other, making it almost impossible for us to act in certain circumstances. Some examples of this type of mind trap would be: "I must find a boyfriend to be truly happy. I am not beautiful enough to have a boyfriend." Or, "I have to be successful to be happy. I am not worthy of success."

With the first three behaviours, we get to be right about what we believe. And, as the ego believes, it's better to be right than be loved. However, it only takes so long before we are acutely dissatisfied with our ego's idea of reality! The fourth condition can be extremely debilitating and cause great suffering.

## Why is self-reflection so important?

Self-reflection is exactly what we need to start making sense of ourselves and our world, and to start transforming our lives consciously. It enables us to see into the shallow illusory nature of our minds, our beliefs and our actions. We begin to see how we are confined by our thoughts, and we create a space to examine them effectively.

With deeper reflection we are able to unleash our authentic expressions and true conscious power. We cultivate a meditative mind. In the process we become conscious of our formerly developed unconscious beliefs. We are also able to see the cause and effect of our beliefs. Through the act of self-reflection, we may begin to see that it is *our* thoughts and beliefs that create our appearing reality.

Most people are geared to constantly look outside themselves, yet fail to realise that *what is seen is produced by the one who is looking.* Subsequently, most people fail to see that *life reflects us back to ourselves.* Because we continue to look outwardly it can take a long time to realise that everything we perceive is generated by our internal map, not by the people or events outside of us.

**Beliefs precede and colour experience.**

*Everything* you encounter was first only imagined or thought, especially those things you believe. Since whatever you deeply believe comes true in your life, you could make a conscious choice to believe whatever would create a happier, more peaceful life. Most people, however, never take conscious charge and do this. Instead, most people unconsciously remain a victim of so-called circumstance.

On the other side of the fence are people who repress negative emotions because they *are* trying to take charge. This repression happens when people 'decide' to empower themselves or improve their lives by thinking positive thoughts, but they don't go about it the right way. Instead of acknowledging and processing negative thoughts, they ignore and repress them, blanketing them over with 'positive' affirmations that are really being directed by underlying conditions of fear and lack. Consequently this results in disempowerment and feelings of disillusion.

Self-reflection facilitates a shift from these disempowered states by cultivating more awareness. It brings us to the part of us that can respond effectively. As the light of *consciousness* shines on the unconscious aspects of ourselves, we are in a very different position. We are able to gain a better perspective. And in most cases, meditation (especially witnessing awareness) dissolves all or part of the emotional charge that corresponds with negative and painful beliefs.

This frees up something deeper in us; the part of us that knows truth. In the presence of conscious truth, whatever has been false simply falls away. It is impossible to continue making the same choices or giving false beliefs the same value. This places us back in a position of conscious awareness and ownership and therefore conscious choice. It puts us in a position of great response-ability! This is the most significant turning point for self-empowerment. We can't continue hoping to rearrange our *circumstances* to solve things; rather, we must rearrange our internal ideas. As Ernest Hemingway wrote, "You can't get away from yourself by moving from one place to another." It is 'you' wherever you are!

Self-reflection reveals the gold mine of potential that lies sleeping within our minds, waiting to be awakened and used for higher purposes. But the real or deeper purpose of self-reflection is for us to know our true Self. As we make contact with our true nature we are able to access the source of limitless wisdom that abides in our hearts and souls. It is through accessing this deeper wisdom and truth that we are able to live empowered and uplifting lives, participating at a level that brings our greater potential to fruition.

With this unfolding comes an unswerving faith in our own capacity to be and do anything.[24] There is infinite potential in every one of us. We also begin to trust our ability to live life consciously. As Oliver Wendell Holmes Sr., an American professor and author, said, "What lies behind us and what lies before us are tiny matters compared to what lies within us."

Largely we avoid the things that we're afraid of because we think there will be dire consequences if we confront them. We are afraid of the pain we will have to face as we journey towards rediscovering our true Self. Sometimes people don't want to know the truth because they don't want their illusions destroyed. But the truly dire consequences in our lives come from *resisting* what is true, from avoiding things that we need to

---

[24] Please keep in mind this is still in accord with your true purpose and universal laws.

address. Avoidance is guaranteed to bring you suffering *for the rest of your life*. Facing the process will see you encounter *momentary* pain as it leads you to great peace and happiness.

Unfortunately most people are still choosing to bury the pain. Using old unconscious habits, or even drugs or medication, to relieve the burden of our emotions bears only the most superficial resemblance to the state of freedom or happiness. Unlike a *meditative* mind, the medicated mind is dependent on something chemical, something 'other', whereas the meditative mind knows there *is nothing outside itself.*

When we choose to face the pain and work with it *consciously* through meditation and self-reflective tools, we begin to develop a 'practiced mind'. The practiced mind constantly learns new ways to trust itself and to discover its own process of liberation, entering into a deeper place of substantial calm. In this way insight is gained every time the practicing mind meets (rather than avoids) challenging situations and emotions.

The more deeply practiced one is, the less one is drawn to the idea of easy fixes, because deeper satisfaction (and more desirable outcomes) arise through transformative self-discovery. We learn that meeting difficulty with willing attention is far less exhausting and significantly more rewarding than employing avoidance tactics. We also discover that we are far more creative and intelligent than we previously imagined. We have *never* truly been confined in the way we have been conditioned to think.

## The art of self-awareness and self-reflection

Self-reflection is born of a willingness to understand more about our fundamental nature, purpose and essence. A person's ability to reflect inwardly ultimately leads them beyond the contemplation of their conditioned 'self' and into the broader contemplation of life as a whole, as something far greater than the mind's perception or identity. But before we are able to recognise these deeper, more expansive aspects, self-reflection is the tool we use to understand how and why we think and act the way we do.

During clear self-reflection you will begin to recognise not only what you did or what happened, but also what you felt, how you attracted or created the circumstance, and the beliefs that generated it. You come to see that all circumstances, and *how you feel about them*, are a mirror to your inner beliefs. Reflection also reveals how the situation served you in a process of growing and becoming more conscious. You can explore what you have gained from the experience and what it gives you to move forward in greater awareness. In fact these perspectives can be put to use as specific questions during self-reflection.

Most people consider themselves too busy to stop and take time to self-reflect. Time is typically our excuse, but it isn't the only reason we don't reflect. Perhaps we don't even think about it, or don't think we know how to do it, or don't recognise the power we can access through it. Maybe we're afraid to acknowledge what isn't working or feels bad. We may think staying busy and *doing* is more important, or that we should avoid all forms of 'thinking' on the spiritual path.

However, self-reflection is the most significant form of 'thinking' we can do, because it is our capacity to inwardly observe that leads to greater conscious awareness and transcendent being. It supports our minds to make the shift from unconscious being to conscious awareness. Self-reflection is integral to experiencing greater fulfilment and liberation. The desire for personal mastery all hinges on our ability to harness the insights gained from self-reflection. Self-reflection equips us to truly take responsibility. It also enables us to strengthen the practice of witnessing. These two skills, witnessing and self-reflection, are enough to divert anyone from continuing a life full of chaos and crisis.

In most instances we react to situations without much presence or awareness, simply acting from subconscious beliefs and habits. However, when we bring conscious awareness into our experience, we eventually start to recognise the very first moment a subconscious belief or fear is triggered, and this enables us to respond to it more appropriately. I call this 'catching the tipping stone'.

When we are not consciously present to the first trigger, we have a knee-jerk reaction and do the best we can to reject it. We kick the stone over the edge of the mountain! The thing is, that stone doesn't stop there. It continues gathering more debris as it gains momentum and oftentimes turns into an avalanche. Most people don't even realise what they have set in motion until the avalanche is looming upon them. It is *much* easier to catch the little stone at the top of the mountain than stop an avalanche!

This is why we need to travel to the top of the mountain, the peak of our awareness, and to be present as the conscious self in the now. It is there that you can master the art of 'catching the tipping stone'. Gradually you begin to catch the unconscious thoughts *before* you validate them or put them into words or actions. Thoughts are easy to transform. Words and actions are much more powerful, creating human realities that can be hard to undo. If we are watchful and mindful we can prevent unkind words from leaving our mouths. Speech should have three gatekeepers: Is it kind? Is it true? Is it essential?

Let us not forget that thoughts *are* very powerful. A collection of thoughts can create a world of war or one of peace. By becoming more conscious you change your thoughts, the way they accumulate, and what they create. In essence, the more conscious you become the less possible it is to continue acting out unconscious behaviours.

**It is impossible to do something harmful to yourself or another, and do it *consciously*.**

Only by remaining unconscious can a person continue to do something that is harmful to themselves or to others. Once we truly understand this, we know why Jesus said, "Father, forgive them; for they know not what they do." So the only real issue in the world, or in oneself, is non-awareness. It is impossible to say hurtful words if you are aware. It is impossible to violate when awareness is there.

**When you make self-reflective meditation a habit, it is impossible to remain unconscious. Awakening is inevitable.**

Most people continue to believe that the mind itself is the place to find answers or validate reality. Ironically, although the mind cannot give us true answers or reveal the true nature of reality, we must first shed conscious light on our minds, especially on whatever we hold unconsciously. Beliefs are usually evaluated by information, which 'proves' something is 'true' or 'false'. If it's true it's worth believing; if it's false, it isn't.

The problem with this form of assessment lays in the limitations of the mind itself and the fact that, essentially, most of what we perceive to be true or false is merely an illusion. A more useful way to evaluate beliefs is by whether they are resourceful or non-resourceful. Does the belief create happiness and peace or something less preferable?

Since whatever you deeply believe comes true, the only resourceful beliefs are those that correspond to the outcomes you aspire to. Perhaps the most important skill you can gain from self-reflection is the ability to choose what you want to believe. You don't have to believe what appeared true based on past experience or continue a belief just because you gave your allegiance to it before.

## Identifying unconscious beliefs

The first step in transforming beliefs is to find out what beliefs you still identify with. One way to begin this is to complete the following sentences:

– I am...
– I can... I can't....
– I should... I shouldn't...
– If I could... If I had... If I was...
– People are...
– The world is...

Pay attention to your deeper thoughts and feelings, or the things you say to yourself in a moment of irritation, not the ones you've learned from self-development books and programs (the things you think you *should* believe about yourself). The positive beliefs don't need attention; they are already contributing constructively to your life. You need to bring your awareness to what you really believe about yourself when things seem the most difficult; for example, "No one will ever understand me. There's something wrong with me. No one will ever really love me. The world is a cruel place..." and so on. These statements are connected to your negative and limited core beliefs. These are beliefs that need to be brought into consciousness, not supressed and ignored!

You can also see what beliefs you carry by looking at what is happening in your life. Since what you believe generally manifests, you can tell what you believe just by looking at the elements of your life. If you are having trouble (or *perceive* something to be a problem) in any area of your life, somewhere there is a core belief about yourself and about that type of dynamic that is manifesting in your life.

When you compare yourself to people who appear more successful or seem to have a better life, you can be sure the difference is that they have different, more empowering, core beliefs. Once you identify your core beliefs, you can then determine what beliefs would create a preferred result and attune to this new way of thinking and feeling about yourself. Importantly, when we are truly aligned with our inner being, what we prefer is no longer about the ego's definition, but about the soul's creative purpose and process.

It is important you attune to these new images (the beliefs, thoughts and feelings) frequently. The only reason the old belief seems true is that you have focused on it so much, which makes it play out in reality, which of course makes you focus on it more, which makes it play out more. Essentially, your beliefs and the degree to which you operate through them create feedback loops in your life.

## Transforming beliefs

The real key in establishing new and more constructive beliefs is to be able to generate the matching type of feeling or state at a deeper level. This is why meditation is such a powerful tool for self-transformation and liberation.

First of all, create a regular meditative space where you can enter a deep state of acceptance of yourself *as you are.* It is important you do this first so as not to attempt re-forming yourself from a space that is already vibrating with self-resistance. From a state of acceptance you can then focus on a new belief. Create a clear vision of how you choose to see yourself and your life. Make it as sensually alive as possible: How do you look? How do you feel? What are your thoughts? How are you acting? How does life look around you?

The more vivid it is, and the more emotion you associate with it, the better. This is not the type of 'emotion' that goes along with a stored conditional belief. It is an *energy* that corresponds with the type of experience you *want* to cultivate in your life. In addition to holding this vision during meditation, replay it right before you go to sleep and as soon as you wake up. Repeat the vision as often as possible.

Doing so may bring up old and uncomfortable feelings, so be prepared for that. Old beliefs are associated with safety and the identity of yourself or the world around you, as you have known it. Because of this deeply stored association, old beliefs fight for their/your life! If you understand this, and maintain the tool of *witnessing awareness*, you don't need to let it bother you when old feelings or thoughts surface. Just see them for what they are, nothing but un-resourceful thoughts and beliefs, and bring your attention back to a deeper state of awareness and focus on what you want.

Though changing beliefs can happen in an instant, in most cases the process of changing core beliefs takes many months or even years to achieve. Most of our thoughts and beliefs have been operating on default for a long time, hidden in the unconscious self. So it takes practice – the *habit* of self-reflection – to bring more awareness to your deeper thinking and feeling self. However, with the correct methods it is possible to transform the old conditions and establish more empowering 'beliefs' in 21 days.[25]

It is important you are patient with yourself. This patience is readily available the more you practice acceptance. Change does take time, especially without the aid of conscious tools. Meditation greatly speeds up the process, because it helps you become much more conscious and aware of what you are creating. It also takes the emotional charge off things in your life, allowing you to see more objectively. The practices of witnessing and self-reflection strengthen this and make the journey of transformation truly worth undertaking.

You may not have realised it yet, but you are already an expert at creating what you believe and focus on. You may not yet trust that anything you focus on and believe *can* (and does) happen for you. But remember, most of what you focus on you did not consciously choose. At the ordinary level, what we focus on was chosen for us when we were small, and it continues to run on automatic. Our experiences were also chosen at the level of our souls (again something most people are not conscious of) as part of the perfect scenery we need to experience, to create and master our soul's purpose.

---

[25] See my website *www.isira.com* for details of free programs, or for a more intensive guided one-on-one process called the Deep Resolution Process.

But the very fact we can adopt and change our beliefs indicates that we truly are not bound to any conditions that are linked to them. Even though the 'map' (our collection of beliefs) is linked to all our experiences, the 'map' is not reality itself. We simply learned to use the map, or identify with it to the point that we believe it to be reality. It has been given power through habit! As readily as we learned the map, we can unlearn it.

All you have to do is to consciously change your attention to a state of aware acceptance and focus on more conscious choices. Once you learn to consciously direct your focus, you'll start experiencing more of what you want. As you gain the ability to understand your beliefs more deeply, you will begin to see beyond them and even understand how to complete with them. As a result, growth and transformation are inevitable.

## TRANSCENDING BELIEFS

The quality of witnessing in self-reflection gives us the ability to see our beliefs for what they are: simply beliefs – constructed *ideas and generalisations* about reality – not reality as it actually is. Every ego is a master of deception, working through distorted perceptions and selective reasoning. With enough rationale you can make *anything* right or wrong. The question is: Can you find the way to make *everything* neither right nor wrong? If you can achieve this you will finally come to peace with yourself... with life. You will be liberated.

Ultimately it is only awareness that will enable you to see beyond conditioned opinions into what truly is. All happenings simply are what they are... there is no right or wrong event... just different versions. The more we see ourselves and our beliefs with the light of awareness, the more we experience our true nature. What naturally follows is the transformation and *release* of our beliefs. When we realise the beliefs themselves are not real, we then know *we* are the ones who have the power to either continue identifying with them or to *go beyond them*. This brings us a sense of calm and deeper understanding, leading us to a place of acceptance. It is then that we begin to realise we already are the freedom we seek.

CHAPTER 14

# PRACTICING SELF-REFLECTION

### Conscious Habit 6, continued

> *The world as we have created it is a process of our thinking. It cannot be changed without changing our thinking.* —Albert Einstein

The journey to renewal is available to anyone willing to embark upon it. But personal change of this order is not easy. Many people respond by trying harder and doing more of the same. That is like turning up the heat on a kettle already in danger of boiling over. The real solution lies in a deeper place of our being. It is this that opens the way for renewal through mindfulness and presence.

Being honest with oneself is the first and hardest step toward renewal. Through mindfulness we learn to reflect, and to attend to both the quiet voice inside and the subtle clues from others and our environment, which can steer us in the right direction. Through hope, we reinvigorate ourselves and inspire others. Through compassion, we spark physiological and psychological renewal, while building strong, trusting and meaningful relationships. Consciously attending to ourselves and to those around us, including the communities where we work and play, can pay important dividends to us, our relationships and the world as a whole.

### Being a Conscious Creator

Self-reflection plays an integral role in enabling us to make the shift from a very ego-centred view of life to one that is more universal in nature. Although self-reflection definitely helps us at the personal level, the ultimate outcome is one of liberation. Through self-reflection we gain clear insight about our own unique attributes, strengths, values and purpose. With greater conscious presence we are able to nurture our highest values and bring these qualities into the world, making our lives truly meaningful and successful in the most authentic way.

By taking the time to reflect, we can start to clarify our own personal vision of what it is that we want to be, do and have in our lives – what is most authentic to us – and most importantly, how we want to feel as we go through life. With this clarity we are able to align ourselves with the consciousness, behaviours and environments that will continue to support us in attaining our greatest potential.

This means self-reflection is *the key to progression*. It is the first tool to transform our beliefs. *In order to transform or transcend beliefs you must first be aware of them. Next you must acknowledge them.* Without either of these, nothing changes. As you acquire a more reflective mind and the ability to witness you develop the 'practiced mind' – the art of *mindfulness*. It is for this reason self-reflection is one of the conscious habits of more enlightened people. *Regular* self-reflection creates the openness and expansion of awareness needed to change the way we think and perceive. By reflecting on yourself and life, you will make your life experiences your most precious source of learning, and your most fertile ground for transformation and success.

## Responsibility

Self-reflection also brings us to another very challenging but significant truth. The bottom line is: We are all responsible for our own experience. Until we take responsibility, the full benefits of self-reflection are missed. By continuously looking outside and putting the 'blame' or 'control' on others, on circumstances outside of yourself, you fail to utilise your inherent power.

If you recognise that your negative or fear-based feelings towards others and situations are mirroring back your own fear-based beliefs then you *can* do something to help yourself. By seeing that 'life' is reflected by you and to you, you generate empowerment, and a greater awareness that provides you with the tools for conscious change and discovery.

As we learn to look for that reflection in the mirror, pointing us back to our inner self, we gain a sense of responsibility for our own lives. In doing so we are able to be present at the causative level of our experience. Essentially, self-reflection is a tool that will enable you to become the conscious creator of your life rather than continuing to feel like the unconscious victim of life. This also allows you to be more restful with 'what is'.

The more you can be okay with 'what is', the more you understand 'what is', 'how is' and 'why is'. This acceptance, however, does not mean one becomes indifferent or insensitive. It doesn't mean you're okay with injustice and suffering or that you would not do anything about them. It means you emotionally accept things the way they are and do not resist what is. This is not a state of resignation either. *Accepting things the way they are means you are free of negative emotions that get in the way of a more conscious response.*

Imagine you are walking through a forest when suddenly you find yourself in a bog. If you resist and react and start thrashing around, the log that was floating nearby is swallowed up and you start to sink. If you simply think, "Oh no... I'm in a bog, there's nothing I can do", you don't even notice there is a log floating nearby, and you sink. But if you accept you're in the bog, you relax and you are mindfully present. You think, "Hmmm... okay, I'm in a bog... now what?" Then you notice the log, climb upon it, and make your way out of the bog.

In fact, a state of acceptance is what gives us true access to conscious response. This means if we can transform or change something for the better we will be capable of doing so from a place that is both consciously wise and unattached to outcome. Resisting what is and wanting to change what is are not the same either. The difference is one of attachment to the outcome. The person who is attached to the outcome suffers if they do not get the outcome they want; whereas the happy, peaceful person prefers the outcome they want but is not attached to it. Their happiness comes from within, and is not dependent on what goes on around them.

This brings us to the problem of depending on what 'happens' to make us happy. And, as we see, most of humanity is fixated with what happens at the material level. As far as true joy is concerned, your football team winning, wearing the latest fashion or winning the lottery is completely irrelevant.

Peace is the same. Whether you have your house one day and not the next is, at the deepest level, irrelevant. During certain periods in my life, I lived with almost no belongings. I even lived in a tent under a tarpaulin, with my few belongings in boxes. Nearly everything was destroyed by a mini-cyclone and I was as joyful and peaceful as ever. At the other end of the spectrum, I was also graced with a millionaire's lifestyle, and I never lost any sleep worrying if it would come to an end. It did eventually come to an end, and I moved on with the lightness of self-born happiness.

It just doesn't serve to tie your happiness to things that will eventually come to an end. True joy and deep peace cannot be achieved through dependency on transitory material events. Nor can they be manifested by an act of will, especially if that will is based on a goal or need from the external world of circumstance. That will lives in the same world where the rich exploit the poor and hyper-consumerism destroys our natural environment.

True happiness and peace actually derive from an essence beyond form. It is consciousness itself that is always the supreme essence of who you are – complete, needing nothing more or nothing less, having no conditions. Simply being. And this 'being' is love. When we know this, the real love affair with life begins. As Helen Keller said, "The best and most beautiful things in the world cannot be seen or even touched – they must be felt with the heart."

Most people are not only unhappy as a result of what goes on around them, but because of what goes on inside of them – not in the heart, but in the mind. Unfortunately, when we look around we can see that this universe, according to most people on the planet, is often not a happy one. However the truth is you can always create a new and happier world for yourself, at any time. And this happiness is not at all dependent on anyone else or the rest of the world.

To adopt a position of power, one in which you have conscious direction over your destiny, you must take full responsibility for your responses or reactions towards whatever is happening. This opens up the possibility for you to do something more constructive with your situation and create something different. The main source, then, of both personal power and peace of mind is in taking responsibility for what happens. Once we realise that responsibility is really showing us our response-*ability*, we can pause and take the time to actually *reflect*.

First, you must acknowledge that, whatever your experience, it is *your* response that gives you either peace or suffering. Life may provide the stimulus, but you provide the response. Until you develop greater conscious presence this response often comes from an unconscious part of you, one you have little or no control over, or so it seems. Resistance is simply the part of you that is trying to change (or protect against) what is happening. However resistance is both an unconscious and dysfunctional tool. In most cases resistance was learned as a way to feel safe and protect against further pain.

For example, you may have become an overloaded, stressed, unhappy workaholic because, in your family, you were taught "you only succeed through hard work." But now meditation, or the natural progression of your life, is dislodging the old pattern and creating new possibilities to be more relaxed, to take a path of less effort and more leverage, or to be happy with simple pleasures. Consciously you may want this, but since letting go of the old defence mechanism feels unsafe to that unconscious 'inner child' part of you, you resist.

Whatever the discomfort, whatever the upheaval or issue, some part of you is trying to grow and evolve and another conditioned part of you is not willing to let go. Yet life will continue demanding change and growth. Only if you resist will you create discomfort. And you can only continue to resist if you continue to unconsciously hold onto the inner belief as being something valid.

## THE LIBERATING POWER OF ACCEPTANCE

Acceptance is directly opposite to resistance. Resistance creates more agitation. In resistance there is no space for conscious awareness. Acceptance creates a state of stillness. In this stillness one is able to see the belief (the cause of an experience) for what it is. It is simply a belief, something that was taken on, something that served as a tool for a while, and of course, something that can be released. It can be released or transformed because through the stillness found in witnessing or acceptance, there is also the realisation that the belief is not *who* or *what* you truly are. Greater options can be considered and appreciated.

Acceptance already indicates the workings of a more conscious mind, a mind that has the capacity to self-reflect. And it is during self-reflection, with the 'witnessing' mind, that the grip of unconscious responses is softened. It is self-reflection that leads to the realisation that *you* are the creator of your life. With this realisation come two great gifts.

The first gift is your conscious ability to use tools that serve you for the best experience you can have. The second is that you liberate yourself from your unconscious attachment to thought-based identifications (the ego) and your authentic self begins to shine through. The more you are present as your authentic being, the more you will experience life as it truly is. And, you'll get a lot more out of your life if you're more conscious about what you're creating.

Given that our conditioned beliefs are usually the real source of our suffering, it follows then that suffering is not a necessary element of life. There are definite ways to change your life from one containing suffering to one that is happy and peaceful all the time. It is important, however, to differentiate between pain and suffering, because pain *is* an integral part of life, corresponding with the natural process of life as it evolves. Yet it is when pain is present that most people go into a state of resistance. Therefore, understanding the nature and role of pain in our lives is integral to our ability to go beyond suffering.

## Pain, suffering and self-reflection

One of the greatest challenges arising with self-reflection is that pain and suffering become more evident. This often causes the spiritual practitioner to recoil or avoid the deeper work. However if we understand that our lack of self-reflection keeps us unconsciously bound and causes suffering, we can more readily understand the role and distinction of pain in our lives. We can even meet it with a greater degree of tolerance.

Pain is simply a label for the energy that occurs when we are undergoing a *process of change*, whether physical, mental, emotional or spiritual.

Pain is also the signal telling us we need to pay attention, become conscious of something that was buried in our unconscious self, and make some changes in order to evolve and regain a state of harmony. This signal is actually a tool of our innate intelligence, raising an alarm, trying to tell us we need to address something consciously.

The more we live consciously, the less we create circumstances that cause pain, and the subtler the pain signals become. However, pain doesn't ever disappear altogether because it is part of our natural makeup, a functional energy that serves the process of evolution. On the other hand, suffering is a condition caused by deeply set states of resistance or attachment by the mind. Pain and suffering are neither mutually inclusive nor the same symptom. They are not occurring for the same reasons in life. We have a choice: How we respond to life determines our ability to transcend suffering. *Pain is inevitable – suffering is optional.* It is possible to experience great pain yet not be suffering. In fact one can even experience peace, joy and freedom whilst being in pain.

When I was in hospital with a life-threatening illness I had this very experience. Indeed I could feel the pain energy of the body going through a transition from illness towards wellness. Yet as I was in a surrendered state, I had no resistance to what was happening. I chose to be consciously present. I was in a state of total acceptance. Whilst being at one with the pain, I felt profound peace – in fact, bliss – and in this state I encountered incredible insights about my condition, which led to a 'resurrection' of my whole being. Pain was an inevitable part of the transformative process, yet I did not suffer.

When we continue to resist the 'pain signals', we create even greater tension and confusion until our circumstance is overwhelming. We lose the conscious ability to respond and spiral into deeper states of suffering. We push the pain and suffering (and ourselves) into the unconscious realm. Our attachment, identification and resistance to our conflicting states make it hard to see clearly or act wisely.

Developing tolerance is part of spiritual maturity. We gradually learn that *it is better to tolerate short term pain to make long term progress than it is to resist short term pain and experience long term suffering!* Tolerance is not about being comfortable with what is happening, but the willingness to be *uncomfortable* and still stay present. This tolerance gives us the key to unlock something very powerful. When pain is buried in the unconscious realm its transformative power remains locked up. When we let go of our minds' resistance, when we accept the process we are in, we can yield with what is happening. In this yielding, wondrous and remarkable things happen, albeit not always immediately. It's in these moments that witnessing awareness is our greatest friend!

The spaciousness found in awareness itself reveals a surprising reservoir of energy and clarity that is far greater than the predicaments we face. The intensity of our anger, grief, fear or shame is a gauge of intense meaning that has been locked down, alienated from the aware self, waiting to be released. In the space of awareness, of letting be, the transformative power in the 'pain energy' is unleashed, set free to do its work. We then begin to understand what the pain is telling us, and we can be carried through by its power. We transcend suffering and allow pain to transform us.

Actually, we don't need to *do* anything other than consciously allow. It already is the intelligent energy that will carry us to a renewed state – we just need to let it happen. We also discover that awareness itself is not in pain. Awareness of heat is not hot. Awareness of tension is not tense. So the more deeply seated you become in awareness, the more freedom you discover... To your surprise you will realise that *you* are not in pain at all! This is profoundly liberating. It gives you the space to truly let the process happen.

The art of non-resistance is central to our journey of liberation and awakening. Attaining greater acceptance in our lives brings us greater peace and freedom and enables us to make even deeper contact with reality as it is. Through complete acceptance we can live a life that is deeply centred in the present moment. Actually, in truth, as far as transformation is concerned, there is nothing 'you' can *do* about it. 'You' cannot transform yourself, and you certainly cannot transform anybody else. All you *can* do is create a *space* for transformation to happen, for grace and consciousness to arise.

It is then that we truly re-engage. Whenever someone asks me what to do with pain or conflict I always say 'get engaged'. This means you need to welcome the situation *as it is*. In this way you can open the space for deeper insight to arise and engage in a way that leads you with, through and beyond the apparent 'issue'. The mind usually resists this because we think it will only prolong the conflict, when in actual fact it takes us beyond the threshold of fear and into a place of true responsive awareness. Transformation happens rapidly, even instantly, in this space. By being truly engaged we can access our true Self that is the source of divine awareness, higher intelligence, uninhibited creativity and even seemingly supernatural powers.

As you discover more about yourself through self-reflection, you will gradually understand the nature of your mind and the conditions you have lived by. As you balance the process of clarifying your thoughts and adopting more resourceful ones, you will find it a lot easier to relax into 'no-mind'. It is only because you live in conflict with your thoughts, and because you hold conflicting beliefs, that you struggle to be relaxed within yourself and life.

As we enter more deeply into our true nature it simply follows that our thinking is changed. However, this doesn't mean we leave thinking behind. Yes, we can and do transcend our identification with thoughts and beliefs, but once we realise this, we are free to continue working in harmony with this wonderful tool, the mind. Gradually you will discover the perfect balance between the ever-present Self that is no-mind and the vehicle of this little human self – your mind – that enables you to navigate your way through life. You will soon realise that you, that all of life, is truly wondrous… and what a magical journey it can be!

## GETTING STARTED WITH SELF-REFLECTION

Below are three lists of questions that will help you to initiate the process of self-reflection.

### Life up until now
- What are my happiest memories? What are the beliefs surrounding these memories?
- What are my saddest memories? What are the beliefs surrounding these memories?

- What were the most meaningful moments?
- What were my biggest tests? How did I think about it when first faced with the 'problem'? What was the belief attached to the problem?
- What did I learn? What did I achieve? Consider at least three things you have gained.
- What do I want to accomplish that I still haven't achieved? What are the beliefs and behaviours around this?
- What do I feel acknowledged for?
- What do I feel unacknowledged for?
- What did I feel I couldn't do?
- What did I discover I could do? Think of something you once thought was not possible.
- What are my greatest strengths?
- What were the things I avoided? Which people or circumstances do I still avoid?
- What bothers me still?
- What am I still holding onto? What am I afraid to let go of?
- How well have I communicated my feelings? What remains unspoken? What needs to happen for me to create better communication?

I suggest you spend two weeks reflecting on this first list of questions. Reflect on all of the questions in week one. Use a journal to help the process of deepening self-awareness. In the second week, revisit each question, and see if there is anything new that surfaces, perhaps something that was held unconsciously.

## Changing current life patterns

- How do I feel about myself? Make a list of the feelings and stories you have about yourself. This will help you to identify core beliefs that you are still operating with.
- How do I feel about life? Again, make a list. Identifying your beliefs will help you make greater conscious choices towards life.
- How do I feel limited? What are the beliefs around this? How can I transform my limitations?
- What am I holding onto that no longer serves me? What do I need to see, feel and understand in order to let go?

- What do I tell myself to explain my 'failures'? These stories are important; a mirror to your underlying false and limiting beliefs.
- What does not feel aligned in my life? What do I need to see, understand and do in order to realign?
- What are my strengths?
- What am I achieving?
- What am I learning?
- What do I love doing? What do I find meaningful?
- What are my values? What matters a lot to me?
- In what ways am I giving to others? How can I give more to others?
- When do I feel happiest and most peaceful?
- What am I doing when I feel loving?

Again, I recommend two weeks of reflection. Each day, take time to reflect on each question. Go through the whole list and make journal notes to help yourself gain a clear picture. The following week, simply recognise feelings and thoughts as they arise. At the end of the week revisit the list again, adjusting or clarifying any further insights you may have.

### Moving forward

- How do I want to feel? How do I generate these feelings? What has already happened in my life that I can use as a guide?
- What are my personal values? What is most important to me? What drives me?
- What do I want to achieve? What do I want to do that I have not done yet?
- What are my goals? Which thoughts and habits will best support the goals I have?

Make a clear list of your goals and the feelings you want to have first, and then connect with your inner being in self-reflection to identify which thoughts and actions will best help you achieve your goals. It would be beneficial to take at least two weeks to self-reflect on these questions. Take time each day as you reflect carefully on each question. After the first week you may continue the same daily contemplation, or let a few days to a week pass before you revisit your contemplations. Be clear to make a list of feelings and actions that you need to put in place in your life to support a more conscious creation. When you feel you have achieved clarity with each of these questions, ask yourself one final question:

- What do I want to accomplish and what do I want my life to be like in the coming year?

## REGULAR SELF-REFLECTION

The following is a list that you can use for regular ongoing self-reflection. This will help you to maintain the process of self-awareness and the ability to consciously monitor your perceptions of yourself and your relationship with life.

- *What did I learn last week?* There is always something to be learned or discovered. Paying close attention to this also increases our sense of gratitude and fulfilment.
- *What did I accomplish over the past week?* Reflecting on your accomplishments develops a greater sense of self-achievement and contentment. It's also an effective way to acknowledge and keep track of your development.
- *What do I still want to accomplish this week?* What is my priority or first on my list? Everything else is secondary, and should be treated as such. Nevertheless, this question will also shed light on other noteworthy tasks and goals.
- *What was the most memorable moment for me last week and why?* As you begin to notice more of these moments, it may lead to greater awareness of your strengths (or weaknesses), passions and values.
- *What can I do right now to make the week flow with greater ease?* Remember the conscious habits: breathing, meditating, etc. What else can be done to be more organised and efficient?
- *What have I struggled with in the past that might also affect the upcoming week?* By understanding your struggles you can better equip yourself for future encounters. What can you do to be better equipped?
- *How did I waste my time and energy?* Set clear goals and strategies to disengage from these sorts of habits. Remove things from your life that are potential distractions or establish clear boundaries and schedules for more appropriate use of your time and energy.

- *What am I holding onto that I can choose to let go of?* Whether it is physical, mental or emotional clutter, it is important to consistently clear out. Eliminate the unnecessary things so the essential things in your life may shine even brighter.
- *What have I been avoiding that needs to be done?* Schedule a time for yourself to focus on completing things that need doing.
- *How can I help someone else this coming week?* Helping others keeps us aware of our interconnectedness with each other and with life. It also gives us the opportunity to develop our strengths, put our talents to use and our values into action. And, it brings us happiness.
- *What is my number one goal for the next year? What are my top three goals for the next three years?* Achievements are born out of clear visions. Keep re-assessing and reflecting on these visions, and you will see them manifest.
- *What are the strengths and actions moving me closer to my goals?* These are the things you need to focus on to give your visions grounded energy.
- *What am I looking forward to during the upcoming week?* The answer can act as a great source of motivation.
- *What are my fears?* Schedule the time to sit deeply in self-reflection, practice witnessing and do energy work to aid yourself in moving to a deeper place of acceptance, understanding and transformation. Consciously address your fears each week and you will gradually transform them.
- *Who or what can I give thanks to?* Take time each week to express gratitude. Gratitude develops greater fulfilment and contentment.
- *If I knew I only had one week to live, how would I spend my time?* Simply a helpful reminder... life is too precious to lose sight of the things that mean the most to us.

## How to reflect more effectively

Firstly, make time. We all have the time, regardless of how busy our lives are. You can take moments for self-reflection when you are driving or sitting on a bus, train or plane, or when you are in the bathroom. You could go to bed 15 minutes earlier to reflect, reflect with your family over dinner, or give up some television time. Your inner world can be more entertaining than television and is essentially much more important!

Secondly, ask questions. Aside from the specific list of questions already outlined, it is important to use questions to be actively aware each day. Self-reflection involves a process of inward thinking, and questions help our brain tune in to our deeper thoughts and feelings. Here are some examples of questions that help you to be more aware and conscious in your moment to moment living.

- How do I feel about what is happening?
- What does this situation remind me of?
- What is working? Why?
- What isn't working? Why?
- How can I use this experience? How does this experience relate to other situations I've been in? What can I learn from this situation?
- Knowing what I know now, what would I do differently next time?

Thirdly, think more broadly. Look for the underlying patterns or principles that arise in different settings yet require the same sort of aware response. When we think more broadly, we make our reflection time infinitely more beneficial to our lives. When faced with a challenge or something you are judging as negative, try to look at it from different perspectives. I call this the 'Five Windows' technique.

Let's say your partner comes home and ignores you for half an hour. Your first response might be: "He/she doesn't really care about me." What are five other ways you could see the situation? For example:

- Maybe he/she has had a tough day and needs a few moments to gather him/herself.
- Maybe he/she is just day-dreaming.
- Maybe he/she is hoping I'll come to him/her first.
- Maybe he/she thinks I'm not in the mood to talk and is giving me space.
- Maybe he/she is thinking through some important plans.

Notice how in the first example the thought had a definitive tone. This is typical of the mind that is seeing through its own lenses and beliefs. There is no openness to other possibilities or to uncertainty. The interpretation has already happened, having been generated automatically by the subconscious self. In the second example, the perceptions were all open possibilities, leaving room for variety or discovery. The Five Windows method allows you to open the window of your mind to the other as they really are, rather than stay stuck in the interpretation created by the lenses of your own mind.

This approach helps shift the mind from automatic responses generated by the unconscious self and opens the way for more authentic interaction. Ultimately it will allow you to be more centred and open and perhaps simply ask your partner what is happening for them rather than going through your own conjecturing. The truth is that most of the time what is *really* happening is very different from what you think!

Once you realise this, you will notice how much more aware you can be. You can be aware of your internal stories and fears. But you can also be aware that these fears are really great signals. With awareness you begin to recognise that there is always something above and beyond the limits the mind has set. With awareness fear asks us to trust in a bigger picture and to open our eyes, ears and hearts. Pain asks us to surrender to a process of conscious growth and change. Blame asks us to take responsibility for our own experience. With awareness we are led from resistance to openness. Everything is transformed with awareness.

The more you step into awareness, the more you will realise that every conflicting feeling or thought is asking you to come home to your true nature. If you were to ask *the awareness* in you how it sees and feels about different circumstances, you would be surprised by the depth of your own wisdom... and freedom.

## THE GREATEST GIFT OF SELF-REFLECTION

In the same way that being conscious leads to witnessing, which leads to awareness and pure consciousness; self-reflection leads to self-awareness, which leads to self-empowerment and self-acceptance. And it is only with empowerment and acceptance that a person is able to let go of limiting beliefs.

At the highest level, witnessing enables us to let go of *all* attachments to outcomes and judgments of circumstances. This paves the way for a journey through life that is truly unconditional. If we have no belief system for or against anything we can be open to the organising intelligence of life itself. There is no need for us to be bound to labels – be it political, scientific, theistic or atheistic. For what you label you limit. To let go of *all* beliefs, to be able to adapt your current thinking to new information while holding no bias or attachment, is to be truly unlimited... and free.

The most wonderful side effect of this is pure joy. When we live in this way, free of all beliefs and the need to assert our opinions, we discover the true wonder and beauty of every moment. We live fully in the Now. We also discover that it truly is possible to be happy every day.

This brings us back to Attunement #1

### *I AM consciousness*

Take a few moments with your eyes closed, breathing into your heart centre and reflecting on the words. Then state the words clearly, silently in your heart or out loud, repeating the attunement three times. Continue to feel the state of your being aligned with the attunement for a few more minutes.

CHAPTER 15

# BEING IN THE NOW

CONSCIOUS HABIT 7

*Let us not look back in anger, nor forward in fear, but around in awareness.* —James Thurber

Shrouded within and beyond the appearance of form is something more – something that cannot be named, something ineffable, some deep, inner, sacred essence. It is a numinous beauty, radiating from somewhere deep within. This beauty reveals the true nature of our being and all of life, as perfection, peace, oneness and sacredness. But this beauty, this sacredness, only reveals itself to us when we are present... in awareness.

Really, it is our yearning to reconnect with this ineffable essence that drives our desires and all our seeking. It is because we are not seeing the true nature of what is, what we are or what is happening, that we hold a negative view of the world and ourselves. Because we are trapped in our attachments to non-essential things, we miss the most essential thing of all – the living Now.

Our true home *is* the Now. To live *in* the present moment is to know our eternal home, to know that we never left home, and therefore need not return home. When we realise this, when we live this, we experience a profound security in our being, in life. Nothing can disturb us. We realise that every moment is perfectly made for us and that all things are perfectly placed. Everything, in every moment, is at home.

We don't need to wait or pray for a miracle to happen. All we need to do is be present to the miracle of each moment. Then our whole life is miraculously touched.

The beauty and power of the present has always been available to spiritual seekers, but, ironically, as long as we are *seeking* it, we are not available to the present moment. This 'seeking' implies that we are looking to the future for some answer, or for some achievement, spiritual or otherwise.

Nearly everybody is in the seeking mode, seeking to add something to who they are, whether it is money, relationships, possessions, knowledge, status... or spiritual attainment. We also seek to remove things from what we are, the things we deem unacceptable. Sadly, all this seeking prevents us from seeing how deeply attained we actually are... in every single moment. This 'attainment' is found in the wholeness of simply what is present, as it is.

**Every moment of now is a state of fulfilment. In fact, fulfilment is the constant flow of creation.**

There is only ever attainment. Yes, life is being and becoming. Yet even that which is springing forth into the next moment, transforming, is doing so as an act of complete fulfilment.

## The Illusion of 'There'

**When you realise there is no there, you will awaken to this which is already here.**

Through fixation with what appears as external to ourselves, humanity remains trapped in the illusion of non-attainment. We feel incomplete, and hence are constantly driven to look into 'the future' to try to get somewhere else, to get over 'there'. But this future does not exist. Nor does the past. How many people do you know who live for tomorrow? How many times do you think to yourself, "If I can just get 'there', then everything will be ok"?

It is because a person is not centred in their own being that they project their experience outside of themselves. This is what creates the appearance of past and future. It is what drives a person to look for fulfilment 'over there'. *Yet, there is no 'there'. There is only ever here.* By projecting reality into something perceived as 'outside', you place your being in the *image and concept* of the experience, rather than being centred in the experience itself... the fullness and completeness of the moment. As a result, the moment is not fully experienced and a feeling of lack ensues.

Consequently you cling to the images of the 'past' and strive for the images of the 'future' in an effort to feel more whole. But it is in-between these two extremes that reality exists, that our true self is being, that wholeness is radiating. And this wholeness can only be known and felt in ourselves as we are *being*... truly being. Yet many spiritual seekers have projected this 'being' into images, again, somewhere outside of the moment, outside of the self – 'the higher self', or the ascension realm, or heaven, or the enlightened self of the future.

This 'being' is not some *thing* or somewhere 'beyond'. It is deep within every form as its innermost invisible and indestructible essence. It is accessible to you right now as your own deepest Self, your true nature. Do not, however, seek to grasp it with your mind. Don't try to understand it. You can know it only when the mind is still, when you are deeply present to the moment as it is.

When you are present, when your attention is fully and intensely in the Now, being can be felt, but it can never be understood or explained mentally. What happens is far more astonishing. With this utter presence unfolds a state of all-openness in which life – *reality* – reaches in to rearrange the mind. Wonder and knowingness permeate our whole being. We are returned to reality as it is. This is why it is called *real*isation.

Our whole experience realigns with all that is real. The wholeness and perfection of this 'moment' is so complete it is impossible to find a single thing that is 'wrong' or needs changing. Consequently we are freed of the ever-restless mind. By embracing the inherent perfection of each moment, we naturally elevate the vibration of our whole being. We return our being to a whole state.

**To regain awareness of pure Being and to abide in that state – deeply present, consciously feeling and experiencing – is enlightenment.**

The whole quest then to know yourself must be surrendered into the moment of now. Knowing yourself is to be rooted in *being*, to be authentically present instead of lost in your mind. Chogyam Trungpa, a modern Tibetan Buddhist Master, stated: "The cause or the virtue that brings about authentic presence is emptying out and letting go. You have to be without clinging." Knowing the Self, knowing existence, is to be rooted in the Now... not in the illusion of the past or future. Realisation happens only *now*.

Life *is* now. There was never a time when your life was not *now*, nor will there ever be. Nothing ever happened in the past; it happened in the Now. Nothing will ever happen in the future; it will happen in the Now. Now is the real 'end' point of time. It's being here now that's important. Time is a very misleading thing. All there is, ever, is the Now. We can gain experience from the past, but we can't relive it; and we can imagine the future, but we will only experience it as it is in the living *now*.

This reveals something very significant. If now is *not* time-based what is it? Isn't it you? Isn't it life? Isn't it our planet, our universe... right here? When you remove your eyes from that so-called certainty of time strapped to your wrist, you discover that actually time is you, life... being... and you cannot be anything other than 'this' that is continually becoming yet always being. Contrary to popular belief, time isn't precious at all because it is an illusion. You constantly fret over this thing called time. You even tell yourself you don't have enough time, when in actuality you *are* seated in that which is *all* time... the eternal *now*.

The more you are focused on the past and future – time – the more you miss the Now, the most precious thing there is. You have projected your past judgments onto the moment, making it appear to be an obstacle you need to overcome. It is as if there is inherently something wrong with *this* moment. Yet, since the present moment is *life* itself, it is an insane way to live!

All of this is the grand illusion of time.[26] To be caught in time is to be asleep, unconscious. To be in the Now is to be fully awake, consciously present in eternity. Eternity is not something that begins after you are 'dead'. It is going on all the time. Forever is composed of 'nows'. Now *is* forever life. Death is not the opposite of life. Life has no opposite. It is only in the duality of the mind that we see life as having opposites – birth and death.

---

26  This is what ancient Vedic texts refer to as 'maya': to be trapped in the illusion, to be caught 'in time'.

Most people are so terrified because of this polarised illusion that they are shrinking back from life. As Mark Twain wrote, "The fear of death follows from the fear of life. A man who lives fully is prepared to die any time." It is exactly because people fear this thing called death that they do not truly live. Yet even according to the mind, the opposite of death is birth – renewal. All the while, life itself remains eternal.

The fear of death is only exacerbated through our denial of impermanence. Because we are not awake to our eternal self we despise the changing nature of reality. Just like the non-opposite nature of death and life, 'impermanence' sounds like the opposite of permanence. However, upon close observation, one can see that impermanence has no opposite because there is nothing to oppose. Impermanence is *continuum*. The fact that all things are passing through and nothing remains fixed is the broadcast of the universe in every one of its elements.

We cannot step outside the ceaseless movement of one thing into another because *we are it!* When we bask in this truth, we liberate ourselves from the illusion of bondage. In a universe where nothing is fixed, there is no such thing as bondage! With this realisation comes the sudden revelation that 'you' have always been free. That tremendous fight against your true nature can finally be put to rest. You can finally wake up and truly live. You can dare to dance and revel in your own precarious nature without reservation. You can be taken up in the thrill of a universe that is entirely free. And yes, it is dangerous. Yes, the clouds are in danger of becoming a river, the river is in danger of becoming an ocean… and the ego is in danger of enlightenment! But as Helen Keller said, "Avoiding danger is no safer in the long run than outright exposure. The fearful are caught as often as the bold."

Life asks that we rigorously meet it, that we give up the dream of self as separate from the rest of life and exempt from unavoidable transformation. We may have resisted this for so long, but when we finally choose to meet this precariousness, life in reply gives us our *whole self*. It gives us the wonder of existence as one perfectly, profoundly, radical being without any degree of hesitation.

*All* things are passing through the mysterious interchange from no being to being to not being – from formlessness to form to formlessness.

The universe itself reveals this self-nature within its every detail. All that is shall pass. That which we are, we will cease to be… that which we have, we will lose, and in its place our being will be recreated.

Upon close observation we can see this very phenomenon all around us. The Now is 'rivering' and life is forever 'momenting'. Walk through a forest and you will see that the decomposing foliage and rotting leaves not only give birth to new life but are themselves full of life. Tiny insects are teaming within. Microorganisms are at work. Molecules are rearranging themselves. Plants nourish creatures, excrement becomes soil, soil becomes trees, trees nourish the air and the air is nourishing the planet, the planet is made of stardust and stardust spirals throughout the entire cosmos. So death isn't to be found anywhere. There is only the metamorphosis of life forms. The way one thing insists on becoming another is beyond prejudice; it is just the way life is. And all of this is *now.*

## THE WONDER OF LIFE, HERE AND NOW

The reality is that truth, as we experience it, is both ever-changing and constant, something which cannot be explained or defined. It is alive in the ever-transient dance of life, never the same from one moment to the next; *and* it is the constant presence, the source of life itself. Because humanity is so conditioned to explain things, we are constantly attempting to define existence and to make truth known.

We have become obsessed with this quest, looking for the 'right' answer or the 'right' path. We are so driven by the fear of 'not knowing' that ironically 'our path to truth' becomes a mechanism in itself to protect us or to solve the 'not knowing.' As long as we are attempting to follow the 'right path' to truth we are following a line in the map of the mind, referenced by the past and trying to live in the future – and in doing so we perpetuate our problems.

**All the problems that humanity is burdened with are the *mind's* inventions. They are not reality itself.**

To experience the truth of life fully, we must be utterly transparent and unattached to definition and explanations. We must be surrendered to the unknown, the unexplainable. We must be surrendered to the present moment. As the Zen Master Dogen said, "If you cannot find the truth right where you are, where else do you expect to find it?"

When we do step into the 'unknown', something radical happens. In this surprising space is an aliveness. Here is a wonder that is met, that is touched, yet remains totally unexplainable *and* is totally satisfying! We release ourselves from a life burdened with disappointments, because we have no mind expectations of what 'should' and 'should not' be. Expectations arise from explanations. The moment we say 'this' is the truth, 'that' is what you, me, 'it' really is, we are full of expectation. We imagine that this 'truth' will deliver us all we need. We expect that it will provide everything we want, solve every problem of life, and show us how to deal with time-bound events.

The moment multi-dimensional existence does not conform to our uni-dimensional mind's expectations, we are disappointed. We even fight to uphold our 'true' path or perceptions against other people's 'false' paths or ideas! Why do we need to impose our minds upon the wonder of existence? We cannot place a religion on a river, nor can we patent the planet. Why not allow life to have its dance, its song, without any explanations or expectations? Existence is a tremendously beautiful mystery. Life itself *is* truth. Mistakenly we have thought that because existence is a mystery we need to solve it or explain it. But really, *the mystery can only be lived and experienced.*

The moment one even starts to explain existence one is no longer *being* the experience. To experience the wonderful endless truth of life as it is, in its purity, we are to be fluid like the river. We are to be as light as a feather and as colourful as a rainbow. Instead of needing explanations or solutions, or the 'right path to truth', only one thing is required to see and know truth as it is: an open heart of conscious presence, living in the Now.

As this open heart, we *live* what we have been seeking. We are fully alive, completely at one with the mystery, experiencing so deeply that we feel the radiant truth of every moment. Then we are no longer on a path *to* truth, we are the living life that *is* already truth. This is the essence of what all the sages have been teaching… *I AM the way, the Truth and the life eternally.* Truth is existential. It is experiential. Truth is not a concept, nor an object. Truth is alive. And aliveness is only ever *now*. The bottom line is this:

**If you're not in the Now, you are lost. You are afraid.**

People live in fear because they bring all of their past judgments, the images of the mind, into the present moment. When you look through the screen of these images you do not see reality as it is. You attempt to imagine a future that is really based on images of your past, and thus you never really experience the Now. Living this way, you will never experience the perfection of the present moment.

As long as you live in the mind you will have judgments and disappointments. And as long as you have judgments you will crucify yourself between two thieves: regret for yesterday and the fear of tomorrow. Perhaps the most tragic thing about human nature is that most people tend to put off living... *truly* living. We are all dreaming of some magical garden over the horizon instead of enjoying and tending to the one we are standing in. If you continue worrying about what might be and wondering what might have been, you will ignore what *is*.

It is good to learn from the past, but the future can only be positively fulfilled by focusing exclusively on the present. That's where the fun is. And it's the only place you can truly live from and be *efficient*. As the Dalai Lama said, "There are only two days in the year that nothing can be done. One is called 'yesterday' and the other is called 'tomorrow', so *today* is the right day to love, to believe, to do and, mostly, to live."

We forget that any action that supports life, that enables everything to be the best it can be, all unfolds from and happens only in the Now. This is where your real power is. This form, this version of you, will not last forever. You only have now to live it, to enjoy it, to make the most of it. Don't let the past steal your present. Opportunities fly by while we sit regretting the chances we have lost, or mourn the moments that have passed. Of course 'when one door closes another door opens', but we so often look so long and so regretfully upon the closed door that we do not see the ones which open for us.

Perhaps you think you need to keep looking into the past to make sense of yourself and life. Perhaps you think this is the only way you will know yourself. But, in truth, *you cannot find yourself by going into the past. You can only find yourself by coming into the present.*

## Being fully present

The present is Life's eternal gift to you. When *you* are present, you can allow the mind to be as it is without getting entangled in it. The mind in itself is a wonderful tool. Dysfunction only sets in when you seek and validate yourself *in* it and mistake it for who you are or what you perceive life and others to be. Unease, anxiety, tension, stress and worry – all forms of fear – are caused by too much thought about the future and not enough presence. Guilt, regret, resentment, grievances, sadness, bitterness – all forms of non-acceptance – are caused by too much attachment, too many judgments about the past, and not enough presence.

As long as you are unable to access the power of the Now, every emotional pain that you experience leaves behind a residue, an impression of pain that lives on in you. But this pain can only continue as long as you identify with it. True 'salvation' is freedom from perceived negativity, from the images of past and future *as a psychological need*. When you are freed of these psychological attachments or rejections, the past and future have no power over the present moment.

Therefore, whatever the present moment contains, accept it as if you had chosen it. Because in truth, even though you may not realise it yet, you did. Always work with it, not against it. This applies equally to the power of accepting your own being. There is no point in trying to be something or someone else, because you simply are what and who you are, right here, right now.

The pain that you create now is always some form of non-acceptance, some form of unconscious resistance to what is, what was or what might be. On the level of thought, the resistance is some form of judgment. On the emotional level, it is some form of negative response, a mechanism to deal with the resistance. The intensity of the pain depends on the degree of resistance to the present moment, and this in turn depends on how strongly you are identified with your mind.

So, the key is to always say, "yes" to the present moment. What could be more futile than to create inner resistance to what already is? What could be more insane than to oppose life itself, which is now and always now? So, simply, surrender to what is. When you say yes to life, you will see how life really is working with you rather than against you.

As the Roman Emperor and philosopher Marcus Aurelius explained, "If you are distressed by anything, the pain is not due to the circumstance itself but to your own impression of it; and this you have the power to revoke at any moment." You have this power because that impression is only a thought; it is not reality itself, and because it is *you* who chooses to occupy the thought.

Sometimes this appears terrifying, because you have mistakenly come to believe your thoughts are real… that they represent yourself or reality as it is. You are terrified that you may lose yourself in the process. But a thought is only something you *had*. It is not something you *are*. You can only lose something that you had. You cannot lose something that you are.

Realise deeply that the present moment is all you have… all you *are*. Make the Now the primary focus of your life. When you do you will discover that what you really are is *love*. When we are deeply centred in the Now, free of our mental projections, we are in a state of total acceptance. When we are in a state of total acceptance, we experience unity with our being and with life. In this oneness there is only the realisation of love, loving, lover, beloved. Life is something we live, and love, fully.

Being in the moment involves giving maximum appreciation and love to your present experience. It also allows you to recognise the perfection of every preceding moment. Every event that has taken place in this universe has led you to this moment. Every exploding star, every quantum occurrence, every birth, every death, every being that has ever lived, every thought, every single event of your life, has all been the orchestration that gave you to this now. The real question is: What will you do with this moment?

It is the quality of your consciousness in *this* moment that shapes the future, which, of course, can only be experienced as the Now. Realise that now, in this very moment, *you are creating*. You are creating your next moment. The future is always beginning now. This is what is real.

Not only is this moment the only thing that is real, but it is the only place you can make your life one that is truly meaningful and fulfilling. Today… now… is the moment in which to express your noblest qualities of mind and heart, to do at least one worthy thing which you have long postponed, and to use your divine abilities for the enrichment of others. Today you can make your life significant and worthwhile. The present is truly yours to do with as you will.

It is when we are rooted in being that we are our most authentic selves. We are no longer the product of our minds' creation, but the living expression of loving presence. However, we tend to put so much energy and focus on how we 'present' ourselves – the way we appear, what we wear, the title we bear, what we say, what assets we own – that we forget about the real value of our existence. If we put even a fraction of that energy into ourselves on the mental and emotional levels, we could greatly reduce anxiety and increase our vitality.

**So, at the least, the ability to be in the present moment is a major factor for mental wellness. At best, it is how we realise and embody our enlightened nature.**

In every moment we each have the option to *be* loving. Making a less conscious choice will not only affect us adversely, but can negatively affect those around us, as well as the planet. The most caring choice is conscious presence in the Now, which is love! When we are truly present in the moment it is impossible to have a negative feeling. It is also impossible to be unconscious. Being in the Now is integral to our ability to live a conscious life and to realise our most enlightened nature.

In most instances even the notion of this opportunity leads a person back to the mind and the idea of 'doing' something more conscious. Yet 'doing' is the active state through which people are 'trying' to become a more loving or conscious presence, which is also tied to the deeper belief that they are not already this. As usual, this 'efforting' is the result of the mind and the ego's projections.

Conversely, 'being' is the state in which an individual is centred in Self and present in the moment. In this state, you are so connected with your true nature and the true nature of what is happening that a flow occurs. You are in both a state of stillness (surrendered and being) and flow (acting and becoming). By being deeply centred in this way we are able to be truly connected with life and participate consciously in a state of ease and grace. We simply respond consciously, lovingly, with awareness in each moment. This is what the sages mean by the words: "It is in being that all is done."

## Applying yourself in the Now

There are various activities that assist us to stay present in the Now and to experience the true nature of each moment. This may sound overly simple at first glance, yet the more you choose to engage in and with *aliveness*, the more you will see, feel and know the freedom and certainty of life in every moment. The more you will engage in the Now.

If you seek to understand yourself then ask, "What is alive in me?" If you want to know what is true for you, then be aware of your nature, your passions, and your motivations in the here and now. In any given moment you might notice a feeling. If you pay attention you will notice how that feeling is constantly changing and reforming as you bring your awareness to it. Everything continues flowing with the river of life, moment to moment.

And the more you pay attention to everything that is truly alive, the more you will realise how quiet the mind is, that in fact there is little place for the mind and the stories of the past or future when you are engaged with all that is alive. You may also notice that curiosity has awoken again, and that there is no need to define anything, for the experience is already fulfilling and true in itself.

I encourage you to try the following experiment with yourself – with life – for at least a week:

Make it your intention that you will give your full attention to the aliveness that is in you and around you. Notice your breath, your heartbeat, the light in your eyes, the movements of your body, the workings of your consciousness, the unfolding of the blossoms, the songs of the birds, the engaging with friends and loved ones... all illumined in the living now.

This means you really need to see, feel, listen, touch, taste, smell, observe, engage and respond to what is occurring in the very present moment. If you are successful in staying engaged for most of the week, you will get wondrous glimpses of the freedom and certainty that I mention. In fact you will feel the depth of peace and wholeness and truth that is always present, that is life itself – alive here now – within you and all around you.

The most important thing is to stay connected to your feeling body and the senses as they are occurring in the moment. For example, really watch the colours and movement of shapes, feel the energy of what is happening and listen to the sounds that are flowing. See Chapter 11 to refresh your memory on utilising the senses to be more deeply anchored in the Now. Make a firm determination to *feel* what is happening in the moment rather than to *think* what is happening in the moment. This will enable you to engage with what is happening at a more conscious level, present in the moment.

As a fast way to re-centre yourself, start practicing the attunement... *I AM here.*

Make this statement to yourself regularly throughout the day. You can also keep asking yourself questions like these:

– Where am I?
– What is here?
– What is the feeling of this moment?
– What is the energy of this moment?

Also remember the power and clarity of consciousness that is available through the breathing exercises outlined in Chapter 8. Putting your attention into the flow of breathing and maintaining this concentration for at least 20 minutes will not only calm your mind and enhance concentration and awareness; it will also bring you deeply into the present moment.

Remember, the living moment is all you have; it is all you are. Make it your priority and habit to be centred in the Now, and you will live a more enlightened life.

Perhaps we could all think a little more like Winnie the Pooh.

"What day is it?" asked Pooh.
"It's today," squeaked Piglet.
"My favourite day," said Pooh.

## Attunement #6

*I AM here.*

Take a few moments with your eyes closed, breathing into your heart centre and reflecting on the words. Then state the words clearly, silently in your heart or out loud, repeating the attunement three times. Continue to feel the state of your being aligned with the attunement for a few more minutes.

Part Three

# AN AWAKENING WORLD

In this section you will celebrate the truth that your awakening is inextricably linked to humanity's purpose as a whole – to awaken, to love and to serve. Through awakening, we are able to embody pure awareness and love, and to extend this love to all beings for the benefit of the whole. As a natural consequence, we create harmony on earth. You will discover that *your* process of enlightening informs and influences the collective as we awaken together as a human family. You will begin to understand much more deeply that through awakening YOU, the whole world changes with you.

CHAPTER 16

# HARMONY ON EARTH

*If we have no peace, it is because we have forgotten that we belong to each other.* —Mother Theresa

A world of harmony may seem like an impossible dream. However as we awaken, we feel our undeniable connection with the earth and every single being. When we realise we are one with the very fabric of life, everything changes. We cannot help but take responsibility. We gain a new perspective based in love and awareness, which opens us to creative potential beyond our greatest imaginings. When this creative potential is shared and amplified on a collective level, harmony on earth can become a reality.

## A THRIVING ENVIRONMENT

As we face an ecological crisis of unprecedented proportions, a crisis of our own making, we are challenged to consider our response. How do we even begin to reverse the destruction we have created?

First, we must *welcome* our plight with eyes wide open. Yes, *welcome* it. It is our plight and we must own it. We must let it deeply and consciously into our hearts. We must step outside the closed habits of the mind and into an awake presence with exactly what is here, before what is here is no longer viable.

It is only when we regain our sense of interconnectedness that we *will* take responsibility again for the wellbeing of our environment. True caring emerges when we have a direct conscious and emotional experience of our interconnectedness. When we don't have this connection, we as human beings do not take responsibility. It is why our politicians make short-term decisions based on economics and expediency. It is why, as individuals, there are many moments we still find ourselves acting against our conscience.

It is essential that we *feel* our interconnectedness with all of life. There is even physiological evidence to support this. Our mental processing is largely conducted within two primary regions in the brain. The neo cortex deals with rational information and is concept oriented. The limbic system is emotional and feeling oriented. It is the limbic region that controls *all* behaviour and decisions.

This profoundly underlines the importance of a *feeling* experience of our interconnectedness. And this doesn't happen behind books and computer screens, it happens in our wild rambling moments with nature: sitting beneath a giant gum tree in awe of its majestic presence, watching the sun rise and the night fall, listening to the song of a river, tasting the rain and losing ourselves in the flow of life.

I know, without doubt, that I can attribute my deep sense of knowing and interconnectedness with life to the interaction I have always had with nature. I *feel* the earth and the earth *feels* me. I *see* the earth and the earth *sees* me... Indeed I, you, and every other thing are products of the earth. When we are immersed in nature we can no longer see isolated events... for where do the leaves begin or end when they are the product of the sun's rays, the cloud's raindrops and the soil's grains? Where do I start or end when I am drawn out of every breath I take from the winds that caress the earth and forests?

When we enter a natural environment in its most complete ecological state, we sense its completeness – its *togetherness*. This is its numinous power. And, within just a few moments of immersion, earth caresses us, she speaks to us... she reveals what *is*. She tells us that there is but one great intelligence flowing freely through all living things. To be awake *is* to be alive; to be present, engaged and empathically connected with every part of the whole right here, right now. Earth *is* our birthing – our waking up, our return to this empathic connection with all life. Suddenly, we not only imagine our way into the plight of every other being – we *feel* it.

And indeed, if there is no beginning or end to 'me', then the empirical fact is this: There can be no end to that which *I must accept as my responsibility*. I am responsible for the whole... I *am* the world, *we* are the world. It is through such a *feeling* state of interconnectedness with life that our moral conscience is restored. We are able to act consciously with a clear understanding of cause and effect, and with a clear understanding of how integral *we* are to the balance of *all* life.

Dr. Seuss understood this when he wrote in *The Lorax*: "UNLESS someone like you cares a whole awful lot, nothing is going to get better. It's not." Our ability to care is central to our process of transformation. Every one of our thoughts and actions *is* rippling through life, shaping and stirring it in ways that bear future results.

Awareness of the web of all-connectedness was once integral to all people, safeguarded in the stories and rituals handed down by elders for each generation to stay awake and aware in the dreaming of creation as a whole. There was an acute awareness of the interconnectedness of all actions throughout all time. It was common Aboriginal lore that whatever was taken from nature, enough must remain to sustain the next three generations. Not only that, but the trees, the birds and the animals were seen as brothers and sisters – all life was seen to be one living whole.

I remember stories my 'Aunties' and 'Uncles' would tell of the earth talking to them.[27] I know exactly what they were saying because I too had this communion from the very beginning. I also remember the aunties telling 'white fellas' they needed to go 'walkabout': "Just walk on the land, find a place that calls you and then sit. Sit there and say, 'Hello... I am this fella'. And wait. And listen. And watch."

It is time to recover our part in and connection with creation, and awaken to the call of earth that is telling us *we are wanted and needed here... now*. Our intelligence and awareness are needed to take care of this wondrous planet with its miraculous web of intricately all-connected life. This strong sense of belonging is utterly critical. It impels us to become present again and listen to what earth is asking of us: to remember, to respect, and to act for all – *to uphold the lore of connectedness*.

---

[27] In Aboriginal communities it is common to refer to any man or woman older than oneself as 'Aunty' or 'Uncle'. This stems from the basic principle and understanding that we *are* all related!

Opening ourselves again to the story of the universe, and our responsibility as part of that, begins with our willingness to stop and be silent. We need to be deeply present to see and hear the *reality* of life's interconnectedness. We need to disentangle the conflicts in our minds. As Gandhi said, "In the attitude of silence the soul finds the path in a clearer light, and what is elusive and deceptive resolves itself into crystal clearness."

So what is it that disentangles the mind?

Meditation helps us develop this quiet open mind, this reciprocal spirit – one that is sensitive and awake to life's interconnectedness and capable of participating with the deepest regard for the wellbeing of all. Meditation clears us of all our mental noise. It cultivates a mind of awareness and tolerance for what is actually happening, unclouded by personal agendas. It delivers a conscious calm that no longer conforms to the dramatic story of 'self versus world'. It heightens our sensitivity towards genuine danger and injustice, providing us with far greater skills to respond in a timely and effective way. It enables us to move beyond our childish denials and resistance, to in fact embrace our situation.

It is only when we welcome our circumstances and ourselves in this way that we can begin to respond with greater intelligence, to bring ourselves as mature, conscious participants into the universal story. As we participate again with this all-interconnected story, we become ecological in spirit, we become the true custodians of earth, capable of ushering in a time of environmental renewal. We restore our relationship, not only with ourselves, but also with each other... *and with every living thing.*

If we look around at our blue-green planet, we will realise that we never really left Eden. We just fell under the spell of the mind's mistaken idea of separation, of being cast out, which is profoundly strange given that when you look deeply enough, it is evident that all of life is *in*. It is inside existence. It is inside the life force that produces all things. It is only when we let go of our mind-made walls that we can begin to live beyond fear and in accord with life as it is, as an interconnected whole. It is only then that we can truly let life in again. So how can you deepen your own emotional experience of interconnectedness?

**This experience of oneness is not, and cannot be, born in your thoughts and concepts alone. It must be based in heart awareness.**

Heart awareness unites us with the three essential dynamics of interconnectedness. The first is *awareness*, pure consciousness. The second is *energy*, the manifestation of spirit. The third is *empathy*, the feeling and awareness of connection. The first two dynamics are the essence of life itself, the very nature of existence. The third dynamic enlivens us as humans, making us aware and responsive to the connectedness of all things.

Through the activation of heart awareness, we stimulate and activate our 'mirror neurons'.[28] These neurons play a direct role in our capacity to sense the suffering or joy of others, pointing to a sentient consciousness that is all-unified. When these neurons are active we are able to feel another being's experience as if it were our own. And, in actuality, at the deepest level – it *is*.

**Heart awareness allows us to truly see, feel and experience the interconnectedness of life.**

With such an experience, the mind-made walls are seen for what they are: an illusion. As this illusion dissolves, the dream of separation vanishes, and instead of seeking a way out, we discover we have always been, and always will be, immersed in the whole. We have *always* been and always will be this whole, vast, unspeakable beauty called existence. This becomes a consciously embodied experience, not simply a sentiment or concept. Once we encounter this more directly, we naturally begin to align our thoughts and actions with our feeling experience.

Our ability to stimulate these expansive and unified states of consciousness is easier than we might think. Try hugging a tree, for example. Yes! There's a reason people hug trees, find out for yourself. Introduce yourself to the tree, and spend at least three minutes in the embrace. What do you feel? What do you hear? Or, find an open space outdoors and walk barefoot, slowly, upon the earth. So slowly that you can feel every element of the earth touching the soles of your feet and every part of your feet touching the earth. Feel her calm power. Be aware that she feels you just as you feel her.

Regaining a sensitive relationship with the natural world around us is

---

28  For more on mirror neurons, see the 'TED' talks by neuroscientist Vilayanur Ramachandran: https://www.ted.com/speakers/vilayanur_ramachandran.html

rewarding in ways we may not always realise. Earth *is* our home. Why make ourselves a stranger in our own home? We mustn't be afraid to embrace the elements, to tilt our heads at the sky and feel the rain on our cheeks. Counter to what we may have been taught, the more we immerse ourselves in nature, the more resilient we become. This returns us to our true human strength, one that is powerful but profoundly sensitive, in touch with every creature.

Nature is always embracing us, supporting us and providing all our needs. The more deeply we understand this the more grateful we become. When we understand our place within this perfect system we discover a peace that we can never find within the confines of our offices, our lounges… or our minds. The more we nestle in with nature, the more things make sense. We discover that we don't really need to know the answer to everything, or control everything. Everything in nature has its perfect rhyme and reason, of which we are a perfect part. The more we are connected with our natural world, the more readily we are able to care for it. And harmony is something that arises effortlessly when we find our true place again in the world.

Remember to attune: *I am GRATEFUL for this moment.*

## COMMUNITY IN HARMONY

Common to us all is the desire for peace. Yet we often go about our quest as if it is something we have to acquire for our separate selves. The truth is, the harmony we seek is not something we can discover in isolation. Individual peace cannot be measured without taking into account every other person. Indeed, we suffer the discord of our conflicts because we continue to behave *as if* we are isolated. Discovering how irrefutably we belong to each other can at first glance be enormously confronting. Yet the more deeply we look into this, the more we discover a hidden power that, once tapped, unleashes enormous potential for us all.

Whilst we attempt small steps towards better relations, we often miss the most important point: the place we need to start from. A group of Australian politicians was shocked into muted stalemate during 'Reconciliation forums' in the 1980's by one blunt truth: "I don't hold with this talk of reconciliation," said Uncle Max, an indigenous elder from the Yuin country. "How can you have reconciliation where there's never been a relationship in the first place?" With that he leant down, grabbed a handful of dirt and said, "Reconcile with this! And you won't need any reconciliation after that."

Uncle Max's words are two-pronged. He's reminding us that we are trying to reconcile differences without having true human relating, let alone a true relationship with earth herself. To reconcile with the earth is a work of profound social healing. It pushes us to the edge we all share, that illusory line in our own minds called 'separation'. We begin to see that establishing peace is inseparable from the empathy we can generate for each other and for every living thing.

**At the heart of breakdown is the desire for unity.**

It is quite common for many people, including the spiritually-minded, to want to turn a blind eye to what is really happening. We *are* in a passage of breakdown. Of course in the scheme of the universe, it is all transformation; it is the perfect and natural sequence of life being and doing what life does. What looks like chaos and collapse is the dynamic that necessarily precedes reorganisation and evolution.

Every passage of breakdown brings with it the necessity to reflect, to reassess, to gain new insight and to re-organise, based on a more aware and evolved state. At the heart of this shift is the quest to regain a state of connectedness. Everything we are facing is telling us this. Hidden in every disaster is the power to respond. When faced with a tipping point or moment of tragedy, great things emerge in humans and we witness a sudden shift towards unified efforts. The suffering and needs of others can grow helping hands and compassionate hearts.

This I call the state of 'empathy in disorder'. We have entered a time when the common sense of our connection generally only arises under adverse circumstances and our actions are based on a 'clean up mentality' of reaction after event. Many of these events were caused by a state of disconnection to start with, including the alarming rise in natural disasters due to climate change – something that *we* are significantly accountable for. In the end, it all comes down to us.

Although society at large may be happy to continue nonchalantly ignoring these signs, what is really needed now is a way to *step back into our causative power.* We must access our greater intelligence that knows how to create from a state of harmony to prevent unnecessary conflict, rather than expend our knowledge dealing with the effects of unconscionable actions. We must be willing to use the opportunity that comes in the presence of hardship at a global scale. We must learn to feel the connection between our choices of comfort here and now, and the longer term suffering of children in Africa or of orangutans in Borneo.

**In the end, greatness is not measured by the size of one's bank account, house or career, but by the size of one's heart.**

Letting go of our conditioned lifestyle can be quite demanding. We must not fall back into the pettiness or self-fulfilling dramas of the ego, but instead be willing to endure what it takes to be worked by great transformative powers. We must see that we are responsible in *every* moment. Only then can we use the true power of empathy to its greatest capacity, a power driven by the truth of originating oneness. When we most deeply recognise this unity, we are moved by the needs of every other living thing.

To grow forward as a society, we also need to harness the collective power of humanity, working in united harmony, guided by a vision that benefits the whole. As Einstein explained, "The most important human endeavour is the striving for morality in our actions. Our inner balance and even our very existence depend on it. Only morality in our actions can give beauty and dignity to life."

**What is needed now is empathy in oneness. We need the true vision of our oneness to be our master and guide, to navigate our way to restored harmony.**

Remember to attune: *All is ONE.*

Unless we start with ourselves, all efforts will falter at best and fail at worst. As Lao Tzu said, "If you want to awaken all of humanity, then awaken all of yourself. If you want to eliminate suffering in the world, then eliminate all that is dark and negative in yourself." Truly, the greatest gift you have to give is that of your own self-transformation. Trying to create better communities on an existing foundation of ego-based identity will only create a repetition of history.

**The leader we are looking for is Consciousness.**

Remember to attune: *I am Consciousness.*

Inevitably this does involve a journey of interaction with those things and people that evoke greater consciousness. This is why 'teachers' are still so profoundly relevant. As the old saying goes, the blind cannot lead the blind. It is conscious presence that evokes more conscious presence. It is *consciousness* that awakens us again to our true Self, that empowers us, awakens our hearts and shows us the way back to truth.

In short, the wellbeing of our human communities will be reflected through a return to wholeness, to consciousness, in each individual. Consequently, all efforts to change our world through the usual measures, without changing our individual perceptions, will result in further failure. At some point this 'me', this individual, must be willing to risk opening, to become a courageously open heart and mind. There comes a time when we can't afford the risk not to. Now, more than ever, is such a time for humanity.

**Without regaining the clarity of an internal enlightened reference, all our external efforts lack true awareness.**

What, then, do we do? Firstly, we must have enough humility to recognise our misplaced beliefs and efforts. Then we must have a willingness to let go. We must cultivate enough courage to step into the place we call the unknown and to simply… let ourselves *in*.

That place we call the unknown, however, is not really the unknown at all. It is simply the forgotten, the ignored. What we really discover, when we do give ourselves time to let into our innermost being, is that it is a place of profound familiarity. We have a feeling of returning home, because it *is* home. It is the Self we truly are and always will be. Whilst we may have the body to experience for a while, within a matter of blinks it, too, returns to its source. Every physical experience we have is absorbed again into the endless field of life's energy. However, whilst we are here having this human experience, it is possible for us to imbue our lives with a conscious presence. It is possible for us to live in a unified state of love, peace and harmony. It is possible for us to create thriving communities and, ultimately, a world of joy.

**The shift to enlightened community begins with awakened individuals.** We must begin to share a story that includes us all, the cosmic story of life as *one*. With this personal commitment to awakening, each individual is beginning to build a conscious and harmonious community. With a reawakening to unity comes a reawakening of peace and harmony – within and without.

**If there is unity within, there is oneness in our being. If there is oneness in our being, there is peace in the mind. If there is peace in the mind, there is awareness in action. If there is awareness in action, there is harmony in community. If there is harmony in community, there is peace on earth.**

Playing our part is integral for global wellness. To do so we must also understand the way we function as a collective, because our world is governed largely through the power of groups. With world problems threatening to spiral out of control it is easy to want to continue blaming 'others' for what is going on. We cannot solely blame capitalism, corporations or governments for the problems we currently face. We may point to unethical systems in which economic advantage seems to dominate all other values in decision-making, but we can easily overlook our unconscious contribution or acquiescence to these systems. And furthermore, because we are not aware of our connectedness with everything else we don't tend to take broader causes and effects into account in decision-making.

Societal problems are often attributed less to those in charge and more to basic facets of group dynamics, so understanding how groups do or do not work effectively can facilitate us with our community efforts. It is no secret that groups create norms, producing expected or accepted behavioural markers and further reinforcing these within the group. These norms can even violate the needs of individuals or group members yet remain unchallenged. Take, for example, the concealing of gross violations within the Catholic Church, vigilantly protecting perpetrators of child sexual abuse at the expense of the victims' rights. The ability of groups to continue functioning in this way is founded on two basic features: the dispersal of responsibility and depersonalisation.

When responsibility is dispersed, *each individual feels less personal responsibility and is less inclined to associate themselves with the consequences.* This leads to the 'tragedy of the commons' where shared assets or problems are neglected because we think they're someone else's responsibility. The same dynamic is often observed at the scene of accidents or in the face of organised corruption. It is also why relatively empathic people are more likely to fall prey to cults.

Depersonalisation occurs when individuals lose their personal identity and instead merge with the group. Ironically, we could say this is most of humanity. We are taught to conform and mould ourselves into certain groups in order to belong or simply to be good enough. Consequently we lose touch with our own unique selves and our individual response of 'right or wrong', 'good or bad'. The more we are absorbed into the group, the more our ideas, opinions and ways of thinking are set according to the group norm. Not only are the decisions and views of group members unconsciously shaped by others, but the group is prone to make decisions that are more extreme than the views or needs of the individuals themselves.

Groups always have a certain level of 'sameness' and tend to operate on consensus, often leading to the rejection of less conventional ideas. Some even have solid regulations and goals around which their norms are based. This becomes a significant issue when these goals are based on abstract values like 'profit' and are regulated in a way that makes them isolated and often exempt from external circumstances. Conversely, the group dynamic becomes very powerful when 'sameness' is based in the principles of oneness and consciousness. Each individual in the group is supported and elevated, and the benefits flow on into the wider community, to every being on the planet.

It is important to make group regulations, goals, objectives and strategies transparent. When external entities maintain a watchful eye, any dysfunctional norms are more likely to be exposed and addressed. External feedback can provide much needed fresh insight, perhaps even genius, allowing a leap in evolution. With greater transparency, greater consciousness will arise. Along with it, the 'individual will' may be realigned with a more soulful conscience, a unique intelligence working in harmony with and for the whole. Inevitably it is up to each of us to play our parts, and to do this we are best equipped by having a stronger connection with our own being.

Ironically, the more we try to grasp onto a fixed individual identity, the more we trap ourselves and lose ourselves in generalisations, even becoming lost in group norms. Yet the more we let go into our essential Self, which is free of distinction, the more present we become to our own uniqueness and authenticity. We come to really know who we are as an individual in each moment. This is the gift we can bring to our community and to the whole. Without this we may remain caught in our apathy.

If we look closely, this 'apathy' is actually grief and disempowerment. Most people *do* care deeply but think they can't make a difference. The realisation that we are all connected and that our inner states and our actions ripple through everything is enormously significant. This awareness is the very thing that can lift us out of grief and disempowerment and into a greater trust in the value of our own individual efforts. Once we establish a more aware connection with the true Self, we can establish a more aware connection at a collective level, paving the way for greater balance and harmony.

CHAPTER 17

# AWAKENING TO LOVE

*Love is the voice under all silences; the hope which has no opposite in fear; the strength so strong mere force is feebleness; the truth more first than sun, more last than star...* —E.E. Cummings

Love. It's what unites us, literally. When we look beyond our differences, we discover that in love we are the same. We all seek love – to love and be loved. It is the one thing that can transform us forever. Love is the only power that can dispel our fears and elevate the darkness of our unconscious self into conscious light. It is the only vibration that can completely clear the toxic symptoms of our false conditions. Without it, we simply exist. With it, we blossom and thrive.

## What is love?

Love is the essence, consciousness and source of all that we truly are. Just as white is the sum totality and presence of all colours unified, love is the totality of all energy, the essence of all creation unified. It is the all-inclusive state of life.

The *realisation* of what love truly is comes from a *state of consciousness*. We experience this when we truly surrender, when we no longer hold on to an image or feeling of separation from the whole. In a state of wholeness we let go of the belief that love is something created by someone or something outside of us.

As children we were much closer to this innocent, natural state. We were simply being the experience of life and love, moment to moment. We could love the boy with different coloured skin, the insect on the leaf, our mother's imperfections and the mud between our toes, all because we were innocently and unconditionally in touch with life. But gradually it changed. We were taught bias. We were taught judgments. And as a consequence we learned to confine love, to reduce it to emotions and select situations.

Yet love is not actually an emotion or a sentiment. Love is a dynamic state, it is a 'presence with', not a 'falling for'. It is beyond the mind and emotions, which is why when it is felt, we find it impossible to truly describe or articulate. Emotions and sentiments are just fleeting moments of perception relating to an instant. For example, when we meet someone and feel close to them, we lose our sense of boundary. We experience the feeling of our true underlying nature – that which is not separate – yet we project that feeling onto the person and circumstance and mistakenly call *'it'* love! We are not even aware that we are actually feeling our very own true nature.

Sadly, most of humanity mistakenly perceives love as something confined to specific circumstances, when, actually, *love is the constant power and intelligence of every moment and of the entire universe.* There is no cause for this love; it simply *is*.

This power is one absolute all-connected being. It is more than the energy and the potent life source of all things. It is the very blueprint and intelligence of all things. It is the essence of all things. Contrary to how it seems, this essence is not a tiny part of us – some tiny fragment hidden between the folds of our conditioned mind, or tucked in a corner of our heart – it is the *whole* of us. This essence is the totality of our eternal, ever-present being, which is forever *one*. Essence is not a small thing. It is immense! It is immeasurable. It is our essence that shows us the way and delivers the true help that we need – the answers we seek, the peace we yearn for, the love we long to return to.

When we understand this, we do not see our world through dualistic measures. Nor do we seek love as something external or separate from what we are, or from what *is*, in each and every moment. However, we do become *loving* in every way. And we become the living experience and expression of oneness. With this we transform every so-called problem we think we have. Why? Because every 'problem' is caused by the fundamental belief in this illusion: that we are separate from creation and each other.

When we live in this dualistic state, we live in fear. When we resolve this illusion, we resume a state of perfection. We *get* that everything is our one Self and that this is love. We *get* that if there is only our one Self, there truly is nothing to fear.

Through fear we seek to protect ourselves and provide for our own individual needs. We don't believe we have enough for ourselves, let alone for anyone else! We don't realise that the answers and resources for everything we seek are within our very being – the totality of our 'self' as the individual and our Self as the whole of life. We live in constant conflict with 'the other'. Ironically, we are only in conflict with ourselves, creating a life of profound suffering. When we realise we *are* love, we realise we are at one with all things, with all resources, with all intelligence. We awaken to our infinite Self and discover that life can be dramatically different just by the realisation, "I am love."

Then it is impossible to be anything but a living state of harmony. This is the solution to every problem. Actually, in this state we no longer see a problem. We see that every experience we face, and indeed life as a whole, is a living *process*. Knowing this, we are able to respond consciously, lovingly and peacefully. Every one of our thoughts and actions is generated by love. In this way, we become a truly loving presence capable of bringing extraordinary love to the world.

When we think of famous enlightened beings, it is easy to think of their love. Most people think this love to be super-human, an exclusive divine power brought to us from some distant heaven or God, or perhaps see these enlightened individuals as the exclusive personification of God. But really this is like a tiny seed looking up at a giant tree and saying... wow... *you* are God! You are something greater than me! You have come from somewhere different than me! You are the power over and above me...!

Of course an enlightened being can look like this. Yet it is only because they have fully blossomed into dimensions far deeper and greater than the common mind of humanity, that we make them an even greater giant in our own minds. Enlightenment and the realisation and embodiment of true love are the same thing. Even when we understand enlightenment or love with a more level perspective, the 'greatness' of it can seem like a distant dream. And, in the moments we *are* deeply engulfed in this love, we also become terrified of it... as if we cannot possibly hold it, as if it is too much for us to bear. Yet the truth is, *it* is holding us!

No matter where we are, no matter how evolved or un-evolved we may consider ourselves to be, the journey starts at the same place: here, now, wherever we are. The journey follows the same path: from the head to the heart. And that journey leads us all back to the same place: our Self.

This can seem contradictory to our usual approach to love. We mostly think of it as something we are supposed to give or get. We think if we are to 'be loving' we must focus on others. Yet essentially we must first *realise* we *are* love before we can truly love others.

If we do not realise we are love, we are shut down to ourselves and to life. We become suppressed and perceive ourselves as lacking love. This causes a great distortion in our energy and the way we see things. Literally, we become incapable of giving love to others because it feels as if we are empty of it to start with. At best we give a conditional version of love. By realising we *are* love, we can drop our self-judgments. We can let go of self-doubt, guilt and the tendency to deny ourselves the beauty of experiencing life as it really is: a creation of love and joy.

In letting go of our own judgments, we naturally surrender the judgments we have held over 'others'. When we truly let those we 'love' be perfectly themselves, when we cease trying to twist them into something that fits our own image of what they should be, we finally enter the real journey of shared loving. Without this, we *think* we love them when all we are doing is tying our own needs to them. At best, we love only the reflection of ourselves we find in them.

The less judgments we hold, the more truly we experience ourselves and the people around us. We rediscover our true nature is 'this which is always present'. We can't help but become an *open* presence. We feel our natural state as that which is flowing and alive with energy and meaning. We no longer reject life but instead open ourselves up in fullness to all that life presents in every moment. We let life all the way in! And when we do we can't help but be rendered speechless.

We are humbled by the immensity of grace that flows through life. We feel the honour it is to be truly alive, because we realise the true essence that has been hiding inside ourselves, inside all existence, like a jewel waiting to be placed on our mantel. In honouring our own true nature, we become authentic in every way. We no longer deny ourselves those things that inherently support and uphold the integrity of our true being. We become 'loving to ourselves'. In doing so we see the beauty and worthiness of every single thing in existence.

It is from this state that we expand and radiate with the love that was designed to be given to others. And we begin to see that we never really needed to give ourselves anything but the acknowledgement of what we already truly are.

Already we are love. When we know this we cannot but love! We live a life that is centred in the source, the very presence of infinite love, the Self that is eternal and whole. When we connect with this presence, what previously appeared limited no longer exists. Even if we enter this presence fleetingly, a profound shift is instilled in us, bringing change to the rest of our lives.

Now, let's take a moment to consider what we have created in this world, based in fear. Fear is profoundly limited because it is confined to the realm of 'finite' thinking. Yet, even though our world is primarily driven by fear-based mentalities, incredible things have been achieved... perhaps even in your own life.

Now, imagine a world centred in the consciousness of *love*. Love is *limitless*, for it is unity and all-connectedness. Imagine what can be, and is, created through the power of conscious love! *The power of love far outweighs and supersedes every collective fear in this world.* We simply need to awaken to this truth, each one of us within ourselves, and we can truly change the world.

'Enlightenment' therefore invites us to the ultimate quest…to enter the place within our being that is free of any perceived separation: LOVE.

As we connect with the love that is our true nature, we become capable of greater and greater things. And, we become more loving as a person. This is why every truly 'enlightened' person has been known for their extraordinary capacity to be loving and compassionate... unconditionally.

## LOVE IS BIGGER THAN THE MIND

To love unconditionally, we must go beyond the usual parameters of our minds. Love invites us to cultivate more conscious qualities through right awareness, right attitude and right action. I am not referring to 'right' from the usual polarised perspective, but to the very real factor of cause and effect. If you want roses, you don't go to the old boot shop; you go to the florist! In the same way, if you want to cultivate more conscious qualities, you must point your mind in the 'right' direction, which is towards awareness. You must establish the 'right' attitude of openness, acceptance and unity, and your actions must be born from these qualities of 'right' awareness and attitude.

This requires us to access something that is other than just 'mind', because our mental perceptions are based on defined points, which in themselves are limited and polarised. This does not mean that our thoughts cannot be useful to move us towards love. Just think of the power in the attunements! *Love is here. I AM Love.* In fact it is our recognition of a higher possibility that opens our awareness to move beyond the mind map we have been attached to. It allows us to tune in to our greater nature.

If we are to connect with this higher possibility, we must move our thoughts to that which is whole. This wholeness is the very life essence of every one of us. It is the unified field, our oceanic Self. It is the consciousness that is free of identity. It is the vitality of love that is all-embracing. If we look closely at our experience of life we can distil it down to two distinct states: fear or love. However, fear is *not* the opposite of love. Love is wholeness, absolute being, all inclusiveness. It has no opposite. Fear is simply the by-product of a misplaced perception based in the illusion of separation.

Fear continues to be perpetuated by our belief in separation and our addiction to identification. The many conditional attitudes we hold keep us at a distance from the experience of what love truly is, which is unconditional. Love truly is the Self beyond and preceding all conditions. Whilst we may feel somewhat controlled by our fears, the more we come into presence the more we realise how non-essential most of our fears are. Eventually we come to see that *fear is optional… whereas love is essential.*

Love is cultivated by a state of accepting and embracing the true nature of life. I am not simply referring to love as an emotion but to the innocent state of our true being. This innocent state of love is simultaneously profoundly intelligent and humble, powerful and yielding, surrendered and responding. In this state we embrace all and relinquish our rejection and resistance to life.

Buddha stated that there were three 'sins': ignorance, attachment and aversion. Ignorance is our false view that we are separate from 'God', the limitless Self that is love, and of course the misperception that we are separate from one another. Our attachments arise from this limited view of separation, as a desperate effort to acquire a sense of security, control or safety. Given that our perception is distorted to start with, our efforts only lead to the self-validation of fear and the feeling of lack, conflict and suffering. The resulting doubt, judgment and mistrust leads us to the aversions we hold, and to deeply reject and resist life.

## Love's limitless power

In order to regain our faith and certainty in our true power, we must attune to the nature and intelligence of love. By understanding this divine intelligence, we begin to resolve our ignorance. As we resolve our ignorance, we no longer perpetuate attachments or aversions, for we see life in its true state of wholeness. And as we become witness to this, we generate the power we need for a profound shift. Our whole quantum field takes on a different order.

Love is an *all-connected* presence. It is literally the unified field. As we align our thoughts, feelings and beliefs to the unified field, we literally generate a state of profound connectedness. Our whole being is elevated. Our energy field is open and flowing. We are able to recognise and align with limitless possibilities, through which our entire organism may respond in constant harmony with the greater whole of life. As a consequence we are able to cultivate and sustain a deeper state of balance.

I had a personal experience of this quantum field shift at the age of twenty-eight when I was critically ill. I had 'passed through the death tunnel' three times. During these events I recognised the body/mind's cellular and atomic level that was vibrating to thought patterns (genetic, inherited and collective) of rejection and resistance to life. As I witnessed this I was simultaneously aware of the eternal Self – the presence that is free of fear, pain, illness, aging and death. I realised that the play of life in the atoms of the body was not actually separate from this Self, but a vehicle for the potential of spirit and the creation of life.

I saw the whole Self, from the vibration of particles to the infinite ocean of light. In that witnessing was a profound realisation that actually 'life' itself (the world of form) is not suffering, but that our rejection of it, because of limited perception, creates the energy contractions which result in illness, dissatisfaction and suffering. And these patterns are the result of 'heritage'. This heritage can be from a series of lifetimes, and/or from the patterns passed on genetically through our DNA, as well as simply the nature of being part of a human collective mind.

After long periods in hospital and unsuccessful operations, the series of realisations I encountered gave me the power and certainty I needed to check myself out of hospital. I underwent a radical and instant conscious shift that brought about total healing. With the connection to the presence of wholeness, I manifested vitality in my body that was like that of a 12 year old! And to this day I continue to live with the vitality of someone who feels much younger than the average person of my age.

What was most startling was that the actualising energy, the energy that manifested a healed and renewed state in the body, was not in the recognition of wholeness but in the *love* of the self within that wholeness. The 'realisation' of wholeness was like a key, but the *love* was what actually *turned* the key. Love *is the vibration* – the *energy* – of unified Self.

At a more basic level it is our thoughts that most powerfully affect our physical wellbeing. The cells in our body react to everything the mind generates, consciously and unconsciously. Negativity (literally lower vibrations) brings down the immune system and the optimum function of the body is compromised. Positivity (higher vibrations) sustains health and wellbeing at every level. *Love is the highest vibration.*

With our own direct connection with love as an inner experience, we can really know truth beyond our previously limited perceptions. With love, we unleash even greater consciousness. Once we realise we are *love consciousness*, we are changed forever. Even just a brief glimpse of this love gives us more than we can imagine. We establish a clear conscious response to life, one that is aligned with the true nature of existence. Effortlessly, then, whatever appeared as disharmonious rights itself. Life becomes filled with ease and grace.

If you can't already see that love is the greatest power you could champion, consider this: It is only love that holds the certain power of total wellbeing. Through the power of our vibrational alignment with the limitless love/Self, we are able to manifest our highest possible expression of vitality on all levels. Yet remember... it is a journey.

## LOVE, THE CERTAIN PATH

The moment we are conceived we embark on the journey of potential. It is the potential within us that fills us with a vision of what we are to become. When we discover the spiritual path, we are told that our highest potential is infinite joy and love; the fruit that waits to ripen. Yet as we begin to see this more clearly, we become painfully aware that where we are standing is in contrast to our vision. We see a distance between the two. That gap beckons us to find a path from the ground of our potential to the fruit of its vision.

Certainly a seed already contains within it the life force of a thousand fruits, yet it still trembles at its path, its metamorphosis – to die as the seed and to be born as the fruiting tree. Likewise, as humans, we all share the same journey. As we embark on the path of love, our ego shakes in its death throes. Although the passage may at first be dark, love's power breaks us open, lifts us into the light and nourishes our spirit. It gives us the roots to dig deep, stand tall and bear the fruit of loving wisdom.

Whether knowingly or not, we are all cast into our own plot, yearning to grow into the greatness we are destined to be. Everyone who recognises this possibility always asks, "How? How can I become all that I can truly be?" The answer to that always remains the same. By following the path that is lit by love.

Sadly, humanity feverishly attempts to deny love as the one and only true path. Yet, no matter how many routes we may take with our minds, all the knowledge in the world cannot dispel the illusions of the ego or heal a single wound when love is absent. The path of love is the most significant and important factor in every way for humanity's advance, healing and liberation. It is the *only* path of certainty. Every religion is essentially based on this truth. Take, for example, this passage from the Bible:

> *Love is patient, love is kind. It does not envy, it does not boast, it is not proud. It does not dishonour others, it is not self-seeking, it is not easily angered; it keeps no record of wrongs. Love does not delight in evil but rejoices with the truth. It always protects, always trusts, always hopes, always perseveres. Love never fails. But where there are prophecies, they will cease; where there are tongues, they will be stilled; where there is knowledge, it will pass away. For we know in part and we prophesy in part, but when completeness comes, what is in part disappears. When I was a child, I talked like a child, I thought like a child, I reasoned like a child. When I became a man, I put the ways of childhood behind me. For now we see only a reflection as in a mirror; then we shall see face to face. Now I know in part; then I shall know fully, even as I am fully known. And now these three remain: faith, hope and love. But the greatest of these is love.*
>
> (1 Corinthians 13:4-13)

No single one of us is outside of the path of love. Yet many choose to turn from the light and truth of love, and instead live in the shadows of its impostors and substitutes where fear rules and disappointments abound. So it is that our longest journey is from the head to the heart. It is our one and only path. To recognise this consciously and to make a commitment to all that steers us in the direction of our goal is the moment we *walk* the path.

**The goal of the path is to transform the mind from belief in separation to the awareness of unity – to lead us from judgement to love, from pain to joy, from war to peace. When we arrive at the awareness of unity, there is only the reality of love.**

For this inner transformation to occur, we must have an 'outer' path to sustain it, one that is authentic and approachable from wherever each of us stands. Therefore, the path must be inclusive of our diversity. It is only love that can achieve this.

**Love is the most important attribute of humanity.**

No matter how many names we may give the path, it is the vessel of love that carries us across the sea of fear to liberation. In understanding and following the universal principles of love, we may take a discerning route through and beyond our fears to fulfil our highest potential.

Every human suffering can be cured by the medicine of love. This quality is the ultimate source of human happiness, and the need for it lies at the very core of our being. It is therefore totally natural to every human being to take a path. For what human being is absent of the quest to be fulfilled in love? That journey is inevitable. It is not a matter of *if* – it is a matter of *when*.

## AWAKENING TO THE TRUE NATURE OF LOVE

For most of humanity, love is a sentiment, an act, an event, a relationship or a series of these. And it is a story that requires certain conditions. This dependence on conditions is a limitation, a misplaced perception, like seeing a well as the whole ocean simply because we may draw water from it. If we mistakenly think the well is the source of our water, then of course we will get attached to that well! And if it dries up, we will cry and say we have lost our water.

In the same way, humanity mistakenly identifies the act, the body, the marriage, as the source of love. We mistakenly attribute love to the little self – the well – forgetting the ever-present one that is love – the oceanic Self. It is why people think they are in love one day and they are not the next. Love is mostly considered to be an elusive thing that we can never capture or rely on. This is because of our belief in a fundamental illusion: That love comes and goes, and that when we finally have it, it will only depart again.

Consequently, people are afraid to feel love because they are confusing it with the impermanent events of life. And, ironically, without this impermanence, we would not experience the *expressions* of love. We would not delight in our lover's touch, in the adoration of life's beauty. Without impermanence there is no rarity or surprise. Yet love itself is not impermanent. Love is the constant quality of the deep conscious Self. It is the vital power, the moving energy and the stillness *behind* the transient fabric of life.

It is when we are open enough to see and feel from this state within us that we *feel* love... true love. In this state, subject and object merge. We are not divided from our object of affection. We encounter the profound fullness of knowing unity in its endless nature whilst encountering it through the state of the witness: Self meeting Self. Self feeling Self. Self engaging with Self.

It is due to the appearance of duality (two 'separate' bodies) that the One Self – the unified field – can actually experience *its Self*, the love that it is. It is also because of this appearing duality that humanity gets the idea of love profoundly mixed up! We see the 'other' as the actual source of love, instead of simply the reflection of our Self/love... That which appears as two is actually *one* being.

When we awaken again to what love truly is – the deeper state of our true conscious Self, the constant eternal essence of life – we also awaken to the freedom and beauty of the ephemeral dance of the world. We no longer see endings, but constant renewals. We see the constant rhythm, the coming and going of form as the 'always present' dance. We see that all of this is occurring in the endless field of life, which is love. We know that all these fluctuations are never outside of love. They are all held *in* love. Love itself never ceases.

In this way every moment becomes a living expression of love, an opportunity to express the love that is our true nature and to be *loving*. We discover that *love is only experienced and expressed in the present moment*. Once we know this, we realise that the only real opportunity of this moment *is love*. Love is never about how long we can hold onto a moment or a person, it is not about attachment, getting and having... it is about *being*. When we understand this, we realise that *love is complete freedom*.

Of course, love will express itself in many ways. There are many different forms of love: the type we feel for family, for intimacy and universally. Essentially it is not that the essence of these types of love is different... it is that the way of *expressing* love varies according to the type of form we are interacting with or as.

By being at peace with the transient nature through which life – love – expresses itself, we can celebrate ourselves as that which is eternal. We can feel the constancy of love, and celebrate it in our transient world rather than mourn over it. We are no longer afraid of the passing waves on the ocean because we realise we *are* the ocean. We realise then that it is because a rose blooms in the morning and fades at night that we can celebrate its beauty. It is because a child is born and a man dies that we encounter the endless rhythm of life's eternal symphony. Without the appearance of objects and events coming and going, we do not experience the wonder, the newness, the discovery of life's endless possibilities.

The ever-changing landscape of life is what we are in love with, not the fixed object. We are in love with life's continuous transient play. If it remained the same we would die of boredom. In fact, if life *did* remain the same it *would* cease! And, if love were confined to the actual event then love would die. When we draw into the heart of love we know that indeed we... it... *is* the eternal. For while all else passes, love is the only thing that remains. Love is the endless power.

In lesser awareness it is not really impermanence we fear, but 'endlessness'. We fear something our minds cannot measure or hold onto. We no longer have a secure reference. Yet when we actually let go, when we surrender our fixed ideas and cease all clutching, we encounter a state of wholeness in that endlessness. We discover love's constant presence through constant renewal. We encounter true love as the open state it is; a state in which we embrace that which cannot be measured, our infinite being. It is the state of *letting in*, in which we allow ourselves to fully experience self as Being. And in that being is the vast overflowing essence of indescribable bliss...

It is, however, incredibly common for people to feel completely overwhelmed when they are struck by divine love. It is so immense that the poor little mind thinks it can't possibly handle this vast ocean that seems to have engulfed one's whole being. But when we realise that what we are *is* love, we no longer measure things in finite degrees. We realise we are not the body that tries to hold love, but that *we are the love that is holding the body*.

But as long as we give our finite perceptions a greater sense of validity, we struggle to trust that we really can open so far that we let every being into our heart. We spend so much time and energy protecting our fears because we think if we let someone or something in, we are also going to lose them or be hurt. But actually we are being given endless opportunities to love, to let love in, and to ultimately regain our true state of love: the wholeness, liberation and dance of life that we are.

So maybe you could ask yourself what could be the *worst* possible thing to happen to you if you were to fully let go and surrender to love? And what could be the *best* possible thing to happen to you if you were to fully let go and surrender to love, to let into the opening? You will be amazed to discover that both questions (and outcomes) will actually lead you to *more love*!

It is only a false idea that can keep the story of fear alive. When we realign with the state of our Self as love *we realise we never left it*. We realise that it can never be taken away from and that it is so complete it needs no other thing to be added unto it. We realise that love is our eternal Self. It is but a recognition rather than a change. This is enlightenment.

And this brings us back to Attunement #2

*I AM Love.*

Take a few moments with your eyes closed, breathing into your heart centre and reflecting on the words. Then state the words clearly, silently in your heart or out loud, repeating the attunement three times. Continue to feel the state of your being aligned with the attunement for a few more minutes.

CHAPTER 18

# THE EMBODIMENT OF LOVE

*Where there is love there is life.*— Mahatma Gandhi

If human beings are here on earth for any good reason at all, it is surely to learn about love! The purpose of awakening is to remember our true Self, and in doing so, bring its loving power into this world.

There were times in my life when this truth was profoundly highlighted. The most vivid and comprehensive realisation arose once after nearly dying. I had almost crossed over, and during a passage of 'limbo' was witness to the great divine workings of human life. When I came back from the 'death tunnel', I realised that every single lifetime of every single human is about love. It is about the discovery, remembering, expressing, giving, receiving, being and becoming of love.

Sometimes this is very painful. During less conscious passages we can feel so divorced from love that we act from a place of great torment. But this torment will always, eventually, be met by love. Every single act of violation is actually a cry for love. It is love that gradually mends our fractured self. It is love that grows us into greater peace and wholeness. As we grow through each experience of love – through giving, receiving and being love – we come to truly realise love in its totality.

All of this reflects our conscious evolution. The more conscious we are, the more open and present we are to love. Realising the love we are is truly about the journey from the head to the heart.

## The four pillars of love

The four pillars of loving expression are forgiveness, empathy, inclusiveness and gratitude. Understanding the core behaviours that support us in this journey is essential. These core behaviours reflect love in its distinct qualities and strengths.

### Forgiveness and acceptance

Most people think of forgiveness as a forgetting of something you believe was a wrong done to you: figuratively speaking, 'to forgive and forget'. However, as long as you still hold the view that something was *done* to you, and you hold a *judgment* for the person who 'did wrong', you will not experience a state of true forgiveness. Nor will you forget, at least not at the subconscious level.

True forgiveness brings us to a new level of awareness that liberates us *from the judgment* of the wrongdoing. The event is completely transformed in our consciousness. This may seem difficult. But it is possible.

When I was sixteen a man raped me and attempted to murder me. However, during the incident I was able to hold such a deep state of presence that I was in a state of unified consciousness. I experienced *every*thing as the same *one* Self, and was so deeply present as Self, that I was able to see the event at every level. This meant I was able to see the man's (ignorance) innocence, and that his actions were born of a state of deep unconsciousness and a *disconnection from love*. It was because of the extreme suffering, the lack of love he felt, that he acted so violently and unconsciously.

Because he felt such a lack of love – *and lack of control* – he was willing to 'take' love and kill love instead of being 'rejected' by it. As he brutally bashed me and screamed, "I'm going to kill you! You're going to die, bitch!", I drew into a deeper and deeper state of focus. I could feel my body slipping towards death and knew that I had to focus completely, with full conscious attention.

I put every bit of concentration into consciousness. In such a deep state of awareness I was completely free of any judgment towards his 'wrong' action. I was in a complete state of oneness. Instead I felt overwhelming love and compassion. All I could feel was a complete desire for him to know that he *is* love; that he is lovable, that he *is* loved. It was as if my whole being prayed for him to awaken to love. All I could feel was immeasurable love.

This love was so astonishing, so powerful. It felt as if I were the infinite ocean of love, of all existence. To this day I still struggle to really convey in words the fullness of what happened. This love was not just a thought. It was an all-present, all-penetrating, boundless energy. This love was the *infinite* me. It was a vibration that filled the entire room, and believe it or not, was accompanied by a thousand angels. Yes. The room was full of angels!

As love overflowed, the room literally lit up, and this man fell to his knees and called out... "Oh God, help me... what have I done?... I've killed an angel! Please help me!! Please help her... you have to save her..!" It was the power of that love caused the man – the murderer – to *see*! In that instant he woke up! It caused him to stop trying to kill me and to become the saviour. Although he called for help, by the time my body was in the hospital I had been so severely beaten and damaged that I slipped into a coma.

However, 'I' was very much awake. 'I' was the presence of the eternal, unbreakable Self... the spirit of absolute *oneness*... the pure conscious presence of all existence. I knew myself absolutely as this – indestructible life. And I knew that before this body I was this. When I came to this body, I was this. As I lived through the changes of life, I was still this. I am and have always been this. And in each moment forever... I will always be *this*.

While my body lay unconscious, I continued to witness. I witnessed the body and all the following events. I was able to see that the man's soul yearned to re-awaken – *to encounter* pure unconditional love – which was exactly what happened to 'him' through his encounter with me. I was able to see that 'my' soul, the person I incarnated as, was here *to demonstrate* absolute unconditional love – not just as a concept, but as *the living embodiment* of it – which I did through that encounter with him.

In seeing this I realised the *one* self in the individuated aspects. I was able to see the 'Self' creation that it was... that this event was a perfect creation of love, of one being, and that I had chosen to participate in it.

I was the creator of the event. In that witnessing, there was no judgment, no pain, no victim, no perpetrator. There was *no thing to forgive. There was only a purpose.* There was only *love*. All I could feel was profound gratitude. And, in that pure state of love, the body healed 'miraculously'. To this day I remain radiantly free of any of the 'would be usual' physical, emotional or mental scars.[29]

This is a potent demonstration of the power that is within us when we embody love *consciously*. It is why masters have said that *LOVE is the power that overcomes all enemies*. Love *is* the greatest power! It is the single power through which we can transcend divisiveness to regain unity and harmony. It is *the* power that shifts us from fear to certainty, from the unconscious to consciousness, from conflict to peace, from separation to oneness.

Ordinarily, however, a person must understand how to transform the feelings more typically experienced as the perception and the state of *being a victim*. Whether you are feeling victimised because of a specific event or person, or more generally as if all of life is somehow against you, it is important to *regain and reach* the understanding I have outlined through the above example.

By revisiting one's own thoughts and feelings about life's events, it is possible to see life in a new way. It is possible to see that *everything* is the creation of the *one* Self, and that *we* are this self, we are a part of it, and very much the creator of every one of our experiences. Indeed there *is* a purpose to each and every event. And that ultimate purpose is to realise and fulfil love.

**Not forgiving means you still wish it could have been different. But it wasn't, and it won't be. The only way you will find peace with it is to find a higher meaning or purpose within it.**

Now, this does not mean that we are to condone violent actions or certain behaviours (I certainly did not condone the violating act of rape and attempted murder), but it does mean that we can see how and why such acts are created and experienced. The reasons for the event will vary according to the people involved and the level of consciousness that is occurring.

---

[29] To read more of the story, see my autobiography: *Buddha on the Dance Floor.*

However, in every case, whenever we *understand* the creation, and we realise that we *chose* the experience (even though at the time it may not have been consciously) we reach a state of true understanding, acceptance and completion. We attain a true state of forgiveness. We are able to see that either we, or the 'other', (or both) did not know any better at the time, and that each was in a shared process of growing towards greater conscious awareness… and *love*.

We are able to see that indeed we are each playing a role for each other to fulfil our own goals of life experience and mastery. Each event is actually the vehicle we are using to *become* or embody that which we seek to know or be. Ultimately, *every* event is leading us to greater consciousness and love.

The experiences we have are all the tools of our soul. Our soul is using specific life settings as the stage on which we can play out our process of evolution. Through each event we take the journey of consciousness. We move through the layers of our unconscious self and begin to awaken, moving into greater conscious realisation and more aware manifestation.

The more conscious we become, the more we are able to see that life is not something separate from us, and that life is not being *done* to us. Rather, *we* ourselves are the process, the co-creator, experiencing and awakening through the events we call 'my life'.

As we realise this, we no longer need to hold on to the emotional energy that was associated with a past experience. And in doing so, we release ourselves from the judgment which kept us bound to suffering and victimisation. Instead, we are able to use the experience as insight, as material that supports our ongoing purpose and process of growth or awakening. We undergo a true assimilation of all we have encountered, and from it comes real maturing and the most wondrous of blossoming – a fully loving human being!

Freedom from our past is essential for us to know the love we truly are. We need to connect with the real essence of love in order to know it. This is why the ability to expand into witnessing awareness is so essential. It creates the shift for us; our ability to shift from the head to the heart (from what we think love is or isn't to what it *actually* is); and from unconscious and closed awareness to conscious and expanded awareness. It is with the power of witnessing and reflection that we can revisit the images of our past with clear consciousness and gain insight.

And, with witnessing we are able to dispel the emotional charge that has been stored in relation to a past event. We are able to literally release ourselves from the energy that has kept us bound to the past. Whatever occurred is integrated through awareness and love. In doing so, we can finally be fully present and available to the moment of *now* as it truly *is*... as that which is forever new, whole, perfect and purposeful... forever truth.

## Empathy, kindness and compassion

The more we are able to release ourselves from our judgments and see into our unconscious experiences with higher awareness, the more we develop empathy. This in itself is a journey as we grow through our own personal experiences.

In basic terms there are two forms of empathy. One is more self-reflective, in that we empathise with another in terms of how we might feel in their situation or how it makes *us* feel. The other form of empathy is being open to how the *other* person feels, with substantially less self-referral. Although the latter is a truer form of open care for another, we can only truly feel and understand another's experience through understanding our own.

The more we understand our own unconscious experience, the more we are able to see ourselves in every other person. We are able to relate more consciously to our experiences of pain and the process we undergo as we shift from unconscious states of suffering to more conscious states of resolution and liberation. As we ourselves undergo this, we cannot help but feel more empathy for others.

We feel tenderness for each and every person we meet when we can see that they too are undergoing the same journey; the shift from *unconscious* being to more *conscious* being. We understand in many moments that the 'other's' behaviour is where we ourselves have been, less capable of feeling and acting from a place that is in harmony, empowered and aware. We understand that these limited states cause suffering. *We understand* what it is to suffer. And just as we know our own desire to be liberated from suffering, we cannot but wish for others to be free of suffering. As we wish for our own happiness it is natural to wish for others to be happy.

As a society we often disregard compassion, considering it to be irrelevant when faced with situations that demand intelligent responses. Paradoxically, compassion is essential for us to attain the most relevant and intelligent responses – those based on caring. We have even come to believe that compassion is somehow unnatural in certain situations, for example in business or the workplace. Yet by our very nature we are compassionate beings. Why? Because compassion begins with curiosity about other people, what motivates them, and how the world outside of our own actually works.

As any parent knows, children are naturally curious. It is only as we age that our natural curiosity is often replaced by learned conditions masquerading as worldly sophistication. We become so certain that we know other people, and how the world works, that our ability to be pleasantly surprised and even delighted withers away or expires. Compassion, then, by definition, involves a renewal of the innate curiosity we were born with.

It is this openness, this curiosity, which enables us to be in tune with people. Being in tune with others involves *caring* about them, and caring is what invokes the respect, consideration and empathy that constitute compassion. Compassion is defined by three components: understanding and empathy for others, caring for others, and the willingness to act on those feelings of care.

Being open to one another enables us to face conflicts and life challenges with creativity and resilience. Empathy enables us to connect with others and understand what moves them. It helps us to grow, evolve and negotiate our way through this shared mystery called life. When we consistently act based on real understanding of others, and with care and concern, our relationship with the whole world takes on greater depth and significance. We discover all of the things that make it evident we are truly connected.

Instead of feeling separation due to our differences, we begin to feel a deeper connection because of our sameness. We see how truly interconnected we are. We are absolutely related to each and every other being we encounter. And, in some way, we are playing a role in their lives. No single one of us lives in isolation, even when it may appear as such. In recognising our interconnectedness, we begin to realise just how profoundly relevant all thoughts and acts of kindness are.

**The ability to perceive other people's actions and existence as meaningful is critical for altruism.**

This shift in our perception is fundamental to our personal and collective fulfilment. Various studies in social behaviour have come to the clear conclusion that people's happiness is influenced by the happiness of others with whom they are connected. This highlights a fundamental truth:

**Happiness and wellbeing is a collective phenomenon.**

With the awareness of our interconnectedness and the significance of every single being, we shift from being an egocentric person to being allocentric, extending our interest equally to others and the wellbeing of the whole. Our sense of *awakening* also shifts from the notion of something that is self-centred (fulfilling the self) and isolated to something that is collective (fulfilling the whole) and interconnected.

Awakening brings us to the true shift from the egocentric to the allocentric self. There is still a 'self', however it is no longer identified with the ego, driven by fears or motivated by self-gain. As enlightened being, we realise we are the presence of love consciousness, interacting and corresponding with life – *giving* to life – fulfilling a role for the benefit of the whole.

As a natural consequence, we become a truly civil, sharing society of individuals acting in aggregate rather than in a self-absorbed manner. We become a compassionate collective, united through a deep emotional bond and the trust we invest in each other. Naturally then compassion *is* the most relevant human quality. Compassion is the currency of our connectivity, shaping our truest relationships and holding us all together. Whilst still primarily motivated by economic return, even our corporate world is beginning to wake up to the relevance of all of this.

With unified efforts in awareness we begin to see the true flowering of our humanity. We discover the wisdom that lies in the heart of each and every one of us, waiting to be harnessed for the greater fortune of the whole. It is this wisdom that reveals the true nature of ourselves and others. With this, the veils of ignorance are lifted. We have awoken again to the love we truly are. Our motivations begin to align with a more realistic gauge of 'global profit' as something reflected in the equality, health and wellbeing of people and the planet, rather than pure economic gain.

Rather than feeling pity for others, we are able to see their divine essence. Compassion is not the heaviness of pity. It is something much lighter and much more significant. It is the realisation that we are all powerful, we are all love and we are all deserving of wellness and harmony. In knowing our own divine essence, it becomes our wish for others to be awake to this, and in doing so, to be able to transform their suffering.

**A compassionate heart and mind then naturally asks: How may I help?**

With compassion there is no thought for personal gain, nor projection of what we think another person needs, but rather a direct response to the other's *expressed* needs. Naturally, then, our heart centres, those most luminous chakras of human beauty, blossom and expand. We discover that indeed we are truly caring, gentle, sensitive, generous, compassionate and altruistic beings.

It is easy for us to actively generate love consciousness. If we make a commitment to practice more acts of kindness – particularly random acts of kindness – we increase our sense of connectedness significantly. Kindness as an act in itself generates a shift of consciousness. We literally create the energy and space for greater awareness to enter into our hearts and minds.

We create stronger threads of aware connection with 'strangers', only to discover that in every moment, around every corner, we are meeting our Self. It is then that we realise: All we do, we truly do to ourselves. This realisation leads us to live a conscious life of respect and sacredness. It is through this compassion that we can truly change the world for the better.

### Inclusiveness and unity

To love oneself is in the beginning… to love another is in the middle… to love all is in the endless. Inclusiveness is in fact a very human, deeply spiritual need. When we take a close look at our most inherent needs, we discover that, other than food and shelter, our most common need is love – to love and be loved. We only have to look at our hopes and fears for confirmation of this. Just scratch the surface and we find one of our biggest fears – the fear of being alone. This runs deep in our shared psyche. The fear and perception of being separated from the source, from our true mother, and from each other causes us to generate protective beliefs and behaviours. Despite the deeper truth that separation is an illusion, for we truly are an all-connected field of life, we deeply feel the need to belong. We only have to look at the success of online social media to see that need in action today.

That we perceive separation, consciously or unconsciously, causes us to feel great anxiety. We are compelled to behave in ways that make us distinctly human; we may become possessive, jealous, controlling, hateful, violent, or depressed and withdrawn. It is a false perception to feel apart from others and the world, and it doesn't have to be like this. We can also be motivated for the good of the whole creation; we can be kind, generous, supportive and compassionate.

Psychological research has revealed that one of the greatest fears we share is most deeply linked to this need for belonging. At some level we are terrified of being ostracised; judged as unacceptable and rejected by those we most want to belong with. Perhaps this explains why social media platforms like Facebook have become so successful, as they respond to the innate human need to connect and belong. Facebook is evidence that we are not separate. It is a tool through which we, as individuals and a society, are perhaps trying to re-awaken ourselves to the truth that we really are all connected.

The work of artist Marina Abramovic is a particularly telling demonstration of our potential. She performed two significant pieces of 'live' art. In the first she wanted to test the limits of human relationships. Marina placed upon a table 72 objects that people were allowed to use on her in any way that they chose, including some objects that could give pleasure and others that could inflict harm. Among them were a rose, a feather, honey, a whip, scissors, a scalpel, a gun and a single bullet. For six hours she remained passive and un-engaged, avoiding eye contact and allowing the audience to do as they chose.

Initially, members of the audience reacted with caution and modesty, but as time passed and the artist remained passive, people began to act more aggressively, ultimately reaching breaking point with someone pointing the loaded gun at her head. This became a poignant example of the strong inclination for humans to regress to destructive behaviour when *personal and engaging connection* is absent. The same thing happens with mob mentality.

In stark contrast, Marina performed another live piece called 'The artist is Present' in which she invited spectators to sit and gaze into her eyes. The dynamic was so overwhelming, bringing tears to many people's eyes, that it sparked the need for support groups to be established. The most commonly reported feeling was one of a deep, unexplainable soul connection.

Like these two performance pieces, social media also straddles personalised connection and the impersonal, reflecting the diverse range of our human behaviours. Despite its limitations, including the tendency to remove us from direct living interactions, its enormous success proves that our need to connect is very real. It is our awareness of this need that paves the way for us to enter into a more meaningful life.

Our ability to connect, and the depth to which we connect, is dependant on the *way* we connect. When we are deeply present, centred in our being, centred in the moment, we are most capable of being deeply connected with another and with life as it truly is. The encounter is one that is unifying, uplifting and enriching. It is also the only way in which we feel a power that is greater than our individual sense of 'self', one that contains the sense of a unified soul.

When we are connected in this way, only love flows, and it is impossible for feelings or acts of violence to arise. This is what *ahimsa*, the Sanskrit word for non-violence, really means. It is not in our effort to stop our acts of aggression that we achieve ahimsa, but rather in our ability to be truly connected, united by the inherent power of love that flows through our souls. Our ability to foster more deeply connected encounters with each other could be the very thing that steers us towards a world of greater peace and wellbeing. And our ability to foster a more deeply connected state within ourselves will inevitably re-awaken us to the truth that we really are *one* life.

Self-awareness without connectedness with the whole can be quite unfulfilling. However, self-awareness *combined* with communion provides the foundation for real hope. It gives us a glimpse of the potential we really have… to live a love-filled life. Perhaps this is why the Buddhist faith espouses the virtues of *sangha*, living spiritual community, as the highest principle for human development. And, whether we are 'spiritual' or not, it is evident that the more connected we are, in ourselves and with each other, the happier we are. Perhaps then it is time to prioritise real life relationships over virtual connection and to reconnect with the living world, where reality *is* in the ever-present *now*.

**Love is what holds everything together… because it *is* the everything.** As we create a stronger thread of connection with others, we create an even greater field of connectivity and magnetism. We become so open that we can welcome all of existence – as it is – unconditionally, into our hearts and into our awareness. In fact, by making it your intention to allow *every* thing – every person, every thought, every belief, every event, every atom – to have its place and purpose in existence, you will find yourself in a state of total unity. You will find that your whole being has become the presence, the energy, the expression, the field of *love*. You will realise that there is no single home for love, for it is an infinite ocean with no beginning or end.

## Gratitude and praise

By simply pausing and paying attention to your life you will be able to acknowledge what a gift it is in each moment. You may not always feel grateful, especially when you are challenged, but the truth is, there is always something you *can* be grateful for. The human mind has a tendency to veer towards the things it is not satisfied with. However, once we begin to recognise the things we *do* have, we discover there is a lot to be thankful for. Remember to attune: I am *grateful* for this moment.

Even if we can't see the perfection of each and every moment, practicing gratitude and praise will soon lead to a very loving and unified state. In this loving state, we are able to see things with higher vision. We are able to see that love is at work in each and every moment. We are able to see that each situation, each and every little being, is designed perfectly in accord with the whole. We can begin to praise life for all we have.

This awakens our universal heart. We find ourselves in the middle of the wonder of existence, in love and in awe of this astonishing creation. We can't help but praise all that is.

## BEING THE PRESENCE OF LOVE

There is one simple guide to follow whenever you feel unsure or like you've lost your way: close your eyes, listen closely and attend with your heart. Your heart will always guide you more wisely than your head. Following are some simple points that are easy to put into action, yet capable of generating immense love. These activities have the power to completely change your life!

### Be love

Meditate daily. Cultivate peace and loving awareness in yourself, and bring this to everyone else in your life. Accept that love has nothing to do with another person, rather, love is the true nature of your own heart. It is about you showing up in your heart every day. In essence your quest is to *be the presence of love*. You can use the seventh attunement as a way to focus your loving intention into action: *I am the Presence of Love.*

Love is the way *you* live, the way you walk, the way you talk, the way you interact with every aspect of your world. Start immediately – be loving *now*. If you wait for the right person or the right moment to give love, then you will never give love. 'Fall in love' with life every day. Give thanks for the things you love, and make it a point to look for and participate in the things you love. *Be* loving and peaceful… and watch the ripples spread.

### Voice love

Speak carefully and kindly. Develop your skills in communication and conflict resolution. We must cultivate loving and co-operative language for a life of unison. Be willing to apologise, as it conveys a genuine care, respect and love for others. And speak up. Make your voice heard through groups, polls and petitions for conscious and peaceful policies to be implemented by governments. Write to politicians to express what you feel is most equitable for the greater good. Every voice does make a difference, *know yours counts*. Remind people of their own love and beauty. Remind them often of their best attributes, and the ones you see them aspiring to. Sing freely and often... even if it needs to be in the shower. It opens the heart! It also brings more love into your words.

### Think love

The power of intention is magical. You may start with affirmations such as:
- I AM love.
- My body and mind are filled with peace and love.
- This moment is peaceful and loving.
- My day is filled with peace and love.
- The world is filled with peace and love.

Read books and material that centres all of your thoughts on a peaceful and loving reality. Give thanks for the perfect and all-unifying power of love. Honour all types of love. It isn't only romantic love that leads to a marriage that matters. Friendship love, familial love, neighbourly love, divine love, self-love and universal love, are all essential and equally important types of love.

### Inspire love

Bestow genuine compliments. Every day, give three thoughtful compliments, each to a different person. If you can't find three people to sincerely compliment, open your eyes – and your heart – a little wider. Beauty, both internal and external, is abundant and worth acknowledging. Come up with creative ideas about how you can help cultivate love and wellness in other people's lives. Encourage others to join you in these creative aspirations and share your energy with as many people as possible.

### Feel and act through love

Connect with others and life through your heart. Make a daily effort to lighten another person's life. Join a group dedicated to service for others, or gather regularly with a group to meditate on peace and love together – collective intention is more powerful than our isolated efforts. Listen to music that inspires loving feelings. Smile and laugh everyday, especially if you find a bad mood grabbing hold of you! Fill your place with objects that represent love and peace.

Tell the truth, the whole truth and nothing but the truth, however do so with sensitive consideration. The smallest lie can erode the foundation of love, and unnecessary 'honest' thoughts can do the same. Relationships will endure and flourish with an honest and sensitive heart.

Abstain from criticism and judgments, they close down your heart and close others out. Accept loved ones as they are. Nothing feels less like love than somebody who corrects, judges, and tries to 'reform' you. We all long to be treasured despite our flaws, or even better, we long for our flaws themselves to be treasured. Start the cycle of acceptance by treasuring every part of every person you love, including yourself!

Remember important events. Celebrate birthdays, wish good luck before an interview, ask about stressful meetings and offer assistance during illness. Showing genuine interest in the major events in the lives of those around you will endear you to them for life. Call just to say "I love you." Small gestures of affection toward lovers, friends, family, neighbours and co-workers can turn an average or even gloomy day into an extraordinary one.

### Share love

Give freely and eagerly. Love is not like money. Love does grow on trees, it *is* the tree of life! Love is plentiful. It is infinite, actually. You don't need to store your love away and save it for one perfect purchase. Let love burn a hole in your pocket and set your life ablaze with joy!

Do not project your hopes or perceptions onto others, or impose your beliefs onto their words or thoughts. Listen quietly without interrupting or offering advice until it is requested. Give gifts that awaken the heart and inspire the soul. Simplify your own life, cut back on material luxuries, and make it your commitment to share a portion of your earnings and time with others who have less. Give time and energy to support nature and the environment, or an organisation committed to a world of greater peace and love.

### Unite loving power

If the world can rally hundreds of thousands of people for war, the world can rally *millions* of people for love! Become a member of an organisation committed to the vision of a world of *love*. Regularly join groups and events dedicated to the vision of a more loving, peaceful world.

Get to know your neighbours, co-workers and community. It's when we bond with others that we feel a common purpose to achieve greater good for the whole. Remember it starts with you and your local part of the world. Keep that link alive. Know that in uniting with others through the inspiration of peace and love you are bringing unity to the world.

And remember the power of simple gestures. Smile warmly and offer a gentle touch of your hand. Hug often and like you mean it. Embrace warmly and with intention, and feel the unity. Last but not least make it your sacred commitment to:

– Select at least one of the suggestions above as your daily love action.
– Select at least four of the above as your monthly love quota.
– Select one of the above as a love goal for the year.
– Select a major love tool as a life-long purpose to fulfil.

Or, create some of your own.

Today is your day. This *now* is your moment, the one and only place you can be all you can be; so let it be great. Let it be a smile, a kind thought and a loving action. You have an infinite supply of everything you can give! And remember, your whole life changes with the one realisation: "I am love." All of life is the creation of love. *You* are love. You always have been and always will be.

Repeat Attunement #7

### *I am the Presence of Love.*

Take a few moments with your eyes closed, breathing into your heart centre and reflecting on the words. Then state the words clearly, silently in your heart or out loud, repeating the attunement three times. Continue to feel the state of your being aligned with the attunement for a few more minutes. Make it your intention that your words, thoughts and actions are based in love.

CHAPTER 19

# IN SERVICE OF THE WHOLE

*The highest destiny of the individual is to serve rather than to rule.* —Albert Einstein

Although awakening may be initially driven by the desire for personal liberation, its real purpose is to serve the *whole*. As the Roman philosopher Seneca said, "We are all members of one great body, planted by nature. We must consider that we were born for the good of the whole."

We may think of 'purpose' as something unique to each of us, but in reality we all share the same common purpose – to awaken, to love, and to serve the whole - and it is only the vehicle for its expression that is unique to each of us. To fulfil this purpose is to live our highest potential, and ultimately, to embody a more enlightened self.

Enlightenment is not about escaping the world; it is about being in the world *consciously*. It is about bringing the gift of loving consciousness *into* the world. This is what Buddha meant when he said, "Be in the world but be not of it." In other words, do not be bound by illusions, do not see yourself as an inherent 'something'. Be here with transcendent presence, but in an immanent way. Buddha suggests that we *do* transcend the world as we know it, and as most live it, and to be truly *in* it... with love and awareness. This is why all of the great enlightened ones – the Buddhas – have been calling to humanity to join the journey of awakening.

## Altruism, kindness and selfless service

As you will have already noticed, everything in this book is pointing to one key attainment, and this is it: To be fully here, in the living now, consciously and lovingly. This means to be present and aware. It means to awaken again to the oneness of all life. In attaining awakened presence, we transcend the ego, we go beyond our identified 'self'. In the awareness of oneness, we know and see the interconnectedness of all life.

Then we see and know our true Self as eternal life. And we also understand that this great Self manifested this small ephemeral life for a great purpose. In understanding the purpose of our existence, we can bring compassion to the world, and with it a new reality. As 'individual' aspects, each and every one of us is playing a role in relation to every other part of existence. As consciousness we are the one life, the essence, the love, the power that is behind all things, within all things, moving all things.

Awakening brings us the realisation that what appears as two distinct aspects is indeed the same one being, just as our two hands are part of our one body. We see the absolute perfection and interconnectedness of the 'individuation' of apparent 'selves' created by the one omnipotent being. We discover harmony and perfection in this great play, the infinite one that is simultaneously the eternal multiplicity of creation.

We are freed from our angst, judgments and rejections of all that appears in duality. Instead, we realise it is the magical tool of the one great being. Knowing this gives rise to absolute peace, freedom, joy, wonder, love and purpose. We cannot but see that as a manifestation, we are purposeful to the whole – and that, in actuality, *each and every one of us has been designed to fulfil a role and a function in relation to the rest of existence.*

You are meaningful to existence. Not only does this mean you are worthy in every possible way, it also means you are necessary in every possible way. This is what true altruism is: all-true-ism, or all is true and truth for all. An altruistic person sees, feels and understands that everything is true and purposeful, interdependent and absolutely interconnected. An altruistic person therefore has an uncompromising reverence for all life. There is a knowing of equality. There is love for all beings, and there is perfection and purpose in all beings. Most significantly, the purpose of being a 'self' is *to give for the whole*, to fulfil a role for the benefit of the whole. In doing so, we realise the meaning and purpose of our existence.

Without this understanding, it is very difficult to cultivate compassion or tolerance. Yet tolerance for each other is needed as we make the shift from unconscious to more conscious ideas and action. This is what Christ meant when he said, "Love Thy neighbour as Thyself" – that we should treat others with the same care we give to ourselves. Upon deeper consideration, these words equally mean, "Love Thy neighbour for he *is* Thyself." Other people *are* our very own being, there is no 'other'. There is only *one*, and therefore only one love and one purpose, which is to see, be and give love in each and every moment. With this realisation we are capable of truly loving and serving the whole.

Therefore, altruism is the fruiting of compassion. The writer and mystic Thomas Merton articulated this well when he said, "The whole idea of compassion is based on a keen awareness of the interdependence of all living beings, which are all part of one another and all involved in one another." Compassion rises up out of the seed of understanding, and it generates tolerance and empathy. When we are filled with compassion, it overflows into our desire to put loving kindness into action to serve and benefit others.

If we look closely, altruism and selfless acts of service are central to most religions and spiritual paths. Altruism in the public realm, caretaking of each other and all life on earth, has been left almost entirely to voluntary organisations and religion. Yet the importance of *each and every one of us* playing a role for the benefit of the whole is increasingly critical to the wellbeing of our world.

In Buddhism, the first and most comprehensive of the eight *paramitas* for enlightened action is *dana*, or mutual generosity.[30] It states that if we have something that could benefit another who needs it, then to give it away benefits all. This 'something' could be anything: food, clothing, kind actions, wise words or inspiration. When we live with awareness, we can't help but be motivated to serve in some way. In fact, we see that this is exactly what we are designed for.

---

30 'Paramitas' translate as 'perfections' of completions.

In Sanskrit the word for selfless service, *seva*, translates directly as 'string', implying that all things are connected in the thread of existence. With this recognition, seva becomes a spiritual practice to uplift and assist people through selfless service, bringing benefit to the whole. To engage with one is to engage with the whole. To serve one is to serve the whole. Likewise, *to withhold from one is to deny the whole.*

To continue living our life as miserly, greedy, selfish human beings is a sure recipe for global collapse. Giving ourselves generously to life hurts far less than withholding does. And withholding eventually hurts *all* life. Seva is therefore one of the most profound and life-changing of practices. It is also one of the most imminent necessities. However we choose to express our own unique seva practice, we ultimately test our altruism and put our spiritual knowledge into action.

In essence, seva is an attitude as much as it is an action. Seva is when you approach the world around you with an open and offering heart: "What can I provide to uplift these people, this place, our world?" Then, even going to the supermarket is an opportunity to connect with people in your community with a smile, a kind deed, kind words or gratitude, as well as an act that supports your household. Every action and interaction can become seva when it is conceived and executed without thought to how it benefits you.

At other times seva can be a focused, premeditated activity such as volunteering with a service or organisation, or being committed to a regular voluntary task. *Through the spirit of selfless action,* we attain that height of realisation whereby our minds become absorbed in the divine essence of all – love and oneness. *We become 'holy' – living for the 'whole'.*

In its highest sense, seva should be done with no expectation of reward or acknowledgment. However, seva can equally be a means to transform actions that are self-centred. The mind, like a vessel, needs to be 'cleansed' of egocentricity if it is to fulfil the spiritual purpose. This cleansing of the mind can be done with the 'soap' of humility. In seeking humility, there's no need to blindly wade through religious tomes. No penances, no fasting, no retreats, no lofty attainments, no certificates of mastery or Godliness. There's a simple, direct and effective way - seva.

Nothing grandiose is necessary for this inner cleansing. We don't have to build monuments, or light a candle atop a mountain, or even go on far-flung crusades fighting for world peace. In fact, the greatest power of seva is most often fulfilled through the most menial tasks. Just serving those who are in need puts us on the right path. At home, with our neighbours around the corner, in the community we live in. The concentric circles can be as wide or as narrow as the situation presents.

Feed the hungry, clothe the destitute, shelter the homeless. Sweep floors, clean toilets, wash dishes. Put stamps on the letters, pack the boxes, file the papers. Simply be willing to do whatever needs to be done in order to help another or the collective. You simply do it, and you do it to the best of your ability, and nothing else matters.

Anonymity helps and is a key ingredient for this humbling process. Doing it without fanfare or a pat on the back is a definite plus. Doing things that others do not want to do, or cannot do, is at the heart of seva. Sweeping the floor or cleaning bathrooms are therefore bound to be very effective. Ultimately the practice of seva becomes a path to self-realisation, a return to the Self as One.

Put simply, altruism is the complete opposite of selfishness. It is the renunciation or transcendence of the separate individual self, and an exclusive concern for the welfare of others. And this rides on the back of the realisation that all is one. Pure altruism is giving up something of value (such as personal time, rewards, money, or goods) with no expectation of any compensation, benefits or recognition in return. We serve simply to serve and for no other reason. No strings attached.

Make yourself invisible and do acts of kindness with love and without expectation of return. If any of the following underlie your actions then it isn't truly seva:
- If it isn't done with honesty and integrity, or if your heart and soul aren't in it.
- If you believe that mediocrity is all that is expected of you and that you needn't do more, or you fit it in only when it suits you.
- If it's for building your resume, getting a tax-deductible receipt, or used as a means to bigger and better things.
- If you need to tell others, now or later, that you did it, or it distresses you that others take credit for what you've done.

- If lack of appreciation by others, or their criticism, drives you away, or lack of outcomes makes you give up.
- If you believe that it is your right to do it, or you're the best or only one to do it.
- If you have to compete with others to do it, or you take it away from another.

Please do not be disheartened or dismayed if you notice any of these underlying motives infiltrating your intentions of selfless service. It is important you acknowledge the tainted motivation; however, do not judge yourself and, importantly, do not give up! Understand it simply indicates you are still in the process of 'cleansing' and continue to offer yourself for selfless acts.

## The flow-on benefits of altruism

Despite its selfless nature, altruism in all its forms – kindness, generosity, compassion, volunteering, donating money, working freely for a cause – has the potential to reward the giver as much as or more than the recipient. If an act of kindness or altruism is motivated by any desire for self-gain, it is not true altruism.[31] However, by its very nature, such an act *does* generate benefits as a result of cause and effect. If I cause suffering, I will, as a natural consequence, experience suffering. If I cause happiness, I will, as a natural consequence, experience happiness.

In this regard, the greater benefits gained from altruism are an effect of the action rather than a motivation. Most altruists have held that each person has an obligation to further the wellness and alleviate the pain of others. The same truth reveals that happiness, rather than pleasure, is the goal of life. The real formula for happiness involves doing good to be good, rather than doing good with the expectation of getting something in return.

Altruism is the key to the social connections that are so important to our happiness. Research finds that acts of kindness, especially spontaneous, out-of-the ordinary acts, can boost happiness in the person doing the good deed. There are many reasons for this. Being kind promotes a sense

---

[31] We may, however, draw motivation from the understanding that by advancing the greater good we advance ourselves on an individual level too. This concept has been described as 'enlightened self interest'.

of connection and community with others, which is one of the strongest factors in increasing personal *and* collective happiness. Being generous helps us appreciate our own good fortune, boosts self-confidence and gives us a way to use our strengths and talents in a meaningful way. It also leads us to perceive others more compassionately. We typically find good qualities in people to whom we are kind.

Kindness can start a ripple response of positivity. Being kind to others may lead them to be grateful and generous to others, who in turn are grateful and kind to others. Positive spiritual emotions such as gratitude, compassion and forgiveness create an internal harmony that brings joy and good health in many ways. When we get in touch with our higher Self and we cultivate these qualities each day, it's tremendously good for the people around us, but it's also wonderful for our *own* happiness, health and wellbeing. There is documented evidence that acts of kindness alleviate depression, and that people who do good deeds find it good for their health.[32] Surveys involving thousands of volunteers have revealed that participating in regular, small acts of kindness is beneficial to health, longevity and wellbeing.[33]

Whilst being kind and compassionate is linked to greater happiness, health and longevity, there is one important caveat. Becoming overextended and overwhelmed by helping, as can happen with people who are caregivers to family members, can diminish health and quality of life. Compassion fosters happiness, but being sacrificial reduces wellbeing. This 'sacrificial' nature is distinguished by an individual's inability to know their own limits and honour them. Being generous with an abundance of time, money, and energy can promote wellbeing, but being sacrificial quickly lowers wellbeing. This is a good reason for communities to share the giving and supporting roles for everyone's benefit.

Being able to give is an expression of deep gratitude. Through kind and selfless acts we are able to express thanks for the life we have and the gifts we receive. Seva allows us an opportunity to be fully compassionate and to engage with our world and community in a meaningful and fulfilling way. When it comes to being altruistic and giving back to

---

[32] Layous, K. et al., 'Delivering Happiness: Translating Positive Psychology Intervention Research for Treating Major and Minor Depressive Disorders', *The Journal of Alternative and Complementary Medicine*, 17.8 (2011) 675-683.

[33] http://www.kindnessfoundation.com/research

others, it's important to recognise that everybody has unique qualities and different strengths.

**Because of our diversity, when people unite their efforts, the benefits increase. If and when we pull together as one body we can change the world.**

## Creating a more peaceful world

During these troubled times, the concept of world peace may seem an unlikely outcome. Yet, if we feel powerless to positively influence world conflict, we have in a way resigned ourselves to the situation. To start with, this lack of power is born of our limited perceptions, leading to a lack of motivation and cultivating apathy. The resulting inaction allows such conditions to continue unabated.

I call what is happening here, 'the mountain syndrome'. The mountain appears too enormous to scale. Yet, by setting out with the right attitude, one step at a time, standing on the peak becomes our reality. So if we are to move towards world peace, we must ask ourselves what is within our measure. What is the step that will get us started? In one simple word, in one simple attitude, it is *compassion*. And in one simple act, it is *kindness*.

When you let kindness fill your soul, you effect great change. This is not only our individual power but also our collective power. In fact, it is the link to world peace. With selfless acts of kindness we create more positive, sharing and loving links between each other and all of life. This connectivity is at the heart of peace, individually and collectively. Despite great greed and corruption in the world, there is a great amount of kindness. As research has shown, kindness is at the heart of most people. When asked about what makes us happy, 87% of respondents in one survey said 'acts of kindness'.[34]

If we look closely, we will see we already have the right ingredients and the motivation for kindness. Great things can appear in human beings when disaster happens. Great power is generated when the citizens of the world unite in a common cause. The trauma of the suffering of others can give birth to stronger hands and hearts in people. Our human-created barriers become irrelevant.

---

34  Dr Dan Robotham et al., 'Doing Good? Altruism and Wellbeing in an Age of Austerity', Mental Health Foundation, 2012.

We have witnessed this in recent global events of tragedy and social upheaval. In such situations, we sense a palpable power that ties us all together at some deeper, unbreakable level. In these situations, the power we are witnessing is kindness. People are mobilised and unite to extend help in every possible way. It often takes times of great adversity for our compassionate heart to be awoken.

This phenomenon of people power has been recently dubbed 'the other world power'. We have witnessed the presence of this force throughout our history in the peace marches of the Vietnam War, the ousting of despots, campaigns for social justice like the WTO demonstrations, and disaster relief appeals like the Boxing Day Tsunami, the Japanese earthquakes and the Australian floods.

The clue now is for us to recognise this inherent power and put it to greater effect in our everyday lives, rather than waiting for tragedy to strike before we value it enough. Creating such an outcome is easier than we might think. Initially, we must realise that individuals have within their grasp *the ability to positively influence any negative condition.*

**No single one of us is powerless unless we choose to give our power away. YOU have the ability to effect positive change in the world.**

We all do. When this truth is realised, we can more effectively extend the power of kindness and compassion. We can adjust and arrange our lives to express kindness in many different ways. For example, we can easily make it our intention to be more caring, loving, attentive, courteous and helpful. It is also important to regularly re-assess our values and ethics, ensuring we follow and act in accordance with our highest principles. Even when we find our own lives challenging, we are still capable of offering a smile or a hug and finding something to do, whether large or small, for another person. Each one of us has the capability to be kind; it is simply a matter of making it a priority in our lives. All we need do is remember to extend acts of kindness more often.

In truth, for the good of our mental, emotional and physical health, we should all be eager to be involved in acts of kindness. Furthermore, kind and caring people are not only good to be around, they also feel good about themselves. We all admire kind people. It is proven that when we see a kind act or are the recipient of a kind act, our faith in a better world is restored. But the benefits of being kind extend even further.

Altruism behaves like a 'miracle drug'. It has beneficial effects on the person giving help, it benefits the person who receives help, and it can stimulate healthy responses in people who may view it indirectly. Making the decision to be a little kinder will bring more pleasure, success and direction to your life than ever before. The challenge for our world is to have a sufficient number of people committed to kindness and compassion through daily contemplation and action.

Whether we realise it or not we all carry the power to transform the world... to create a kindness revolution.

**One act of kindness has the power to ripple out and bring positive change to a thousand people. Seven million people acting kindly have the power to affect seven billion people, the entire population of the planet.**

Globally, around 971 million people engage in volunteer work in a typical year and the numbers are growing.[35] In Australia, over a third of the adult population undertakes some form of voluntary work every year.[36] In a world of looming change, this is the most important thing we can all set our sights on and be a part of. It is also a sign of great hope... we are already the change in motion. May you embrace the power you have today, and make it your commitment to achieve at least one act of kindness every day.

See you on the peak!

## Giving and receiving kindness

Here are some ways to cultivate altruism and kindness:
- Listen attentively without interrupting.
- Be respectful to every person and everything in every moment.
- Be understanding and forgiving of yourself and others, don't judge or criticise.
- Have compassion towards others, smile often.
- Offer kind words, encouragement, compliments and praise.

---

[35] Estimate by the John Hopkins University Center for Civil Society Studies. See: http://ccss.jhu.edu/research-projects/volunteer-measurement/about-volunteer-measurement.
[36] Statistics from The Centre for Volunteering. See: http://www.volunteering.com.au/tools_and_research/volunteering_statistics.asp.

- Act when your intuition tells you to.
- Give your time or donations *generously* to a cause.
- Commit to at least one kind and selfless act daily.
- Meditate on compassion and wellness for all beings.
- Prepare a meal or a surprise for a friend or elderly person.
- Give a gift simply to give.
- Remember that all life is connected and the purpose of your life is to fulfil a role for the whole.
- Have faith in yourself and others.
- Remember that there is no such thing as an insignificant kind or selfless act.
- Give thanks every day to the Divine for your life and all you receive, including a kind act bestowed upon you.

In receiving a kind act, it is common to think, "Oh, I must pay this person back." Whether it be about acknowledging the gift, evening the score, or displaying gratitude, this response tends to be centred in the ego. Instead, when you receive a gift, physical or otherwise, remember where it truly came from. All giving is an act of the universe – the energy of the universe is alive and flowing, in and through us.

Whatever we are giving *is* the energy of the universe. It has come from the universe and is being given to the universe... the *one* life. So, make it your practice to first thank the Infinite, the true source of all we receive in this life, and recognise that the person who gave it to you is an instrument of God – the universe. Saying a prayer or blessing for this person is a beautiful way to acknowledge his or her seva. And, of course, a big smile and hug or thank you directly to the person is a wonderful courtesy that acknowledges the circle of life's energy flowing in us and through us.

It is also important to understand that energy is all-connected and never confined to the singular action or person doing the act. In other words, you may give a great amount of time, kindness or help to a particular individual and they never say "thank you" or do anything in return for you. However, somewhere in your life, someone else bestows kindness and gratitude upon you. Or you may feel it is unfair that you keep giving to a cause without being paid for it, whilst you are blessed with a partner who financially supports you or an inheritance from which you can live sufficiently.

The truth is, the universe is a circle of life. You are it and it is you. Whatever you receive will be given back to the universe, and whatever you give to the universe will be given back to you. Of course that doesn't mean if you give apples, it is apples you will get in return. The universe is more intelligent than that. The universe will give you exactly what you truly need. Energy is not time, nor bound to time. You may spend a year giving selfless service and feel there is little return in your life, then discover five years down the track that your life is suddenly full of gifts and blessings in ways you never anticipated.

Most importantly, it is the truth that all life *is* energy. The nature of this energy is flow. That means whatever we have within us, whatever we receive, is ultimately to fulfil a purpose through which it may flow on to others. *Life is nothing other than giving.*

When we realise this, we can let go the fear that we will run out of supplies or that there will never be enough if we keep giving. It is only when we buy into this fear and *contract* that we inhibit the flow of energy through our beings and through our lives. If we hold on to anything for too long, we will notice that very little can flow into us. Literally, by holding on, by not giving, we are closing the doors to the energy of the universe.

Interestingly, if we give to a person for their own singular benefit, there will of course, at some time, be a return flow of energy to us. But if we give to a cause that is for the purpose of the collective, the effect of our giving is multiplied significantly... not just in terms of the personal benefits, but in terms of the collective benefits. If we join together and unite collectively we can change the world. All because in truth... We *are* the world.

Now I will leave you with another lovely Dr Seuss inspiration from *Oh, the Places You'll Go!*

You're off to Great Places!
Today is your day!
Your mountain is waiting.
So... get on your way!

# CONCLUSION

## The Sacred Story

As we have already explored, 'what' and 'how' we think plays the most central role in our personal and collective transformation. Put simply, the ego is a collection of stories we have become attached to. So attached, in fact, that the real sense of self, and life, is lost under a constructed identity. But these stories shape our lives. They determine our wellbeing or our demise, so this is an important area of examination and one that is pressing and relevant right now. This is not just a personal struggle; it is the very thing we face as a collective human experience.

The stories we have been telling ourselves for millennia are determining our relationships with each other and our entire connection to the world around us. We may be able to look to a truth higher than the 'stories', and understand that at a greater cosmic level all is perfectly in order. However, it is quite evident that the stories we hold, tell and live out in this world are indeed a source of great destruction. They also tend to keep us asleep, locked down in unconscious habits.

'Story' is so relevant to our human experience, because it is the way we hold the world in our minds. It is how we grasp the wonder of existence and negotiate our way through life. However, as long as we hold desperately to the small story, the one of fear and separation, we continue to perceive the world as a hostile place and remain in fear of having our lives torn from us. This small self has lost sight of the real story of the universe – one of wonder and of a great continuum.

Now, more than ever, is a time to take stock and re-assess our personal and worldly stories. It is unmistakably evident that many of our most familiar and cherished ideas are no longer viable. True happiness is not found in more money, accumulated possessions and vanity. Yet our billboards tell us these stories every day, continuing to condition us with superficial agendas. Most of our politicians, teachers, and leaders continue to tell the story of 'us and them', of privilege, hierarchy and division.

Although many of these stories try to convince us of our might, they really keep us very small. In reality, most people feel terribly fragile, alone, frightened, cut off and left out. These little stories hold great power over us. But many people are awakening to this and no longer want to be part of these unconscious and destructive stories. You are not alone. In the heart of everyone is the desire for truth, for love and for harmony.

If we are to steer ourselves towards a healthier world, we must let go of the small stories and resume our place in the *sacred story of the universe*, the story that tells us we are *one life*. This is the story that can awaken us all to the truth of our Self and of life. It tells us we are *never* alone and that we are intrinsically interwoven into the fabric of every living thing. This is much more than just a story; it is a remembering, an awakening. It is sacred... it is truth.

We are all connected to this universal, sacred story. And when we listen closely, it tells us we have everything we need to truly thrive. When we awaken to this, when we take up and live this sacred story, we find the way back home to peace, love and harmony.

Our awakening is about rediscovering the great conscious agreement and participation we have with the universe. It is the recognition of the Self – *our Self* – in all things, and of all things in the Self. It is about us discovering that through the very fabric of our being we are imbued with the senses, intelligence and consciousness that can chart the way for harmony between all living things.

But reclaiming our sacred story takes courage. There is always great trepidation when we are faced with the notion of giving up the small story, the story of the little self we have become so fixated with! We are so entrapped and mistakenly comfortable in our small stories that we are willing to defend their false grounds at the expense of greater truths. Or we may yearn for the absolute truth of our being, yet feel afraid it will fill us with more false hope and disappointment. This is especially true for anyone who has had a bad experience with religion. Unless we cultivate our own direct experience of the truth, it can feel conceptual and intangible – we don't yet see or feel it. This causes us to hold significant doubts.

And oftentimes the truth we need to face is not compatible with the 'stories' we have come to believe. We are even willing to give up truly living and loving just so the ego can continue to be 'right'. Or, we feel we have to take a teacher's word for it, yet again bringing up fears of potential exploitation. Guidance is wonderful and most often essential, yet in reality, it is only *you* that can become your process. It is only *you* that can awaken you to your Self. The inescapable fact is that we need to let the little self 'die' in order to truly live. Contrary to how it might first seem, this reveals something extraordinary. We come to our greatest discovery:

**The loss of the small self is the recovery of our greater Self.**

This small self created the illusory boundary between our great Self and existence. By letting go of the little self, we can let reality *all the way in*. Any pain we undergo is simply the breaking of the shell that encloses us from true understanding and from all that we truly are.

We are not cramped at all by the walls of our conditioning, by beginnings and endings, or by birth and death. We extend in every direction, in every place, in every time. We transcend even these apparent parameters and discover that we are being and becoming itself. The entire universe is composed of this beingness. It is not fixed in time or place, is never born and can never die. The small self dies into this eternally present, grand Self.

It is truly astonishing to emerge from the ego to discover that you are empty of all you thought you were. *You* are that awareness that has always been present – the wholeness, the love, the oneness. This revelation is the instant return to the fullness of being. This is what I call 'empty full'. We are truly boundless – all open – all empty and therefore that which contains all that is. Nothing is left *out* of what we are and can be. There is no outside to the universe. Every thing is present. Everything is always *in* life. This is the cosmic story. It is the awesome story of the universe as it is. It is the profound story of each and every one of us, of every being on this planet, of every particle in existence.

This is the only story that can guide us to a place of wellbeing for all on the planet now. It is the only story that can awaken *you*. It is the only story that can mend the perceptual divide we have created between the micro and the macro, between ourselves and all things. And it is only when we take up this cosmic story in person that we can embody a deep enough connection with all things, consciously.

This immense and unfolding revelation has the power to ignite the inquisitive and creative capacity in human beings, to acknowledge what is being made painfully obvious by the earth right now, and to respond skilfully and consciously, instead of denying it and maintaining our course towards self-destruction.

Why is this relevant to us all?

How many times have you heard the complaints that politicians are fixated on short-term solutions? If you look closely at *every* problem we face it is because of this blind, short-term, 'micro' view we have. As individuals and also collectively we enact limited solutions, without care or consideration for the longer-term 'macro' balance of the whole. It is because we are blind to the 'macro' that our collective stories continually teach us to stay attached to, and manipulate, the 'micro'. As a consequence, we ignorantly destroy what we have and ignore the greater reality of what we are and what we truly need.

The attachment to our micro stories keeps our lives bound within the parameters of unrealistic perception and unsustainable needs. We can never stretch far enough beyond our imagined fears to let life in deeply enough. This keeps us rapaciously hungry, like cancer cells, consuming everything in our path at the expense of the whole.

Only through the 'death' of our little self can we re-awaken to the cosmic story and to our whole Self. That death is something wondrous. It is not a loss. It is a great transformation, a great discovery of what we truly are. The discovery awaiting us is that we have always been the source of everything we seek. We are more than capable of living in harmony with the whole. This is the sacred story of life. *This* is a story so worthy of embracing!

This is a story that can equip us with the strength we need to re-adjust life as we are living it now. It is a story that serves us to know and believe in our capacity to act with the greatest efficacy and timeliness, to steer our world towards one of wellbeing for all. The choice is simple. Change nothing and serve the limited ego-version of ourselves at the expense of the whole, or liberate the inherent power of the grand Self for the whole to thrive. This is the cause of awakening. It is why the journey of awakening is the liberator for us all. It is the only passage that can bring us out of our world of destruction and into a world of co-creation.

The story of Mother Earth herself is not one headed for the end any time soon. She will go on without us to slowly return to harmony and wholeness, regardless of whether we join the shift in consciousness to move with her.

The prospect of changing our stories may sound confronting. And that may be a good thing, because this is a matter of urgency. Species are becoming extinct every day, vanishing forever. The fragile essential ecology of our forests wiped out, gone forever. All of this is happening right before our very eyes and yet we act as if we have all the time we want and all the solutions. This is the reality we are facing right now. Yet in the face of this shocking truth, we have a great story that can pull us all together. If we can recognise this, something truly powerful can happen.

The shock at the micro level becomes the charge of energy needed for us to begin to let in the power of the macro again. It becomes the impetus we need to give our priority and attention to the whole again. And the sooner we start, the sooner we realise that in doing so *every* one of our needs is met. The struggle falls away into the grand working of our being in the universe. This realisation has the power to return us to trust once again, allowing us to be guided by the very intelligence and functioning of the universe.

Humanity is embarking on a profound paradigm shift; from ego-centred 'reality' to collective reality, and even further, to universal intelligence. This means we are challenged in every way to extend ourselves beyond our own individual confines and comforts of self-centeredness. It means we are to awaken, to let go of the illusions of confinement. It means we are also to extend beyond the boundaries of our own small family or cultural nucleus to become true global citizens . It means we are to realise that each and every one of us is designed for the purpose of the whole. We are, indeed, one human family and one living earth.

But it takes each one of us to live a more awakened life to bring kindness, love and harmony to the whole, to commit to the journey of awakening as a human family. To strengthen this capacity takes conscious intention, commitment and effort. It requires holding ourselves and our consciousness open towards the unknown, that which we are all unfolding into, in a curious rather than fearful way. It is a practice in process. Practicing in accord with the universe, like life itself, is a work in progress.

This book has provided you with the most fundamental keys of the sacred story and the path to awakening *you*. This is not just another conceptual promise. It is an invitation for you to make a direct connection with the truth, to make it tangible, because it already abides in you. It invites *you* to become the living experience. The attunements literally contain the vibration of each element of truth, of the sacred story of you and the universe.[37] As you continue to work with the attunements and the practices provided, you will realise that *you* have become the sacred story.

You will discover that every part of your life is part of this story... and that *your* awakening is bringing the power and truth of this story back to life, to your life and to the world around you. It takes each one of us to realise that this is our true purpose: To participate in this consciously evolving process, and through our transformation, to offer ourselves as a gift to the world. Through this we will ultimately realise we truly are one.

With this as our navigating story, our lives and our world are destined to return to harmony. The truth is, we are destined to realise once again that *we are* the world. This is the sacred story... awakening YOU.

To complete, let us repeat the attunement:

*I am the Presence of Love.*

---

[37] For a deeper exploration of the attunements see my book, *The Seven Attunements,* and details of related programs at www.isira.com.

# BIOGRAPHY

Isira was born with awakened awareness. Through a series of profound spiritual events, the course of Isira's life led her to follow her greatest passion – supporting humanity to awaken into wisdom and love and transform the world. She is a spiritual counsellor and teacher and author of her much celebrated autobiography *Buddha on the Dance Floor* along with many other published works. She lives in Australia and holds regular public events for the shared journey of awakening.

# ISIRA'S SERVICE

Isira offers a range of programs and services for people to connect more deeply with the path of love and awakening. Through these, she has been a source of great transformation for many people around the world.

Isira teaches that enlightenment does not need to be complicated, it is not restricted to a certain religion or way of life, and it is not a far off future destination. It is simple, available to all, and it can be experienced right Now. Isira's purpose and passion is to help you (yes you!) awaken, flourish and achieve your own self-mastery. And as you awaken to your own wisdom and love, you make a difference in the world. Below is a general outline of some of the programs and services offered by Isira:

## SHORT PROGRAMS

**Satsang/Meditation/Life Answers:** The opportunity to spend time together in conscious presence and exploration of the heart and essence of existence, including meditation and time for your questions and answers. You can participate in many of these events via webinar.

## WEEKEND AND LONGER RETREAT PROGRAMS

Isira offers a range of events that allow seekers of awakening and Truth to more deeply explore and experience their true essence and harmony with life, through simple yet powerful tools of meditation and conscious practices. These teachings and applications are all drawn from Isira's direct experience of the truth at the very core of us all. With grace, humour, compassion and love, Isira has the capacity to lead us into a space that allows the most natural depth of consciousness and transformation to be encountered.

## CONSULTATIONS

**Spiritual counselling**: Isira shares enlightened insight, wisdom and loving compassion in one-on-one consultations providing the opportunity to find clarity and accelerate spiritual and personal evolution.

**Transformative processes**: These individualised processes are able to unblock deep conditioning that has held you back from your potential. Isira uses a combination of advanced hypnotherapy, conscious dialogue and enlightened awareness to help access the root of any blockage. Through bypassing the 'critical mind' and tapping into the innate knowing of your higher self, you will find a deep, sustainable resolution that helps you to maintain a life of balance, wellbeing, happiness and purpose.

Consultations are available both in-person and online.

## BOOKS AND RECORDINGS

Isira has shared a vast body of wisdom through her published work, satsangs/meditations and longer programs. Many of these are available in written, audio and video formats.

www.isira.com

## LIVING AWARENESS

Living Awareness is the vehicle to share Isira's teachings with the world. As an organisation Living Awareness shares the same passion of awakening together as one human family.

www.ingramcontent.com/pod-product-compliance
Lightning Source LLC
Chambersburg PA
CBHW021121300426
44113CB00006B/244